BETWEEN SPEECH AND REVELATION

An Evangelical's Dialogue
with Farrer, Jüngel, and Wolterstorff

by
Joshua Ryan Kira

PICKWICK *Publications* · Eugene, Oregon

BETWEEN SPEECH AND REVELATION
An Evangelical's Dialogue with Farrer, Jüngel, and Wolterstorff

Pickwick Publications
An Imprint of Wipf and Stock Publishers
199 W. 8th Ave., Suite 3
Eugene, OR 97401

www.wipfandstock.com

PAPERBACK ISBN: 978-1-5326-4934-9
HARDCOVER ISBN: 978-1-5326-4935-6
EBOOK ISBN: 978-1-5326-4936-3

Cataloging-in-Publication data:

Names: Kira, Joshua Ryan, author.

Title: Between speech and revelation : an Evangelical's dialogue with Farrer, Jüngel, and Wolterstorff / by Joshua Ryan Kira.

Description: Eugene, OR : Pickwick Publications, 2019 | Includes bibliographical references and index(es).

Identifiers: ISBN 978-1-5326-4934-9 (paperback) | ISBN 978-1-5326-4935-6 (hardcover) | ISBN 978-1-5326-4936-3 (ebook)

Subjects: LCSH: Farrer, Austin, 1904–1968. | Jüngel, Eberhard. | Wolterstorff, Nicholas. | Word of God (Christian theology). | Revelation—Christianity.

Classification: LCC BT127.2 K57 2019 (print) | LCC BT127.2 (ebook)

Manufactured in the U.S.A.   11/12/19

Between Speech and Revelation

To Keri
My prize and my perfection.

Theologie is Rede von Gott.
Von Gott kann man jedoch auf vielfältige Weise redden.
Auch die Bibel, die als Textsammlung für den Gebrauch des Wortes
'Gott' ein maßgebendes, auf jeden Fall aber lehrreiches Buch ist,
spricht von Gott in sehr unterschiedlicher Weise.

Theology is talk about God. But one can talk about God in a variety of ways.
Even the Bible, which is as a collection of texts an authoritative and certainly
instructive book on the usage of the word "God,"
speaks of God in many different ways.

—Eberhard Jüngel, *Gott als Geheimnis der Welt,* 307
God as the Mystery of the World, 226

Contents

Acknowledgments

THIS BOOK COMES FROM the revision of my doctoral dissertation, which I wrote as a student at Claremont Graduate University. As such, it comes at the end of a rather long academic road that has taken me everywhere from conservative evangelical institutions to secular high academia. With the common trials and travails of scholarly life, many people have supported, influenced, and guided me. Accordingly, there is a very long list of acknowledgments that are appropriate, with only a few being allowed by constraints of space.

I first need to thank the professors at The Master's University and Seminary, with four deserving special mention. The late Dr. C. W. Smith can be largely credited with my decision to pursue transdisciplinary work in both theology and philosophy. Dr. Brian Morley, whose academic path I largely emulated, was also influential in my decision to simultaneously undertake education in both fields. Moreover, Dr. Morley taught me what it means to live as a Christian both inside and outside of the university. He always acted towards me with grace, even when answering more questions than should ever be asked a single professor. I must also mention Dr. Trevor Craigen and Dr. Michael Grisanti, who were the seminary professors with whom I did the most coursework, and who were very supportive of my aspirations even though conservative evangelicalism has a history of being suspicious of philosophy. They entrusted me with theological tools and trusted me to use them rightly.

I must also acknowledge my professors at Claremont, with my dissertation committee deserving explicit reference. Dr. Philip Clayton was kind enough to read my dissertation even though I was unable to take him for coursework. His criticisms were of the best sort in that I always felt corrected without feeling discouraged. Also, of significance, was Dr. Anselm Min. His close reading of historical theology and unwillingness to let me make unsubstantiated claims, made for a much better work overall. Finally,

I am grateful to Dr. Ingolf Dalferth, who has left an indelible print on my philosophical and theological thinking. He is the most intriguing blend of the historical and the constructive, the Analytic and the Continental, the ecumenical and the Reformed. He forced me to read widely, think with precision, and tackle issues of historical significance. I recognize how fortunate I was to have him as my committee head.

My current position at Cedarville University requires recognition of many among the administration and my colleagues who supported the final years of my Ph.D. work. Dr. Thomas White and Dr. Jason Lee not only hired me, but also gave me release time to finish my dissertation. I cannot express how much of a relief it was to study while neither worrying about paying bills nor being concerned about the support of my administration. Also of note, were General Loren Reno and Dr. Thomas Mach, who gave me grants so that I had release time to work on the revision of my dissertation for publication. I am grateful, knowing I would not have finished in a timely fashion without their aid. Finally, I must mention Dr. John Gilhooly, who is my primary dialogue partner on the day-to-day basis in the social activity of philosophy, and Dr. Dan Estes, who prayed for me constantly and still does. It is a blessing to work with brothers and sisters in Cedarville who are willing to invest their valuable time in my work and ministry.

To say that my family life, previously and presently, has been formative, would be an understatement. I must thank my mother and father for taking a precocious child, encouraging him to love reading, and supporting him through the madness that is a doctoral program. Before my dad's passing, they continually woke every morning to pray for myself, my wife, my children, and the rest of our family. My brothers have also been encouraging to me (sometimes through mockery) while working through some very theoretical topics. Seeing how they and my sisters-in-law govern their families and serve in the church is always something that gives me hope for me and mine. My children deserve thanks, both for not complaining about living in a tiny apartment so that I can do PhD work, as well as keeping me grounded when my head threatened to float into the clouds. My youngest still does not fully get why people call me "Doctor" since I do not actually help people.

The two greatest thanks need to go to the two strongest influences on my life, work, and faith. The first is my wife, whose patience knows no bounds. Theologians can be quirky, absent-minded, and impractical and philosophers even more so. To be a philosopher-theologian means that she gets the worst of both worlds. Yet, she has always supported my work, encouraged me when I was wavering in my energies, and challenged me to think in a way that will serve Christ and his church. In her, I see what love is meant to be. The last thanks would be to God, without whom this work has no purpose. It is only by grace that He speaks, only by grace that I know, and only by grace that I write. Thus, all failures contained in this book are mine and all victories are His.

1

Introduction

THE CURRENT STATE OF EVANGELICALISM

AMERICAN EVANGELICALISM IS A movement that is insular by nature. Its historical roots in Puritanism, combined with Jonathan Edwards's powerful influence on the systematization of Reformation scholasticism, has often led to a radical skepticism of any ideas coming from different perspectives, with its attendant polemical stance in the broader realm of theology. Such a skepticism is ironic in light of Edwards's own propensity to study broadly and to utilize thinkers that would hold views that are in stark contrast to his.[1] Evangelical insularity can be seen both as a benefit and a detriment to the movement as a whole in that it prevents the dangers of the more drastic departures from orthodoxy with which it is concerned, but also inhibits the refinements of Evangelical theology that is consistent with a perspective that emphasizes the fallibility and sinfulness of humanity. Yet, theology is an inherently risky proposition in that it has, at least historically, been tested, modified, and advanced in the fires of debate. Theological inquiry, with its relationship to philosophy and argumentation, is a conversational activity that is guided by the normative nature of the Christian Scriptures and nourished by those disagreements that force questions of exegesis, systematization, and practice. For this reason, it is incumbent upon Evangelicals to bring their perspective into the larger context of Christendom for the purpose of contributing to a greater narrative, purifying its own perspec-

---

1. One need only look so far as his well-documented reliance on Newton, Locke, and Hume to illustrate this point.

tive, and developing a constructive practice of theology that can address the changing difficulties posed by the movements of culture and history.

Within the turmoil of the twentieth century, many, if not all, of the major tenets of Evangelicalism have come under intense scrutiny. If one were to follow David Bebbington's popular depiction of the movement within Britain, four major facets of Evangelicalism can be discerned.[2] They would include conversionism, activism, biblicism, and crucicentrism.[3] It is the third of these that is of special note, since the particular view of Bible that is propounded means that it has a largely controlling function on the manner in which the other themes are treated. Though an increasing diversity is, in many ways, rearing its head concerning the Evangelical view of the Bible, it has historically held to verbal plenary inspiration. From this view, the words of the text are not just merely to be understood as testimony pointing directly or indirectly to Jesus Christ, but as the words that God Himself intended to be written. Its primary function, from this view, is to provide the message of salvation that centralizes on the life and work of the second person of the godhead (which can be seen in their emphasis on activism/evangelism). However, Evangelicalism believes that not only does it perform this testimonial function, but that it further provides normative content as to what the life of the believer should be like when brought into relationship with the resurrected Christ. Thus, the strain of pietism found both in the Lutheran and Calvinistic sides of the Reformation figure largely on the manner in which Evangelicals approach the Bible.

It is for this reason that the terms "Bible" and "Scripture" often appear to be synonymous in the movement's literature. The belief in a verbal plenary inspiration of the Bible is combined with a particular reaction among Christendom (i.e., its acceptance under the influence of the Holy Spirit), whereby it is treated as Scripture. Thus, whereby some could see the book, the Bible, as being Scripture simply by its usage in the church, the

2. See Bebbington, *Evangelicalism in Modern Britain*, 1–19.

3. It should be noted that the "Bebbington quadrilateral" has often been criticized for not being specific enough, since it could cover many movements before Evangelicalism. Yet, this criticism is attenuated by three factors. First, some such assessments do not give proper credence to the manner in which Bebbington nuances each to display some of the ways in which they are distinct from views that were previously held. Second, Bebbington may not be giving criteria for distinguishing between Evangelicalism and other movements, since he believes that the historical situatedness performs that function. Thus, he appears to be distilling themes within Evangelical theology that are indispensable in understanding projects of the movement as a whole. Last, though none of the characteristics that Bebbington mentions can distinguish Evangelicalism from other historical Christian movements, their particular combination may be able to do so. Furthermore, it could be argued that even if the quadrilateral could be distilled into more fundamental beliefs, the four tenets would still stand as distinctive.

Evangelical would object that church usage is not independent of the quality of the text based on the Spirit's inspiration. How the Bible and Scripture relate to the "Word of God" is difficult to discern, since there is little stress on the revelatory activity found in Jesus Christ. Thus, it may be profitable to put forth a proposal that is not inconsistent with the typical historical views of Evangelicalism, with the caveat that there is no authoritative view within the movement on the topic.[4] It would behoove Evangelicals to recognize the central nature of Christ as the Word of God to any theological endeavor, a view it would share with many in Christianity.

Since Scripture not only provides a message of salvation, but also gives instruction towards the believer's sanctification, the Word of God found in Scripture is primarily Christ while having a secondary sense in the declarations and commands of God concerning His people. Thus, Evangelicals would disagree with Barth on the manner in which the text is inspired, but not necessarily with his view of the derivative nature of the text on the person of Christ and its authoritative function within the church. In this way, Evangelicalism would be able to claim that God primarily speaks concerning Himself in Christ, but also speaks to the believer (directly!) in the words found in the Bible.[5] With the flourishing of literature both in Protestantism and Catholicism concerning bibliology and Christology within the twentieth century, it is intriguing that Evangelicals often find themselves listening in on those conversations from the outside. The aforementioned inward-looking nature of the movement both prevented them from attempting to defend verbal plenary inspiration of Scripture, as well as learning from the broader tradition in its discussions on the relationship between divine speech and revelation. It is these two deficiencies that this work will seek to remedy, not by the provision of a comprehensive theory, but by laying the substructure for a fruitful interaction between an Evangelical view of Scripture and the contemporary discussions concerning philosophy of language and a theology of revelation. This book will also seek to remedy these deficiencies by demonstrating an Evangelical's interaction with differing

4. It should be noted that Evangelicals would likely argue that an authoritative view, in principle, could be found, were a proper examination of the exegetical material to be performed. However, since Evangelicalism has not examined the topic to the degree that it has occurred in other movements (especially those coming from the roots of dialectical theology), there is no clear consensus on the relationship of revelation in Jesus Christ, the Bible, and Scripture.

5. Significant to this argument is that Christ, himself, quotes the text of the Old Testament and treats it as including commands that are to be heeded. Thus, even when the imperatives are meant to point to the need of a savior, they in no way are muted as a text that can speak to the lives of individuals.

perspectives. Thus, it will attempt to encourage dialogue by both providing the foundation for dialogue, as well as illustrating it.

The idea that revelation is central to the religious experience almost goes without saying. Within the five largest religions, the revelatory act plays an important role to both the theoretical and practical life of the adherents. Western religions are explicitly "religions of the book," while Eastern religions have something like revelation even if a particular text does not have as central of a function. Hinduism promotes the Bhagavad Gita, while Buddhism believes that the Buddha "unveiled" the necessary path to enlightenment. With the revelatory act playing such a large role in the various faiths, how that revelation works may be central in distinguishing the religions beyond simply a comparison of their content. This work, recognizing the importance of revelation, will seek the principles necessary to construct a viable philosophy of revelation from a particularly Christian perspective.

The manner of investigation may best be described by a phrase that John Webster uses in his introduction to *God's Being is in Becoming* in describing Eberhard Jüngel's methodology. He calls Jüngel's work a sustained endeavor in "philosophical dogmatics."[6] It could not be considered philosophic theology, since the particularity of the theological stance taken does not fit well with the generality of the moniker. Similarly, this writing will take a perspective that recognizes the centrality of Christ to the theological endeavor and will attempt to philosophically analyze the doctrines and presuppositions that relate to this commitment.[7] For this reason, in a manner similar to Paul Tillich, a transdisciplinary approach will be practiced.[8] In doing so, the groundwork will be laid for how one is to understand and interpret Scripture as a text that claims for itself, and has been communally affirmed as being significant to the contact that the individual Christian has with divine revelation.[9]

6. Jüngel, *God's Being*, x.

7. Such a methodology will, admittedly, show some of the influence of Wittgenstein on the present author's work. Philosophy, though useful for argument and clarification, will not be used as a mode of knowing a God who would otherwise remain unknown.

8. Though similar in its reliance upon both philosophy and theology, this book will differ with Tillich in the directionality of concerns. Whereas Tillich allowed life to pose questions, which would then be philosophically analyzed before finding answers in theology, the present methodology will recognize this possibility while also starting with theology, which is philosophically analyzed before being brought to bear on life. Not only is the scriptural text a book of answers, but it is also a narrative of transformation.

9. It will be admitted that the movement between a theory of revelation to an understanding of a particular text that is connected to revelation cannot be taken for granted. Thus, chapters 11 and 12 will attempt to navigate the between the words of the Christian textual tradition and the incarnate Word which is primary revelation.

HISTORICALLY SITUATING THE DIFFICULTY

The idea that God can speak is not uncontroversial, as the literature concerning the matter will indicate.[10] The objections that are raised are further complicated by the central position that revelation has in many of the world's religions. Christianity, concentrating on Christ who is called the "Word" (John 1:1–18) is in a more precarious position than most. The myriad of arguments against divine speech in the Christian tradition can typically be simplified into the issue of how a God that transcends history (in some fashion)[11] can come down to the concrete circumstances of material life and speak. Though, lately, much ink has been spilled concerning this topic, early philosophical and Christian theological endeavors let the topic remain in its infancy. The Greeks, with a largely anthropomorphic pantheon, did not perceive the difficulty with great acuity until the Platonic movement towards a more transcendent view of divinity.[12] Thus, within the early Greek philosophers, even though a *logos* idea was already present, the manner in which this related to the gods was not always clear.

Early Christian theology, while concerned with the ontological question of how God could become man, as seen in the Christological controversies, did not extend the inquiry into the linguistic-hermeneutical implications of such an activity with regard to Scripture. Thus, even when appropriating neo-Platonism (especially in using emanations and the gradation of being to understand God's relationship to the world), the discussion of the role of a text is underdeveloped. Consequently, various textual interpretation methodologies could be found in the early church, with the Alexandrian and Antiochian attaining places of dominance.

The rise of scholasticism, culminating with John Duns Scotus and Thomas Aquinas, had a very specific set of concerns with language, primarily with the possibility of talking about God. This is not to say that they

10. Wolterstorff surveys the initial difficulty of divine speech, as well as the compounded difficulty of believing that God speaks through a text, in Wolterstorff, *Divine Discourse*, 58–170.

11. It will be granted that the manner in which God transcends history will vary largely within the Christian tradition itself. Yet, at the very least, it is common to understand that divinity is not bound in the same way as humans by the spatio-temporal nature of the universe.

12. It might be argued that such a movement was already present in the pre-Socratics, but the pre-Socratics had a stronger tendency away from anthropomorphism than a tendency towards a transcendent monotheism. Thus, though it is true that Xenophanes had great similarity with Plato in terms of a God that is transcendent and, therefore, not to be conceived of in human terms, it would be difficult to draw generalizations over all of the Greek philosophers who were not directly affected by Socrates.

did not believe that God could speak, but such a perspective was seen as obviously true and the scriptural text was understood as such. Furthermore, the scholastics recognized that Christ was to be understood as Word, as evidenced in their continuation of the tradition of relating the *verbum incarnatum* with the *verbum aeternum* through the idea of manifestation.[13] Yet, the relationship between Christ and Scripture was usually interpreted through analogy. It should also be mentioned that Aquinas's employment and discussion of revelation in terms of the "light" (*lux* or *lumen*) metaphor,[14] becomes significant to the understanding of the possibility and limitations of natural theology for generations after him. This resulted in an impact both on Catholic and Reformed views on revelation, even apart from recognition of how Scripture can be involved in revelatory activity. Yet, as Aquinas, in *Summa Theologica,* dealt with sacred doctrine (*sacra doctrina*) before moving to theology proper, he only used revelation (*revelatio*) to discuss Scripture or the possibility of the natural understanding of God's existence. Similarly, within the *Quaestio, Sententia,* and commentary traditions of Catholicism, revelation was rarely treated thematically.

For the Reformers, revelation began as an assumption that they shared along with the Scholastics. However, as the movement pushed forward, revelation began to be intertwined with other doctrinal concerns such that it became more central to the overall systematic consistency of the five traditional *solae*. Revelation started as a general term for any of the manifold ways in which God displayed Himself or knowledge of Himself, but gained a more technical usage as a way for the Reformers to emphasize God's gracious activity in both salvation and providing the knowledge unto salvation. In this way, they had a polemical basis for attacking any work of man that may be added to Christ's work. Furthermore, the worry of the Reformers concerning the possibilities of human reason, which was combined with a strong view of the noetic effects of sin, caused them to question whether natural faculties could allow one any knowledge of God. Thus, revelation became a necessary idea to bridge the gap between weakened and disordered human reasoning and a God who is too complex in his infinity to be known.[15] Reformed piety and questions of authority made revelation even more central as the Protestant scholars tried to answer the question of how an average individual could know God through Scripture without the need for the Catholic Church. Furthermore, revelation was attached to Christ

13. See Aquinas, *De Veritate,* 4.1.ad6, ad12.

14. Aquinas, *Summa,* 1.1.2, 5, 6:2–4; 1–2.109.1:1123–4.

15. This appears to be one of the reasons that Calvin echoed the scholastics' reluctance to speak of the essence of God, as well as his caution about using theological language. See Calvin, *Institutes,* 1:125–28.

through the *verbo divino* terminology, which set the stage for the Barthian moves of the twentieth century.[16]

Revelation, as the Reformation developed, was how one can rationally sustain *sola gratia*, since it is by God's work alone that one knows Him. It was related to *solus Christus* in that Christ is the primary revelation of God and His work is what allows one to know God at all. It was nourished by *sola fide*, since only God's work in enabling human receptivity can allow for the possibility of transitive revelation. It was foundational for *sola Scriptura*, since God revealed through the text to allow one saving knowledge. And, finally, it was parallel to *soli Deo Gloria*, in that glory was understood by the Reformers to be an issue of manifestation. That God wanted to be seen in glory meant that God would reveal Himself in glory. Thus, as the *solae* became prominent in Protestant thought, so did the idea of revelation. It should be recognized, however, that such systematic necessity of revelation did not carry over into a similar amount of effort being expended on understanding how Christ, the Word, should be related to the textual word. They, epistemologically, knew that Scripture had primacy in *ordo cognoscendi*,[17] but they did not give clarity to the reason why the *logos* terminology of the New Testament was significant and how it should affect one's understanding that God speaks through the words of the Bible.

As modernity dawned in Europe, questions of skepticism and the rise of the natural sciences led to an obsession in philosophy concerning epistemology. Yet, the question of divine speech was largely subsumed under questions of revelation. Thus, God speaking as a source of knowledge was lost with the fascination with God's revelation through the natural world. This remained unabated until German idealism, which not only transformed the ontological categories by which one understood phenomena, but also brought, through Hegel, an understanding of God which saw the divine self as being what it was through its historical activities. Fichte's reconceptualization of reality in terms of enactment gives Hegel the resources needed to reframe the question of divine revelatory activity into an issue of self-revelation.[18]

---

16. Zwingli makes it clear that the incarnation was both to reveal God's salvific intentions as well as to actually effect them. Zwingli, "Exposition of Faith," 249–50.

17. This can be seen in the increasing tendency of the early Protestant systematic theologies to be ordered around epistemological questions. Thus, whereas early works often used loci organization to deal with the particular questions that arose from disputes between Catholic and Reformed theologians, increasingly, especially as the seventeenth century closed, theologies were systematized to place the idea of revelation early in prolegomena and doctrine of Scripture relatively quick thereafter.

18. For a helpful treatment of this movement, see Mezei, *Radical Revelation*, 109–49.

Karl Barth took up Hegelian ontology, especially as it was filtered through Kierkegaardian existentialism. Yet he was concerned with the use of Scripture in light of the perceived failures of liberal theology to make good on its promises of a powerful new methodology to attend to the text. Barth also attempted a corrective of the largely ambiguous relationship between the Word in Christ and the word in Scripture,[19] but did so in a manner that was antagonistic to the Scholastic understanding of the question of God's being, so that he frequently failed to see if there were any insights contained within the Catholic tradition that could be appropriated in the development of a theology of revelation. He knew that Christ was to be understood as the locus of how divine revelation was concretized, but did so in a manner that did not always take seriously claims within Scripture (some by Christ himself) that the words of the Jewish and Christian canons were not simply related to the "Word of God," but actually (in some sense) are the "Word of God." Barth dealt with the important issue of what does it mean that God revealed Godself through the "Word," but not how that played into a theology or philosophy of the Bible.

Within all these movements, a core question can be found, which Jüngel (and indeed Barth) considers to be the central mystery of the Christian faith.[20] What does it mean for humans that they are approaching the divine through *Immanuel*, or "God with us"? This leads to the further question of how a text can be understood as God speaking, while itself not being revelatory in a primary fashion (i.e., in the fashion of the Word incarnate).[21] In other words, the question is not only how can it be that God is with us, but how *is* "God with us" and what is Scripture's role in relating God to us.

FROM "BELOW" AND FROM "ABOVE"

In delving into the issues concerning divine speech and revelation, as well its incumbent relationship to an Evangelical view of Scripture, a peculiar methodology will be adopted in that the investigation set forth will start both from "below" and from "above." It could be questioned as to the validity, especially from a Christian commitment, of addressing the present topic

---

19. Barth, *CD* 1/1:296.

20. See Jüngel, *God as the Mystery*.

21. It will be realized that the idea of "Word" is used in many ways within the Christian scriptural and theological tradition. The relationship between the preincarnate and incarnate Word will be drawn as part of the explication of how the doctrine of the Trinity is related to the revelatory act, but other concepts (such as the Apostolic Kerygma) will be left out with the exception of "word" as text.

both theologically and philosophically. Yet, the subject matter, in its complexity, appears to require such an approach. From the Christian perspective, it is often believed that God speaks to humans and through humans. Moreover, revelation, which is a different phenomenon than speech, appears to be related to divine speaking. Since revelation is primarily (though not solely[22]) an act of God and the speech that God uses is human speech, there apparently needs to be a dual-natured approach. Philosophically, one can analyze speech in order to understand what it means to make the claim that God uses "human speech.[23] Moreover, it may address the question as to the possibility of God speaking in a human manner.[24] Theologically, one can begin to fill out the concept of revelation such that one can lay the foundation for its possible intersection with speech. With these in place, the way in which speech and revelation relate can be examined, with an eye towards the role of inspiration in such a relationship.

The examination of speech, revelation, and inspiration in its multifarious approach will begin with three preeminent thinkers who have addressed the issues. Their work will provide a framework in which the relationship of the concepts can be scrutinized. The three scholars who will be employed are Nicholas Wolterstorff, Eberhard Jüngel, and Austin Farrer. These gentlemen share an affinity for delving into matters both philosophical and theological, which allows them to fit nicely into the transdisciplinary approach of the present work. Moreover, their Christian commitments will allow them enough common ground to enter into dialogue with one another. This is significant, especially in light of the potential Wittgensteinian criticisms concerning the manner in which each scholar is involved with particular language games. That they all hold to the normative nature of Scripture, appears to allow them enough of a shared discourse for fruitful dialogue.[25]

22. It will be recognized that in transitive revelation (to use Wolterstorff's terminology), the receiver must be addressed in her receptivity. For more on an analytic of the term "revelation," see Wolterstorff, *Divine Discourse*, 31–36.

23. This is particularly significant since all but the most fundamentalist traditions of the Christian faith have believed that one must at least move beyond the bounds of the text in the understanding of semantics, syntax, and historical evidence related to philology.

24. It shall be granted that Scripture itself is not concerned with the possibility of God using human speech, since it assumes it in its very ontology. Yet, criticisms from outside of the Christian tradition concerning its transcendental possibilities appears to require a philosophical address, even if the Christian is not concerned with the truth of the criticism. In other words, even though someone who holds to the Christian faith may be warranted in believing that it is true that God can speak in human terms, since they believe he in fact did do so, this does not remove the practical use of defending such a proposition in terms to which someone who does not hold to faith might agree.

25. The current methodology is, in many ways, a matter of expediency. It is essential

Whereas their agreement allows for discussion, it is their diversity which will allow them to fill out the portions of the others' perspectives that remain underdeveloped. Wolterstorff has taken pains to understand what it means that God speaks. In doing so, he provides a philosophical treatment of speech in general and how it is defensible to believe that there exists divine speech even if God does not have a physical presence. Moreover, American Evangelicalism, with its roots in the Calvinistic theology of late Puritanism, will find natural affinities with Wolterstorff's theological commitments. Jüngel attempts to understand what revelation is and how it relates to the ability of humans to speak about and, consequently, think about God. This is of significance since Evangelical theology is rightly accused of failing to pay enough attention to the incarnational aspect of God's revelation and thus Jüngel can supplement the overall perspective. Farrer is concerned with the question of how the authors of the Christian scriptures can be divinely inspired in their textual and oratorical endeavors. In this way, his interest in the manner in which the human and the divine can come together in the production of a text bears similarity to concerns found in Evangelical bibliology.

In the current work, each author will be given, in succession, a section which will include the philosophical and theological backdrop for the scholar, an interpretation of the significant facets of his understanding of the relationship between divine speech and revelation, and an assessment of the benefits and difficulties of his position from a distinctly Evangelical perspective. By using each to alternately critique and support one another, a cohesive perspective will be sought that seeks to relate divine speech and revelation. The final section of this book will use the criticism and adoption of the various aspects of the work of Farrer, Jüngel, and Wolterstorff to outline principles for the construction of a more comprehensive Evangelical view of divine speech and revelation. Though they will provide a grammar by which one can speak about the acts of speech, revelation and inspiration, these rules will not themselves provide the actuality of how such concepts work themselves out in the Christian *Weltanschauung*. It will indeed be argued that even when work is appropriated from the authors under investigation, an assortment of constructive possibilities may be available. Thus, the dialogue between Wolterstorff, Jüngel, and Farrer will provide an

---

to philosophy that individuals of vastly different perspectives can begin to speak on the same issues. However, it will require a greater movement of "translation" to move from one scholar to another if they diverge too greatly in their discourse. Thus, the shared foundation of Wolterstorff, Jüngel, and Farrer will, at the very least, make comparison and criticism simpler.

outline of the considerations that should be central when developing a view of how God can speak and reveal and how that relates to human speech.

NICHOLAS WOLTERSTORFF

2

Wolterstorff's Influences
and Methodology

IT MIGHT BE SAID of Nicholas Wolterstorff, that he is a philosopher of a classical style. Resisting the modern trend towards increasing specialization, he writes widely and continues in an area only until he believes he has provided sufficient contribution. After this, he seeks a new topic of study towards which to put his considerable energies. Consequently, he has written in epistemology, ethics, philosophy of law, aesthetics, philosophy of religion, philosophy of language, and history of modern philosophy. In style, he is the epitome of an analytic philosopher, favoring clarity and rigorous argumentation over sweeping theories and generalizations. He gives preference to the particularities of a topic, which he uses to construct a provisional theory that is revised until suitable in explanatory power. Yet, Wolterstorff is atypical within the analytic tradition in many ways, not the least of which is his willingness to be driven by theological concerns.[1] Though it is not unusual for analytic philosophers to be consumed by linguistic concerns, it is far more uncommon for one to be motivated towards a topic like divine speech. For this reason, Wolterstorff's *Divine Discourse* was a welcome intrusion on a field that had long been swayed by a Wittgensteinian-influenced naturalism.[2] His conversancy with the Christian tradition, along with his

1. It appears that continental philosophy is more willing to place a high premium on theological ideas, as can be seen in Hegel, Kierkegaard, and Heidegger.

2. This is not to say that Wittgenstein was himself anti-religious or anti-metaphysical, with both issues being up for debate. However, his work, at the very least, was foundational for some of the more skeptical positions of the early half of the twentieth century, not the least of which was the Vienna Circle. Yet, Wittgenstein's own position

uniqueness in addressing divine speech philosophically, causes his work to possess a significant role in the dialogue concerning God's speech and revelation. His concern with orthodoxy and Reformed influences makes him a welcome dialogue partner with the Evangelical position. This chapter will provide an understanding of the influences behind Wolterstorff's works, as well as his overall project

WOLTERSTORFF'S PHILOSOPHICAL AND THEOLOGICAL FOUNDATIONS

The strong crossover between analytic and Anglo-American philosophy can often be seen in the influence of Enlightenment philosophers from the British Isles. Wolterstorff is an example of this in that two of his main philosophical influences are John Locke and Thomas Reid. He does not appropriate their work uncritically, for his theological influences often cause him to diverge from the specifics of their systems. Yet, it is not difficult to discern their mark on his scholarship.

Perhaps the manner in which Locke's influence on Wolterstorff can best be clarified is in contrast to another scholar from the Kingdom, David Hume. Both philosophers strongly affected the trajectory of empiricism in the west, but Hume was more extreme in how he pushed the movement. Agreeing with Locke concerning the contradictory nature of innate ideas,[3] he takes a posteriori understanding towards a skeptical turn, by denying any law-like structures at work in the natural world. Where Locke, along with many of the other philosophers in the Royal Society, saw a type of mechanistic nature in the universe,[4] Hume saw causation as a mistaken extension of correlation. Why Locke was unwilling to carry empiricism forth toward the destruction of scientific law, ironically, appears to be more of an offspring of his religious perspective than anything else. He was concerned to defend a type of objectivism that he believed necessary to the traditional understanding of the Christian faith, as well as seeking to defend the rationality of belief in God. In doing so, Locke provides certain ideas that significantly influenced Wolterstorff. First, Wolterstorff maintains a type of

---

is far from clear, especially in light of his belief that Bertrand Russell did not understand his *Tractatus Logico-Philosophicus*, as well as claims by some of his more religiously inclined students such as Rush Rhees and Elizabeth Anscombe.

3. Flew, *Hume's*, 21.

4. It was this mechanism, which influenced later Anglo-American philosophers to conceive of a static view of reality, against which Whitehead resisted in developing a scientific understanding that focused on processes. See Whitehead, *Process and Reality*. For a helpful survey of this movement see Padiyath, *Metaphysics of Becoming*, 23–25.

objectivism, found in his predecessor, that attacks communal understandings of Scripture. Locke's worry about the possibility of the text becoming a "wax nose"[5] is determinative for Wolterstorff and his attempt to provide a normative understanding to the Christian faith. Second, Locke's empiricism, as mediated through early-twentieth-century analytic philosophers, affects Wolterstorff's methodology and his preference to phenomenological description prior to theoretical exposition. Yet, his third and most prominent influence on Wolterstorff is in the area of epistemology. Locke was no stranger to rationalism, but was unwilling to admit that one could only hold a belief if it was rationally justifiable. Thus, Wolterstorff gains from his brand of deontology[6] and tendency to preserve an entitlement to religious belief, a more open epistemological structure than proposed in classical foundationalism.[7] With this belief in place, Wolterstorff uses a modified form of Alston's proposal[8] of doxastic practices to investigate other rational sources of knowledge.[9] This shift in the theory of how knowledge can be justified provides the basis for his well-known adherence to Reformed epistemology.[10]

Thomas Reid, though often critical of Locke, provided an epistemological perspective that overlapped with his, such that he had similar influence on Wolterstorff. Reid had a strongly realist sensibility and a philosophical approach that, in many ways, was a foil for Descartes's methodological doubt. He believed that showing the weakness of systematic skepticism was enough to recommend realism, since common sense provided justification for belief in the existence of one's self and one's world. This view appears to be mirrored in Wittgenstein's criticisms of the foundations of

5. Wolterstorff, *Divine Discourse*, 226.

6. Locke's deontology also has significant consequences in Wolterstorff's ethical writings, especially his recent work on natural rights. See Wolterstorff, *Justice*; *Justice in Love*.

7. For Wolterstorff's understanding of the rationality of religious belief, as it relates to Locke, see Wolterstorff, "Can Belief in God Be Rational?," 135–86; *Divine Discourse*, 261–8.

8. For the difference between Wolterstorff and Alston on the use of the concept "doxastic practice," see Wolterstorff, *Divine Discourse*, 322n4. To summarize, Alston sees a doxastic practice as a function that receives inputs and produces outcomes and is essentially a belief-forming mechanism. Wolterstorff, however, focuses on doxastic practices as those practices which one uses to choose and steer their belief-forming mechanisms.

9. For Wolterstorff's use of Alston's doxastic practice to explain Locke, see Wolterstorff, *John Locke*, 86.

10. It should be noted that Alston was reluctant to use the moniker "Reformed epistemologist," since his denominational affiliation was Episcopalian.

methodological doubt. Moreover, Reid felt that common cultural structures could be analyzed to see the manner in which common sense manifested itself. Thus, Reid was one of the few early modern philosophers who had strong linguistic concerns. It was this focus on language that would eventually influence Austin and Moore and provided significant roots for the analytical tradition in which Wolterstorff was steeped.[11] Not only did Reid supply a considerable backdrop for Wolterstorff's linguistic and realist concerns, but he also attacks some of the epistemic structures with which his successor is concerned. He was unwilling to submit to some of the strictures on what were considered to be rational sources of knowledge. Reid wanted to defend the rationality of traditional ways of knowing, including testimonial evidence.[12] This is a significant theme in twentieth-century philosophy, since some of the previous canons of rationality could not produce a practicable perspective. Since all people require testimony as significant for their appropriation of knowledge, any perspective that cannot permit it must itself be treated with skepticism. Reid's epistemology of testimonial evidence is significant for Wolterstorff in two ways. First, it would provide him with a significant link between his theological dependence on the Bible and his philosophical desire for rationality. If Reid's argumentation is correct, then relying upon the testimonial evidence of the gospel writers would not be irrational. Second, similar to Locke, Reid's work is supportive of resisting foundationalism. With the collapse of foundationalist epistemology, reliance upon religious ideas and practices in the development of knowledge once again received attention. Under this impetus, Wolterstorff wrote *Divine Discourse*, where he states, "And as for myself, I will be wanting to ask what a non-evidentialist epistemology of beliefs grounded on divine discourse might look like."[13] Thus, with his Reidian background, it is impossible to separate Wolterstorff's philosophy of religious language from his epistemic preoccupations.

The last philosophical influence of note, in respect to Wolterstorff, is the speech act theorists of the twentieth century. Since the publication of J. L. Austin's *How to Do Things with Words*,[14] speech act theory has provided endless content for discussion among the analytic tradition. As a movement, it is neither monolithic, nor static. There have been significant developments in the field beyond Austin's original formulation, not the least

---

11. For the relationship between Reid and Wittgenstein, Moore, and Austin, see Ledwig, *Common Sense*, 15–78.

12. See Wolterstorff, *Thomas Reid*, 163–84.

13. Wolterstorff, *Divine Discourse*, 15.

14. Austin, *How to Do Things*.

of which is the refinement of a taxonomy of illocutionary acts. In the latter half of the century, Searle was especially influential in this endeavor, and it is his schema that Wolterstorff largely adopts.[15] Yet, his influence does not end there, in that his de-emphasis of the locutionary act finds echoes in Wolterstorff's work. Though Austin's work sought to differentiate what is uttered from the act it performs, Wolterstorff instead wants to dispense with the utterance and focus on the difference between the propositional content of the utterance and illocutionary act. Not only does this practice of propositionalizing require specific ontological and epistemological backing, but it also leads to one of the more substantial differences between his work and that of Farrer and Jüngel.

Other philosophical predecessors are discernible, but for the sake of space, they will be left to the body of the text. However, a few theological influences deserve mention. Wolterstorff considers himself a Calvinist and takes up Calvin's scholarship with some facilitation from his roots in the Dutch Reformed tradition. This is one of the areas of commonality that he possesses with Alvin Plantinga, with both drawing heavily on theologians from the community, such as Herman Bavinck and Abraham Kupyer.[16] It also appears to give rise to their commonality in terms of skepticism towards natural theology[17] and draw towards epistemological structures and systems that find their affinity with the Reformed tradition. Of great consequence is Wolterstorff's willingness to let religious concerns dominate philosophical ones when he believes there is an area where resolution is impossible or unlikely. Furthermore, Calvin's emphasis on God's sovereignty and independence finds significant reverberation in Wolterstorff's work. Along with this focus, comes a view of God that Jüngel derogatorily calls the "metaphysical"[18] view and which Wolterstorff himself terms the "classical Western concept of God."[19] To summarize the view, he claims that it

15. The most notable divergence between Wolterstorff and Searle, is the former's lack of significant discussion of expressives. See Searle, *Expression and Meaning*, 1–29.

16. For some of their influence, see Wolterstorff, "Herman Bavinck," 133–46; "Liberating Scholarship," 4–5.

17. In spite of attempts to argue that Calvin holds to the significance of natural theology, it is more likely that Calvin, using his "spectacles" metaphor, is rehashing the Augustinian argument that one can see God in the book of nature, yet only can do so clearly and correctly with the help of the book of Scripture. See Calvin, *Institutes*, 1:69–70; 1:159–61. For arguments concerning the structural importance of natural theology to Calvin's position, see Muller, *Post-Reformation*, 273–80; Sudduth, *Reformed Objection*.

18. For one of his more pointed criticisms of this tradition, see Jüngel, *God as the Mystery*, 38–42.

19. Wolterstorff, *Divine Discourse*, 15.

holds "that God is eternal, that God is everlasting, that God is immutable, that God is omniscient, that God is impassable."[20] Intriguingly, Wolterstorff appears to be ambivalent toward the last of these characteristics,[21] as well as loose enough in his Calvinism that open theists have taken to his work.[22] Yet, omniscience and autonomy will play a principal role in the way he conceives of God. He will, to a large degree, reiterate the historical tension between divine independence and theistic personalism.[23] In doing so, he will want to define God's work apart from humanity to the degree he is able.

Two other manners in which Reformed theology forms the backdrop to his work are in terms of his view of Scripture and his understanding of piety. He will stray from a historically influential view of inerrantism,[24] but does agree with later Church Fathers, scholastic Catholicism, and early Swiss Reformers concerning the need to see the Bible as *"one* book of God."[25] In doing so, he will want to stress the continuity of the message of Scripture[26] due to the belief that God uses the diversity of texts within to speak. Wolterstorff also has a pietistic strain moving through his work, which influences the prominence of activity to his philosophy. His political,[27] aesthetic,[28] and linguistic theories all stress acts and activism. This prevents him from continuing with the types of essentialism often seen within Christian theology.

20. Wolterstorff, *Divine Discourse*, 15.

21. Wolterstorff does not appear to believe that God has emotions, but that he is capable of suffering in some manner. See the discussion in Vanhoozer, *Remythologizing Theology*, 387–415.

22. The three primary areas in which he has been appropriated appear to be a temporal view of God (Wolterstorff, *"Unqualified Divine Temporality,"* 187–213) his literary hermeneutics which trends toward taking narrative depictions of God as literal unless one has a good reason otherwise, and his aforementioned belief in divine passibility (see Wolterstorff, *Lament).*

23. For clarity, it should be noted how Wolterstorff defines personhood in God. He writes that he is "a center of consciousness who forms and acts on intentions and has knowledge of entities other than Godself" (Wolterstorff, *Divine Discourse*, 95).

24. It has been argued by influential historians that inerrancy was not the historic view of the church. By inerrancy it is meant that Scripture does not have any errors in it, regardless of whether the material in question is understood as being theological, historical, scientific, etc. Some of the reason for this is the use of the English term "inerrancy," which is obviously a late addition. The greater question is whether there were early claims that pointed to such a view, even if the perspective is unnamed. An example of this would be Augustine, which will be discussed in chapter 9.

25. Wolterstorff, *Divine Discourse*, 53.

26. Following Wolterstorff's nomenclature, no distinction will be made between the terms "Bible" and "Scripture."

27. See Wolterstorff, *Justice.*

28. See Wolterstorff, *Art in Action.*

It is perhaps this willingness that allows Wolterstorff a type of innovativeness in his philosophical pursuits not always found in twentieth-century Christian theologians in the Anglo-American tradition. In fact, it is the de-centering of the theoretical and emphasis on the practical that Merold Westphal considers to be the most noteworthy contribution in Wolterstorff's work.[29] It is the act that takes the place of primacy in his speech act understanding of divine speech[30] and provides the fertile area of continuity between his work and that of Farrer and Jüngel.

WOLTERSTORFF'S PROJECT

In terms of divine speech and revelation, Wolterstorff's goal is to examine the nature of divine speech. He, like Jüngel and Farrer, sees the phenomena as distinct. He laments what he believes to be the historical trend where, "Divine speech disappeared into divine revelation because speaking of God speaking was taken to be a metaphorical way of attributing revelation to God."[31] In attempting to locate the uniqueness of God's speech, he both characterizes revelation, and holds to its separability from the question of divine speaking. Yet, in doing so, he takes a strongly hypothetical approach. In many ways, *Divine Discourse* can be seen as a depiction of how one would defend an understanding of God speaking through human discourse, without providing a spirited defense of the fact that God speaks that way. Though a later chapter is titled, "Are We Entitled?," under criticism from Philip Quinn,[32] Wolterstorff admits,

> I should not have suggested, in a sentence in the introduction to the epistemological coda, that I was going to discuss whether God does speak. For I do not discuss that; Quinn is right to catch me on my loose talk. What I do discuss, as I indicate right away after posing that malformed question, is whether an intelligent

---

29. Westphal is substantially, though not perfectly, correct in arguing that Wolterstorff's work is destructive of the ontotheological enterprises seen in the nineteenth and early twentieth centuries. See Westphal, "Review Essay," 527.

30. With space limited, only a passing mention will be given to the influence of Hans Frei on Wolterstorff. Not only did Frei want to see the singularity of the Bible, but his interaction with tradition, his exposition of a *sensus literalis*, and his questioning of liberalism all bear fruit in Wolterstorff's work. For their interaction, see Wolterstorff, *Divine Discourse*, 179–80, 220–35.

31. Wolterstorff, *Divine Discourse*, 10.

32. Quinn, "Can God Speak?," 259–69.

adult of the modern Western world could be entitled to believe
that God has spoken to him or her.[33]

This hypothetical nature can also be seen in Wolterstorff's early use of
Augustine's conversion experience as an entry point into the discussion of
divine speech,[34] wherein he admits the possibility of alternative interpretations of the event to his preferred view of seeing God as actually addressing
Augustine through the speech of the small child.[35] Though Wolterstorff believes he provides a compelling depiction of how God could speak through
human discourse, he never actually attempts to show that it is the case.

Though Wolterstorff's overall purpose is to analyze one way of looking
at divine speech, he has a particular penchant for focusing on exegetical
issues. For him, movements away from thinking of the author's role in how
a text can speak have been detrimental to the Christian faith.[36] His pietistic
focus on the practicality of the Christian life leads him to both attempt to
develop a hermeneutical methodology that could be done by the layman,
but also relate this to the rationality of using the Bible as a source of knowledge. It is this reason that he reacts against the "preoccupation" with epistemology that he believes "may have reached the point of pathology in the
modern world."[37] Thus, his emphasis on activity compels him to provide an
exposition of how divine speech appears to work, before moving on to the
epistemological questions as to how one can believe she can know or speak
about God.[38] Consequently, similar to Jüngel and Farrer, he begins talking
about God before ever justifying talk about God.[39]

WOLTERSTORFF'S METHODOLOGY

Wolterstorff's methodology is typical of his analytic style, especially in
investigating speech and revelation. Two hallmarks of such a process are
the propensity to analyze normal language usage and the significance of

33. Wolterstorff, "Response," 305.

34. For an in-depth treatment of Augustine's conversion in terms of divine speech,
see Asiedu, "Illocutionary Acts and the Uncanny," 283–310.

35. Wolterstorff, Divine Discourse, 7.

36. Such movement he sees as a hallmark of twentieth-century philosophy of language (Wolterstorff, Divine Discourse, 15). For a more detailed explanation of his criticism, see Wolterstorff, "Resurrecting the Author," 4–24.

37. Wolterstorff, Divine Discourse, 36.

38. This is somewhat parallel to the Scholastic tendency to place metaphysics before
epistemological concerns.

39. Wolterstorff, "Is It Possible and Desirable?," 1–18.

analogy in seeking explanations of linguistic phenomena. Like any philosophical movement, analytic philosophy is a second order discipline that is in want of content. Thus, not unlike other perspectives, it begins with the fateful decision of how to circumscribe the field of inquiry. Following the common sense tradition, which bore its earliest adherents, analytic philosophy typically seeks empirical data to investigate. Wolterstorff follows this tendency, but in a manner that is distinct because of his chosen subject matter. By deciding to explicate divine speech, he is in the precarious position of attempting to explain how God typically speaks, though it appears to lack the empirical phenomena that he seeks. This causes him to make two substantial moves. First, he does not treat divine speech as a distinctive phenomenon, but categorizes it under human speech. He justifies this activity in a few ways. He recognizes that there is a history of believing that God speaks through humans, whether it be in prophetic utterance, the inspiration of the Holy Spirit, etc. Moreover, the fact that the Bible says that God speaks, means that the term "speech" must be applicable to divine activity. Yet, the term is defined in relation to human life. Thus, Wolterstorff feels he is warranted in beginning with the phenomena as it applies to humanity and then moving to divine speech. Second, he carries out his work on the presupposition that Scripture is divine speech. Consequently, to analyze the text is to produce an analysis of God's speaking and also influences Wolterstorff towards the aforementioned emphasis on exegetical matters. Yet, interpretation of the scriptural text, since it is written in human terms, can benefit from a philosophy of language. Thus, the empirical foundation of the analytic tradition means that Wolterstorff finds his content in the text and his methodology in normal language analysis.[40]

Significant to the analytic tradition, also, is the use of analogy to hypothesize concerning areas where empirical evidence is not present. Though Wolterstorff has some interaction with Aquinas, it becomes clear in usage that he is using analogy as methodology in the vein of Locke. Though Reid uses analogies, Locke gives it explicit treatment as a tool for the explication of that with which one has no empirical contact. Thus, Locke claims, "In things which sense cannot discover, analogy is the great rule of probability."[41] For Wolterstorff, the claim that God speaks is literal and Scripture is to be understood as God's speech. Yet, how God can speak through Scripture remains unexplained. Consequently, analogy is required to understand the manner in which it can be understood as God's speech, since God's direct

---

40. For more on Wolterstorff's understanding of normal language usage, see Wolterstorff, "Resurrecting the Author."

41. Locke, *Essay*, 307.

activity is not open for observation. In this way, Wolterstorff mirrors the type of analysis found in the work of William Alston. Alston believed that one could have literal experience of God, but in relating experience of God to other types of sensory experience, analogy was required.[42] It is the combination of normal language usage and analogical examination that provides the foundation for Wolterstorff's analytical methodology.

---

42. See Alston, *Perceiving God.*

3

Wolterstorff's View of Divine Speech and Revelation

CHARACTERIZATION OF HUMAN SPEECH

THE ORDER IN WHICH the following chapters address the issues of human speech, divine speech, and divine revelation will be telling about their respective scholar's position concerning method of investigation. For Wolterstorff, the decision to understand divine speech through human speech places the latter as the primary phenomenon for investigation. Moreover, his belief that the question of revelation is separable from the question of speech is why it is addressed last.[1]

Wolterstorff's examination of human speech, as was mentioned earlier, is primarily derived from an understanding of speech act theory. When thinking of the criticisms of Maimonides against any literal understanding of divine speech, since as spirit he does not possess the faculties for vocalization, Wolterstorff turns his attention to that in a speech act which does not require vocalization. Thus, he makes the significant decision to explore the possibility that speaking should be identified with the performance of an illocutionary act.[2] In emphasizing the illocutiones, Wolterstorff believes that it makes sense in some of the normal ways in which people understand speech. Since speaking is, for him, an intransitive act, then any attempts at

---

1. In *Divine Discourse*, Wolterstorff actually places his chapter on revelation early, but only does so in order to address what he knows will be a looming objection. Conceptually, revelation is superfluous to his theory.

2. Wolterstorff, *Divine Discourse*, 13.

equating it with communication is suspect. He claims, "The reason it doesn't follow is that success in communication of knowledge is out of hands of the agent in a way in which success in asserting, commanding, promising, and asking is not."[3] In other words, the success conditionals for an act of communication will reside within the hearer, since their failure to understand what is being said can cause there to be a failure to communicate. Wolterstorff sees speech differently since the success is dictated not by the hearer, but by the speaker. If, for example, an individual gives a command and nobody is there to hear, nobody listens, or nobody understands, he still successfully issued the command. Thus, he writes, "Speaking is not communication; it doesn't even require communication. It is a fundamentally different sort of action from communication."[4] Thus, he thinks of communication as a perlocutionary act,[5] whereas speech is an illocutionary one.[6]

There are, for Wolterstorff, a few significant implications to treating speech as the production of an illocutionary act. It allows him to understand the manner in which one person can speak for another, such as is the case with a press secretary, a diplomat, etc. It is these cases that will serve as the analogies necessary for Wolterstorff to make the later move towards understanding divine speech. Furthermore, the intransitive nature of speech will later become part of the reason that he separates divine speech from revelation. Seeing speech as an illocutionary action will also have certain consequences concerning the manner in which the identity of the performer of a speech act can affect one's understanding of the act itself. A few notes of explanation will suffice, which will be given later extended treatment. If one's goal in speech is to perform an illocutionary act, then one might wonder what purpose, if any, locutiones serve. Wolterstorff believes that locutionary acts are necessary since, "illocutionary actions aren't candidates for basic actions."[7] This view will become significant in light of the questions of the capacities of speech when referenced to God. At its core, Wolterstorff's takes an instrumental view of speech, such that it is a way to get things done. So central is its instrumentality, that he claims that one

---

3. Wolterstorff, *Divine Discourse*, 33.

4. Wolterstorff, *Divine Discourse*, 32. That it is a "fundamentally different sort of action" is perhaps an overstatement, since one would have to wonder why speech and communication are so often equated, even if such an equation is incorrect.

5. Wolterstorff, *Divine Discourse*, 33.

6. For the relationship between locutionary, illocutionary, and perlocutionary acts, see Wolterstorff, *Divine Discourse*, 33. In summary, Wolterstorff holds that locutionary acts "count as" illocutionary ones and illocutionary acts cause perlocutionary ones.

7. Wolterstorff, *Divine Discourse*, 86.

would not be able to "imagine a human life devoid of speech actions."[8] It is this instrumentality which will provide contrasts with the views of Jüngel and Farrer.

Though Wolterstorff holds that one has spoken if they have produced an illocutionary act, he realizes that he has yet to define what that speech actually is. Similar to the viewpoint on the relationship between semantics and metaphysics espoused by Saul Kripke, Wolterstorff believes that the question of how a word is used is not always to be equated with what that word is or refers to.[9] Thus, after producing an analytic of what it means to "speak," Wolterstorff attempts to provide an ontology of speech. To understand what speech actually is, he attempts to answer the question of why a locutionary act can count as an illocutionary one. He disagrees both with Alvin Goldman concerning conventional generation[10] and with Searle who relies on institutional facts.[11] Instead, Wolterstorff proposes a "normative theory" of language. He states, "To institute an arrangement for the performance of speech actions is to institute a way of acquiring rights and obligations."[12] In essence, when one speaks, they are taking up a normative stance within the public sphere, a normative stance which is normatively attributed to them. Thus, a speaker ought to be treated as if they performed the illocutionary action and the speaker ought to act and believe in accordance with their action. Timothy Ward makes a provocative proposal that Wolterstorff's theory is a corrective of Searle's taxonomy of illocutionary acts, particularly of the declarative speech act. Searle defines declarations as illocutionary acts, such that "the successful performance of one of its members brings about the correspondence between the propositional content and reality, successful performance guarantees that the propositional content corresponds to the world. . . "[13] Whereas assertions attempt to make sure that words fit the world and commands attempt to make the world fit the words, declarations are unusual in that the successful issuance of one guarantees correspondence between the words uttered and the facts of the world.[14] Ward suggests that Wolterstorff seizes on Searle's understanding

8. Wolterstorff, *Divine Discourse*, 86.

9. Kripke, *Naming and Necessity*. Similar concerns are seen in the works of Hillary Putnam. See Putnam, "Problem About Reference," 22–48.

10. Wolterstorff, *Divine Discourse*, 78–80.

11. Wolterstorff, *Divine Discourse*, 80–81.

12. Wolterstorff, *Divine Discourse*, 84.

13. Searle, *Expression and Meaning*, 16.

14. The significance of the declarative to Searle's taxonomy probably explains his focus on institutional facts, since declarations require institutional support for them to be successful. For example, a judge can only declare one "not guilty" with the support

of declarations and applies the understanding therein in a wider sphere. Thus, Ward claims, "What Wolterstorff has done is effectively to show the failure of Searle's categories by demonstrating that what Searle describes as unique to 'declarations' is in fact true of every speech act."[15] What he means is that the normative nature of speech means that reality will be affected whenever speech is performed, since it will institute relationships of rights and obligations. Ward is right in that there appears to be something similar to what is going on in declarations in the other types of illocutiones. What Ward fails to recognize, is that declaratives go further than this in that there intended effect is based solely on the success of the illocutionary act. If someone were to successfully issue a command, they have changed the world in bringing about the normative ascription of a normative stance, but the effect of the command, i.e., to get someone to do something, may or may not attain. However, when clergy, again in the correct institutional position, declares a couple married, the success of the issuance of the declaration will always mean the success of the effect of the illocutionary act, which is that the couple is actually married. Thus, Searle's placement of declarations as an independent taxonomical distinction appears warranted against Ward's objections, but Ward is right to notice that the normativity of speech, as suggested by Wolterstorff, means that speech will always effect change even if the perlocutionary act does not attain.

Wolterstorff's normative theory of speech strongly affects his understanding of the interpretive process. He is clear that intentionalist understandings of interpretation are mistaken, agreeing that one cannot gain an adequate understanding of a speaker's intention by their speech. Thus, he writes:

> But even more important for our subsequent purposes is the fact that to speak is not, as such, to express one's inner self but to take up a normative stance in the public domain. The myth dies hard that to read a text for authorial discourse is to enter the dark world of the author's psyche. It's nothing of the sort.[16]

Thus, not only does Wolterstorff not see speech as an issue of communication, but he also does not see it as primarily a means of expression.[17] Instead,

---

of the judicial system and a priest can only declare "husband and wife" in the context of the institution of marriage.

15. Ward, *Word and Supplement*, 98.

16. Wolterstorff, *Divine Discourse*, 93.

17. Wolterstorff writes, "The essence of discourse lies not in the relation of *expression* holding between inner life and outer signs, but in the relation of *counting as* holding between a generating act performed in a certain situation, and the speech act

speech brings about the normative ascription of a normative stance. In this, a speaker is not expressing their "inner self," but instituting and making public a particular type of relationship. The relationship is one where he and those to whom he speaks has the obligations and rights corresponding to his illocutionary act. Thus, to interpret is to attempt to discern what illocutionary action someone is performing, along with the noematic or designative content[18] necessary to know what the illocutionary act is doing. For example, one needs to know that another is giving a command and also what is being commanded. In this way, Wolterstorff believes that, in theory, interpretation can be separated from the intention of the speaker. He is willing, however, to recognize the possibility that there are instances where understanding a speech act will require one to understand the intention of the speaker. Yet, by seeing speaking as the production of an illocutionary act, Wolterstorff develops a normative theory of speech, whereby speech is primarily a way in which rights and obligations are gained and imposed.

CHARACTERIZATION OF DIVINE SPEECH

Wolterstorff's move towards understanding speech as the production of an illocutionary action provides him a natural throughway to divine speech. He holds that God can produce illocutiones and therefore literally speak.[19] In this way, he has certain similarities with Jüngel's predecessor. J. Muis notices, "*Weiter hat er mit Barth gemeinsam, daß er die Rede Gottes nicht als allgemeines Symbol auffaßt, sondern als ein wirkliches Reden, wobei er aber Reden nicht definiert als Sprechen oder Schreiben von Worten und Sätzen.*"[20] Though not agreeing as to the nature of speech,[21] both Barth and

generated *by* that act performed in that situation" (Wolterstorff, *Divine Discourse*, 183).

18. For his understanding of noematic and designative content of sentences, see Wolterstorff, *Divine Discourse*, 138–39. Noematic content is, for him, the closest concept to what analytic philosophers have traditionally understood as the propositional content of a sentence. The designative content, loosely speaking, would be close to the "reference" of the statement in the secondary sense that Gottlob Frege used *Bedeutung* (the primary being of proper nouns) (Frege, "Über Sinn und Bedeutung," 25–50). For discussion of the primary and secondary senses, see Haddock, "On Frege's Two Notions of Sense," 31–41.

19. Thus, Wolterstorff claims: "So does God discourse—literally so? Well, yes" (Wolterstorff, "Response," 300).

20. Muis, "Die Rede von Gott," 67.

21. Wolterstorff notices, "Furthermore, not all of those who confess that God speaks would grant that the Christian Bible is a medium of God's discourse; Karl Barth would not grant that. *Paulus dixit, non deus dixit*, says Barth" (Wolterstorff, *Divine Discourse*, 131).

Wolterstorff want to take seriously the idea that God actually speaks, without feeling compelled to defend any idea of him vocalizing or inscribing. Though seeing God as literally speaking, Wolterstorff admits that his speech must be "most unusual."[22] This has led Kevin Vanhoozer[23] and Westphal[24] to claim that his view of divine speech is both literal and analogical, owing to the ways in which it both converges upon and diverges from human speech.

In seeing God as capable of producing illocutionary acts, but not seeing illocutionary acts as capable of being basic actions, Wolterstorff is driven to understand God as speaking through human speech. In order to understand how this can be the case, he looks for analogous situations whereby one individual speaks through the speaking of another. He finds several possibilities, which can be placed on a scale as to the degree of divine superintendence. Wolterstorff believes that God could speak through an individual similarly to how a boss would speak though her secretary, whereby the words written by the secretary stand for the words of the boss. Moreover, he feels that God may speak through humans similarly to a politician speaking through a press secretary, whereby the latter knows the "mind"[25] of the former and therefore can speak for her even on matters where he has not been given explicit instruction. Wolterstorff does not discount these as being significant instances, especially in light of his discussion of authorization and deputization.[26] Yet, he is intrigued by the possibility of another analogous situation whereby the degree of superintendence is less and the mode of said superintendence includes greater distanciation. In the case of appropriation, God can take something that is spoken (or written) by another, regardless of that person's relationship to him, and use their words to act as his speech. It would be similar to one finding a quote by someone she does not know personally and using it to speak for herself. In this case, Wolterstorff would not think it was typical for divine speech to come through the words of someone with whom God has no relationship. Nevertheless, just the proposal of this possibility displays some important facets of his perspective. The appropriation model allows the issue of inspiration to be separable from divine speech, since God could, at least technically, use someone who has no activity of the Holy Spirit at work in them. In this way, Wolterstorff is similar to Barth. He is different from Barth, however, in that the appropriation model does not even require revelatory activity.

22. Wolterstorff, "Response," 300.

23. Vanhoozer, *Remythologizing Theology*, 211n118.

24. Westphal, "On Reading God the Author," 273.

25. Wolterstorff, *Divine Discourse*, 39.

26. Wolterstorff, *Divine Discourse*, 41–42.

Muis sums it up succinctly in writing, "*So kann man sagen, daß Gott in der Bibel spricht, und daß die Bibel Gottes Buch ist und Gott der Autor dieses Buches, ohne sich auf Inspiration oder Offenbarung zu berufen.*"[27] Though Wolterstorff does not believe that appropriation is the only way that God speaks through others, its possibility is enough to discount, in his mind, the necessity of connecting speech to inspiration and revelatory activity.

One last significant note concerning Wolterstorff's view of divine speech is related to his normative theory of discourse.[28] Since he believes that to speak is to take up a normative stance, this would imply that God, were he to be able to produce illocutionary actions as Wolterstorff suggests, must be capable of gaining and possessing rights and obligations. Thus, a theory of divine obligation appears to be significant to his view. Keith Yandell is probably overstating the case when he claims, "First, if divine command theory is false, then the author's account of divine discourse is false or vacuous."[29] It is possible that one could have another theory of divine obligation that is not a divine command metaethic. Yet, he is right that such a theory of obligation is necessary if Wolterstorff wants to retain both the idea that discourse is a normative activity and that God literally speaks.[30]

THE RELATIONSHIP BETWEEN HUMAN AND DIVINE SPEECH

Since God can use human speaking to be the vehicle of his discourse, he has an obviously close relationship between divine and human speech. Wolterstorff does not discount the possibility that God could himself produce vocalization,[31] but his emphasis is on the biblical text and, therefore, he

27. Muis, "*Die Rede von Gott*," 68.

28. Space prevents discussion of Wolterstorff's belief that his theory also likely requires that God can directly intervene in the world. He writes, "I think it is very likely, in the light of the preceding considerations, that the events generative of divine discourse cannot all be the consequence of God's implementation of a plan formed at creation—highly likely that many if not most of the purported episodes of divine discourse are the result of direct intervention on God's part" (Wolterstorff, *Divine Discourse*, 123). It is his view of this type of intervention that causes Wolterstorff to provide an apologetic against scientific criticisms of divine action.

29. Yandell, "Review of Divine Discourse," 146.

30. Wolterstorff is attracted to a divine command theory and how it relates to obligation, most likely the influence of Alston and his colleague at Yale, Robert Adams. See Adams, "Modified Divine Command Theory," 97–122; "Divine Command Metaethics Modified Again," 128–43.

31. Though he does, as was mentioned earlier, deal with the Maimonides objection, he never goes so far as to say that God could not produce a locutionary act. He only

focuses on how humans are involved. The relationship between divine and human speech, in terms of Scripture, is termed by Wolterstorff as "double agency discourse."[32] This idea is significant in that it discounts, to a large degree, the Bible being understood as God using arbitrary words and texts to say what He desires. He thinks it central to the Christian understanding that the Bible is viewed as a single book.[33] Implied in "double agency" is that the human author's free subjectivity is involved, such that their goal in speaking is significant to the way that the text is understood.

The manner in which Wolterstorff explains double agency discourse is primarily in terms of the *"degree and mode of superintendence"* [emphasis in original].[34] Yet, it appears more essential to his overall project of relating divine discourse to exegesis, to think of double agency in terms of how God's illocutionary act relates to the human speech act. For Wolterstorff, there are times where God uses a human locutionary action, independent of its illocutionary correlate, to perform his discourse. This would be the case where God appropriates speech whereby his illocutionary act could not match with the one of the appropriated text. In speaking of the analogy of an ambassador, Wolterstorff says:

> That is, it might sometimes be the case that the very same ut-
> terings count both as the performance of speech actions by the
> ambassador and as the performance of speech actions by his
> head of state; these might be the very same speech actions, or
> somewhat different.[35]

Wolterstorff believes that this case, which he terms transitive discourse,[36] is not typical, but admits that it likely occurs.[37] The more common case of divine discourse would be that in which the human's illocutionary action is the vehicle of the divine illocutionary action. In this case, the illocutionary acts coincide, whereby the human discourse is meant to be understood as God speaking. In the case of Scripture, this means that "God's discourse is a function not just of those human acts of inscription but of

---

hypothesizes as to what it would look like if God produced illocutiones through human discourse.

32. Wolterstorff, *Divine Discourse*, 38.

33. Wolterstorff, *Divine Discourse*, 295.

34. Wolterstorff, *Divine Discourse*, 41.

35. Wolterstorff, *Divine Discourse*, 45.

36. Wolterstorff, *Divine Discourse*, 213.

37. Wolterstorff's most pointed example is Psalm 137:9, which states, "Happy shall he be who takes your little ones and dashes them against the rock."

those human acts of discourse generated by those human acts of inscription" [emphasis in original].[38]

That Wolterstorff believes that Scripture is a case of divinely appropriated human discourse has many implications concerning exegetical methodology. Most significant is his belief that any attempts to discern the divine discourse inherent within the text requires one to first attempt to understand the appropriated speech act. Placing himself in square opposition to Ricoeur's text sense interpretation and Derrida's deconstructionism,[39] Wolterstorff wants to once again place the human author in a place of prominence when one is interpreting. Thus, he holds that the "appropriated discourse anchors everything,"[40] such that one's "first hermeneutic"[41] is to discern the propositional content and illocutionary act of the human act of discourse. He provides a brief explanation of how the first hermeneutic occurs, though he understands that he is in no way providing a book on hermeneutics. Wolterstorff holds that if one has no sufficient reason[42] to the contrary, one should "take the noematic content of the discourse to be the meaning of the sentence."[43] If there is sufficient reason, then one should take that noematic content that is most likely what was intended to be used by the speaker. This move is important not only for Wolterstorff's development of a way to interpret divine discourse, but also because it manifests a particular theory of meaning. Unlike Wittgenstein, he sees the meaning of a sentence within the words of the sentence itself, and not in the usage of the words. This will cause his view of metaphoricity to diverge from Jüngel and that of Richard Swinburne, whose book *Revelation: From Metaphor to Analogy*[44] provides much material with which Wolterstorff interacts.

Based on the first hermeneutic is the second hermeneutic,[45] which is, for Wolterstorff, the attempt to move from the appropriated discourse to that of the appropriating discourse. His goal can be seen as an attempt to apply the common sense philosophy of Reid to the manner in which divine and human discourses are to be understood. Consequently, the principle by which the movement to divine speech is made is similar to

---

38. Wolterstorff, *Divine Discourse*, 186.

39. For a summary of the opposition, see Wolterstorff, *Divine Discourse*, 132–33.

40. Wolterstorff, *Divine Discourse*, 186.

41. Wolterstorff, *Divine Discourse*, 183–201.

42. The phrase "sufficient reason" is purposely ambiguous to allow the question of what these reasons may be to remain unaddressed. Wolterstorff does delve into them in some length, but scope prevents any sustained treatment.

43. Wolterstorff, *Divine Discourse*, 191.

44. Swinburne, *Revelation*.

45. Wolterstorff, *Divine Discourse*, 202–22.

that of the first hermeneutic. One should, in Wolterstorff's eyes, take the propositional content and illocutionary stance of the divine discourse to be the same as that for the human discourse, unless there is a sufficient reason otherwise.[46] He recognizes that this will require some "subtlety,"[47] as the immediate movement is not always possible. Sometimes the main point of what is being said by the human author is appropriated, without the manner in which the main point is made being appropriated.[48] At other times, such appropriation will be impossible, such that the transitive discourse will require a completely different illocutionary stance. It might be argued that Wolterstorff does not give sufficient clarity in this progress between the first and second hermeneutic. Yet, he should be defended on this front since the hypothetical nature of his work is not meant to spell out all eventualities of his theory, but to provide the foundation of how one could conceive of the exegetical project. He is, for the sake of brevity, leaving the working out of his perspective to other philosophers.[49] His modest purpose is to show that there is a practical way to move from the speech of the human authors of Scripture to what God is saying through that mediation.

CHARACTERIZATION OF DIVINE REVELATION

Divine revelation is interesting, in Wolterstorff, in that unlike Farrer and especially Jüngel, it possesses nearly no structural significance to his theory of divine discourse. In fact, he laments how large of a role it has enjoyed in Western theology, since it has prevented, in his view, a clear examination of God's speech.[50] For this reason, Wolterstorff spends the better part of his material addressing revelation in showing why it is different from divine discourse and why it is not strictly necessary in the interpretation of Scripture. His discussion begins with an analytic of the term "revelation," where he recognizes some of the typical distinctions and correlates. He points out that revelation requires a sense of hiddenness and converges upon a continental understanding of revelation in emphasizing its foundation on the "hidden self."[51] Wolterstorff goes on to make distinctions between agent and

---

46. Wolterstorff, *Divine Discourse*, 204.

47. Wolterstorff, *Divine Discourse*, 53.

48. Wolterstorff, *Divine Discourse*, 209.

49. It is, perhaps, this hypothetical nature that has caused *Divine Discourse* to be such a highly discussed book in analytic philosophy of religion.

50. Wolterstorff, *Divine Discourse*, 36.

51. Wolterstorff, *Divine Discourse*, 24.

non-agent[52] revelation. In agent self-revelation, he proceeds to distinguish between manifesting and propositional relationship. The former occurs through a natural sign and may or may not be intended by the agent. The latter occurs intentionally, through words, and is termed by Wolterstorff as propositional revelation. It is noteworthy that Wolterstorff recognizes that words are different from natural signs in that they do not require the same type of interpretation. He suggests that:

> Though interpretation is typically involved in the reception of propositional revelation as well as in the reception of manifesting revelation, there's less of it. The revealer has already interpreted the actuality revealed, by way of formulating the proposition; now all we have to do is interpret what he does as the assertion of that proposition. In manifestation, everything needs interpreting, both sign and signified; we are, as it were, confronted with reality raw. . . . We can't, so as to get at the manifested fact, take the revealer's interpretation lodged in the proposition which he knows; we're on our own.[53]

Thus, for Wolterstorff, words allow for the interpretation of one's self for others, such that if they understand the words, they know something about the person who uttered them. In this way, it is not too different from some of the understandings of language found in the continental tradition.[54] What is also significant, in understanding Wolterstorff's view, is that he consciously and purposely sets aside the case of an individual revealing themselves directly, or what might be termed personal revelation. What he is concerned with is the revelation of an "aspect or item of knowledge of the agent."[55] Thus, for him, the propositional revelation, with which he is concerned, is *"knowledge-transmitting* revelation."[56] It is this difference in what aspect of revelation upon which to focus, that sets the stage for some of the disagreements which he will have with Jüngel and Farrer.

---

52. This appears to be close to the semiotic relationship between natural events.

53. Wolterstorff, *Divine Discourse*, 29.

54. The movement from God's self-understanding, as in earlier models of the Trinity, to God's self-interpretation can especially be seen in Barth and the hermeneutical theologians. Jüngel would be in the nexus of these traditions.

55. Wolterstorff, *Divine Discourse*, 23.

56. Wolterstorff, *Divine Discourse*, 29.

SUMMARY OF WOLTERSTORFF'S VIEW OF DIVINE SPEECH AND REVELATION

With Wolterstorff's understanding of revelation in mind, the manner in which he distinguishes between divine speech and revelation becomes clear. In emphasizing propositional revelation, he is necessarily concerned with revelation that is transitive.[57] Yet, as he makes apparent, he believes speech to be intransitive in that one's success in producing an illocutionary action does not rely upon the listener. This is different from revelation in that it would be unusual to say that revelation occurred even if nobody was aware of it. Consequently, Wolterstorff believes that one can use speech acts to reveal, especially in the case of assertorials, and that speech acts may have some revelatory facet of them, but they are not revelation themselves.[58] Since revelation is not divine speech, and the latter is what is of concern in Scripture, then Wolterstorff believes that revelation, though possibly important in other ways, is not essential to a theory of divine discourse or its interpretation.

BENEFITS OF WOLTERSTORFF'S POSITION

A Well-Defined Theory

What might be considered to be a detriment to Wolterstorff's theory, may be one of his greatest strengths. It may be objected that he does not give attention to one of the most significant aspects of divine speech in that he does not address Jesus Christ as the Word of God. Yet, Wolterstorff's theory is both provisional and, by his own admission, non-comprehensive. He knows that his theory will require supplement. Thus, he claims:

> What's true is this: I have not, in this book, focused attention on that mode of divine discourse which Christians regard as central; I have not focused on God's speaking in Jesus Christ. It would, on another occasion, be eminently appropriate to do that.[59]

57. Wolterstorff does take up the issue of "intransitive revelation," but comes to the same conclusion in noting that it is not divine speech. See Wolterstorff, *Divine Discourse*, 34.

58. Wolterstorff, *Divine Discourse*, 19.

59. Wolterstorff, *Divine Discourse*, 296.

The limited nature of Wolterstorff's endeavor means that he is not attempting to provide an overarching theory that can cover all instances of divine discourse. Instead, he is attempting to understand how one could conceive of the Christian scriptural tradition as an instance of God speaking. Whether he keeps to this limited task, is up for debate, since he does attempt to give an ontology of speech. However, he recognizes the significance of the Neo-Orthodox attention on the incarnation, without feeling compelled to move beyond the text.

By restricting his focus to a particular species of divine discourse, Wolterstorff is able to set forth a well-defined theory that is not thwarted by grandeur. Whereas Dalferth criticizes Jüngel for providing a perspective where "metaphor abound[s] and dominates conceptual reconstruction,"[60] Wolterstorff is able to bring speech act theory into profitably clear conversation with theology and scriptural interpretation. In doing so, he begins to make sense of the normative aspects of speech that had hitherto remain unexamined. Moreover, he uses speech act theory as a corrective to previous theories which overemphasize historical studies or intentionality, without completely dismissing them as insignificant in the interpretation a text. He realizes that there are times that a defined designative content may be helpful in understanding the noematic content of an illocutionary action. Thus, historical studies may be significant in knowing what the author is saying.[61] Moreover, though interpretation focuses on what is said, he recognizes that "saying is an intentional action."[62] While many theories in the twentieth-century relegated intentionality to a historical footnote on modern Romanticism, Wolterstorff retains a place for it while resisting the difficulties posited by extreme forms of authorial intention found in those following in Schleiermacher's tradition. In his defense of propositionalization, the relevancy of historical studies, and recognition of intentionality, he proves a formidable ally to Evangelicalism.

Wolterstorff's unwillingness to take extreme positions also helps him to moderate previous reactionary movements. As the twentieth-century saw multiple attempts to move away from intentionality, there was a correlated move away from thinking that one could interpret the speech of another so as to discern their thoughts. The recognition of the previously neglected fact that understanding the psyche of another individual is highly problematic, led to questioning the extent to which the thinking of an individual could be represented in the thinking of another. Wolterstorff, though not

---

60. Dalferth, "Mystery," 95.

61. Wolterstorff, *Divine Discourse*, 200.

62. Wolterstorff, *Divine Discourse*, 199.

dismissive of the postmodern criticisms of previous interpretive methodologies, believes that the pronouncement of the death of "transference" has
been premature. He believes that noematic content is indeed "transferable"
from "one mind, to another."[63] This will be significant as the different theories are brought into conversation, since Jüngel will require something like
transference if God's self-interpretation can become the basis for another's
understanding of divine being.

Practical Advantages

Any attempt to conceptualize divine speech and revelation from a Christian perspective is complicated by the acknowledgment that Christianity is
not primarily a theoretical endeavor. For Wolterstorff, Jüngel, and Farrer,
the Christian life is a lived life. So important is this idea to Wolterstorff,
that in a conference address to academic theologians, he regrets that "the
second-class status of those who work in so-called practical theology, is
but the manifestation of a pattern that runs deep and wide in the academy
generally."[64] Thus, practicality is of consequence to any theory from the
Christian tradition. It is this idea that provides two important constraints to
a perspective on speech and revelation that seeks to be feasible.

First, if a perspective on divine speech as it relates to exegesis does not
even have the possibility of providing a hermeneutic that can guide a lay-
person, then one must question its viability. Perhaps, even further than this,
there must be significant ways in which a Christian should be able to gain
the necessary aspects of the Christian faith from the text without recourse
to a complex theory. If such a theory was necessary, then most individuals
would be forced to rely upon scholars or have little capacity to gain from the
Scriptures. Though there are some sections of Christendom that would not
have a problem with this, Wolterstorff's brand of Calvinism, along with his
pietism, would not tolerate an academic mediator between the believer and
the text.[65] Thus, it is consistent with his theological perspective that he provides a view of human and divine speech that has, at least at the prima facie
level, a simple movement from interpreting the text to understanding what

63. Wolterstorff, *Divine Discourse*, 155.

64. Wolterstorff, "To Theologians," 88.

65. Catholicism would be more willing for this mediatorial role, in light of their
understanding of the work of the priesthood. Though the debate on sacerdotalism is
beyond the scope of the paper, it should be admitted that the Protestant reaction to
the Catholic priesthood can be an untenable belief that study is unnecessary to have a
deeper understanding of scriptural texts or that there is little communal aspect to such
study.

God is saying. To a large degree, if one is a competent language user, then interpretation of the text should be somewhat natural. Wolterstorff remarks that "the ordinary reader can get the drift of many passages of Scripture without much in the way of additional help from scholars."[66] Moreover, if God often, as Wolterstorff suggests, uses the illocutionary stance and noematic content of the human writer, to perform his speech act, then there is little effort to move from the text to divine discourse. In this way, his perspective is parallel to Evangelical hermeneutics, which is why many in the latter camp had sought to appropriate his work towards the end of the twentieth century.

Second, if *praxis* is significant to a theory, then there should be some historical continuity between one's perspective and how Christians have thought and practiced in the past. If a theory has no connection in this way, then one would have to argue that past believers were unable to understand the text in a manner significant to their practice. Thus, if the practicality of the faith is of importance, one's view should have some historical predecessor. Wolterstorff, though offering much innovation, clearly attempts to draw the relationship from his perspective to previously held hermeneutical methodologies. Wolterstorff has strong historical precedence, in that the early disputes between the Alexandrian and Antiochian schools of interpretation began at the same point; in the literary/literal[67] understanding of the text as produced by the author. He claims, likely correctly, that early in the Christian faith, "there was near-consensus around the conviction that when it comes to interpreting the Gospels as a whole, priority must be given to what Frei called the "*sensus literalis*" of the text."[68] Whether one agrees with Wolterstorff's hermeneutical perspective, does not detract from the fact that he has a theory that is practicable, and therefore cannot be dismissed like those theories which are impeded by their own complexity.

One last practical advantage to Wolterstorff's theory deserves mention. Though there is still constant debate as to the extent that critical theories are important in understanding Scripture, there appears to be less debate that a considerable outcome of focus on such theories has been a reduction in study of the text as it is found in its initial form within the church.

66. Wolterstorff, *Divine Discourse*, 188.

67. Though it is admitted that the term "literal" is complicated in that it comes in degrees and has certain difficulties if one recognizes the semiotic nature of all language, it is useful to demarcate certain positions from those that place heavier emphasis on metaphorical, analogical, and spiritual interpretations.

68. Wolterstorff, *Divine Discourse*, 218. Though the Alexandrian school, as typified in the work of Augustine, did believe in other types of interpretation, those other types were founded on the *sensus literalis*.

Historical critical theories have questioned the canonical form, while literary critical theories have often focused on previous forms of the text. In
doing so, the significance of the text itself can be lost. Wolterstorff sees a
trend in recent biblical scholarship in that many different movements are
beginning to "converge around the text."[69] In fact, he sees this as one of the
central commonalities between his work and that of Barth[70] and is, indeed, a
characteristic he shares with Evangelicalism. Wolterstorff, along with Barth,
does not completely dismiss critical approaches, but limits their usage in a
manner that allows for one to attend to the text itself. Furthermore, his view
of how speech can clarify manifestational revelation makes Scripture significant in its textuality. Evangelicalism, admittedly, is much more reluctant
to use historical critical methodologies, since they hold that a verbal plenary
inspiration would not allow the text to assert anything which is not true.[71]
However, it should be noted, that Evangelicals are open to a use of certain
aspects of historical criticism, especially as it relates to the compositional
structure of the Old Testament text.[72] In any case, there is a shared interest
between Wolterstorff and Evangelicalism in preventing Scripture from being treated as solely a human production, with the attendant ramifications.

Diversifying Speech

Any theoretical endeavor is reductive by nature, but such reduction is always
in danger of the type of oversimplification that is distorting. Wolterstorff,
consequently, wants to keep the diversity inherent in speech that prevents
such reduction. Thus, he seeks the possibility of propositionalizing the text,
while allowing the use of the actual locutiones to take many different forms.
In this way, there is simplification in that a text can be investigated to determine its noematic content, but a hedge against over-reduction since the
illocutionary stance towards that content will be diverse. This is significant

69. Wolterstorff, *Divine Discourse*, 16.

70. Wolterstorff, *Divine Discourse*, 68–69.

71. In this work, the notion of truth that is understood within Evangelicalism is
left undeveloped, since limited space would not do justice to the topic. It will suffice for
the purpose of the present argument to note that historical critics, while varying in the
degree they apply their mode of analysis, will typically be willing to claim that Scripture
contains historical inaccuracies, biases, and claims that God would not intend.

72. An example of this would be the work of John Sailhamer, who receives a mediated Wittgensteinianism from Hans Frei, such that he emphasizes the text as it stands
in relation to his community. However, in analyzing the text, he uses compositional
strategies that first found their home in higher criticism. See Sailhamer, *Meaning of the
Pentateuch*.

since the multifarious nature of speech appears important to the manner in which Scripture describes and testifies to God. Wolterstorff's resistance to over-simplification, can also be seen in a few strategies beyond his emphasis on the multitude of illocutiones. He, like Jüngel and Farrer, does not see divine speech and revelation as the same phenomenon. Moreover, Wolterstorff wants to retain the diversity in divine discourse itself. Though some may argue that he is not always accurate as to Barth's argumentation, he resists both Jüngel's predecessor and Ricoeur because of how he perceives their failure to understand the multiple modes of divine discourse.[73] Whether or not his line of reasoning is convincing is less important than his tendency to oppose conflating different areas of divine speech. His view has the advantage of letting speech be difficult and diverse, rather than simplifying speech in a manner that causes it to be a phantom of how it is in actual usage. Speech can be propositionalized, but usage of said propositions is various.

A vital outcome of Wolterstorff's practice is his retreat from a focus on assertorial speech that has been the hallmark of Protestant systematic theology. Westphal characterizes his work as a "decentering of the theoretical, the indicative, the constative: assertion is no longer the privileged speech act. Language is much more diverse than merely telling others what we believe to be the case."[74] In this way, Wolterstorff has a goal that is similar to that of Vanhoozer,[75] though with a somewhat different understanding of the nature of the scriptural text itself. This is not to say that assertion has no place in his work, as he admits that assertions are significant in that they can allow an individual to reveal something about themselves in a direct manner. Yet, if Ward is correct, the central speech act is actually declaration, since all other illocutionary actions perform in a declarative manner. Each speech act, then, will have a declarative element in that they will affect the world by providing the means for the conferral of rights and responsibilities. However, this declarative substructure does not prevent individuals from enacting this conferral in various ways through diverse illocutionary acts. In any case, his brand of activism prevents him from giving ascendency to theoretical matters, with the result that speech acts emphasize the normative and are able to address the diverse manners in which individuals attempt

---

73. Sailhamer, *Meaning of the Pentateuch*, 58–75.

74. Westphal, "Review Essay," 526.

75. See Vanhoozer, *Drama of Doctrine*, 12–15. For a comparison of Woltesrtorff's and Vanhoozer's approaches, see Berry, "Speech-Act Theory," 81–100.

to live out their faith. Thus, the "activism"[76] that is central to the identity of Evangelicalism finds support in Wolterstorff's praxis-oriented perspective.

Wolterstorff's attempt to retain diversity in speech is also significant in that it forces him to place a premium on interpretation within his perspective. He recognizes that there are parallels in his work with that of Alston in *Perceiving God*. Wolterstorff uses similar methodology in investigating an empirically accessible phenomenon that is meant to be analogous to one that is not accessible. Furthermore, he relies substantially on doxastic practice, which was given significant voice in Alston's work. However, Alston's work does not pay attention to the centrality of interpretation, in that its focus is more on perceptive practice than on the interpretation of purported religious experience.[77] Wolterstorff, in recognizing the diverse nature of speech, requires interpretive practice to be significant in the act of speaking and hearing.

Privileging Religious Belief

Modernity, with its confidence in human reason, led to a strong questioning of the legitimacy, epistemically and otherwise, of religious belief. Moreover, it brought the conviction that correct methodology coupled with neutrality and objectivity could lead to knowledge of a high degree of (if not perfect) certitude. In the twentieth century, reactions to such a perspective were both fierce and diverse. Wolterstorff clearly questioned the legitimacy of a view of epistemology that would make religious belief dubious or of lesser significance to one's knowledge. Thus, Westphal, correctly, places him among postmodern philosophers in this regard.[78] Wolterstorff's impetus for this, though, is probably less philosophical than theological. Reformed theologians, especially of the Calvinist tradition, have often questioned the possibility of neutrality. For Calvin, one is either for God or against him. Wolterstorff appears to be in fundamental agreement with this view, occasionally allowing arguments to end with a recognition that there is a clash of fundamentally different perspectives on the world, which argument may be ineffective in mediating.[79] This is a significant advantage to Wolterstorff's

---

76. Bebbington, "Evangelicalism," 10. It should be noted that the activism about which Bebbington writes is primarily applied to the motivation for proselytization of others, but such activism is actually broader in that Edwards's pietism extended beyond the sharing of the gospel.

77. In this way, Alston's understanding of immediate apprehension is distinct from that of Tillich.

78. Westphal, "Must Phenomenology," 711.

79. Two examples of this would be his recognition of difficulty of finding common

perspective in that he appears to defend the possibility of Scripture taking a central role in an individual's beliefs, without any supposed neutral reason passing infallible judgments on its legitimacy. In many ways, *Divine Discourse* is the natural product of the questioning of classical foundationalism found in his brand of Reformed epistemology, as well as his contemplations on the possible centrality of religious belief found in *Reason within the Bounds of Mere Religion*.[80] His epistemology is more open to different ways of knowing and seeking foundational beliefs, with the natural movement towards the possibility of a text, which is considered to be Scripture, providing these types of beliefs. In this way, Wolterstorff defends the historical perspective, to which Evangelicalism subscribes, concerning the importance of the Bible to the Christian way of life.

A CRITIQUE OF WOLTERSTORFF'S POSITION

Methodology and Metaphysics

Analytic methodologies are undoubtedly significant in the investigation of language, but there always must be conscious questioning of the limitations of such approaches. Thus, that Wolterstorff uses simplification, analogy, and focus on particular phenomena is not problematic, but rather whether these techniques will apply in the situation of divine discourse. The difficulty of reduction is a somewhat Wittgensteinian criticism related to the danger of linguistic atomism. Analytic philosophy has often used the pragmatic method of simplifying issues until it can be properly described by a theory. Thus, language is not always treated in conjunction with the web of beliefs and practices with which it is necessarily embedded. Wolterstorff, fortunately, does not make this mistake overtly, as he seeks a type of holism that does not simply tear linguistic usage from the customs and institutions to which it is related. Yet, the difficulty of religious language is that God appears to be an inherently unusual subject. Speech by God or about God does not appear to be normal language usage and thus seeking to use typical interpretive and analytic methodologies may not completely work. Wolterstorff attempts to remedy this by pointing to the historical Christian perspective that holds that God condescends to speak in human terms, thus potentially removing

---

ground or the ability to mediate a dispute between he and Rorty (see Wolterstorff, "Engagement with Rorty," 130) and between he and Derrida (see Wolterstorff, *Divine Discourse*, 164–65).

80. Wolterstorff, *Reason within the Bounds*.

the uniqueness of God from the picture. Whether he is successful or not, it still may be the case that such an analysis will be overly reductive.

Moreover, reliance on analogies only works if there is a requisite similarity between correspondents and there are no reasons that any dis-analogy between them is insurmountable. Some of the comparisons that Wolterstorff makes would require strong qualification or at least defense of their applicability. An example may be illuminating. When describing the appropriation of speech by an individual, Wolterstorff uses the illustration of someone who is authorized and deputized to speak for another, such as a White House press secretary. In doing so, however, there are certain exigencies that remain unexamined. If a press secretary were to say something incorrect, immoral, or embarrassing to the president, the administration could simply distance themselves from the speaker and portray her as someone who spoke without authorization. However, if the president had the ability to prevent such speech, then if that type of speech were to be uttered, the president would be seen as being at fault. Here is where the analogy breaks down. Presidents obviously cannot prevent such utterances, but God, at least from the Calvinist perspective, can. Thus, Wolterstorff's own theological position may require him to consider a model of divine speech that can deal with the disanalogies between human and divine appropriation. One possibility would be to include an understanding of inspiration, but Wolterstorff is reluctant to do this, since he believes the appropriation model is sufficient to answer questions of God's relation to the human illocutionary action. Consequently, he must defend how these analogies can hold regardless of the unusual nature of God and the complications that occur with understanding God as speaking.

Any investigation of particular phenomena will be largely determined by what is the object of study. Heidegger recognized that circumscribing a domain of investigation will affect how one understands a science. More than this, the ability of the science to deal with cases that do not fit well in its domain is indicative of its maturity.[81] Similarly, Wolterstorff's decision to deal with normal language, though not an uncommon practice, must reckon with language that is unusual. Also, he must defend his decision to limit himself to his domain of phenomena. In many ways, Jüngel's work can be understood as a phenomenology of speech when one primarily uses divine speech as the object of study. Whereas his movement is from divine speech to human speech, Wolterstorff is the other way around. At the very least, it would appear that his perspective would be strengthened if he could

---

81. Heidegger, *Being and Time*, 9–10.

show that despite the unusual nature of God speaking in human words, it is still a phenomenon that falls correctly under his domain of study.

Another area of concern with Wolterstorff's position has to do with his relationship with metaphysics. In dealing with what he perceives to be opposing views in Ricoeur and Derrida,[82] Wolterstorff defends, implicitly and explicitly, the significance of a metaphysical position in certain areas. Why he would do so is unclear within *Divine Discourse*, but becomes more perspicuous when his broader concerns are represented. His recognition of the significance of public discourse[83] and engagement with other philosophers[84] makes the possibility of commonality in discussion of central importance to him. Wolterstorff does not subscribe to the type of objectivism found in early Enlightenment era thinking, believing that one can take a position of neutrality. He claims that the common ground for discussion between individuals will often differ. He asserts, "The truth is that, for any pair of believer and unbeliever, there will be shared justified beliefs; but the particular beliefs shared will differ from pair to pair."[85] Wolterstorff recognizes, then, that discussion will seek for common ground, but the common ground will not always be the same. Thus, for him, metaphysics appears to be the principle of unity that allows for discussion between individuals who do not agree. This is likely why his inability to find metaphysical parity with other individuals, such as Derrida and Rorty, often leads to a reluctant recognition that such a different perspective on life and the world prevents not just agreement, but possibly even the possibility of agreement. His specific perspective on metaphysics, as well as its employment, may be understood by some as deficiencies in his program. The Evangelical, however, will agree that a significant portion of his metaphysical perspective has merit, even if it were to be incomplete.

Wolterstorff's Depiction of Human Speech

If one surveys the literature of reactions to Wolterstorff's views concerning divine discourse, one realizes that he is provocative for a multitude of reasons. He unapologetically subscribes to a particular view of meaning, which will not dovetail well with continental philosophy. His understanding

82. Westphal argues that Derrida and Ricoeur are not nearly the antagonists that Wolterstorff supposes they are (Westphal, "On Reading God," 280–9). He has a point with Ricoeur, but does not have nearly as strong of an argument concerning Derrida.

83. See Audi and Wolterstorff, *Religion in the Public Square*.

84. Wolterstorff, "Engagement with Rorty," 129–39.

85. Wolterstorff, "Is Reason Enough?," 24.

of interpretation defies many of the prevailing views in contemporary philosophy. Yet, to delve into these areas would require another book. For the purpose of brevity, this critique of Wolterstorff's position on human speech will focus on instrumentality and normativity.

An analytic of language that focuses on normal usage will typically understand speech in terms of its instrumentality. Whether this practice is legitimate will depend on how one understands the relationship between semantics and metaphysics. Kripke appears to make a good argument that the phenomenological description of something may or may not provide what that thing actually is.[86] Phenomenological description may provide the grammar for proper use of a word (i.e., its semantics), but not what it is that the word is referring to (i.e., its metaphysics). When one deals with "speaking," describing its usage may not, in fact, provide one with the essence of speech. For Wolterstorff, understanding speech as a way of assuming a normative stance may only tell you how speech is used, but not what it is. What speech is may be closer tied to the teleology of speech, which means that understanding speech in a normative way may require a teleological perspective. This appears to be the reason why Wolterstorff, on multiple occasions, brings intentionality into the question of discourse.[87] Thus, while Wolterstorff's normative understanding of speech's usage is not incorrect, it is likely incomplete.

A normative theory is not sufficient to describe the ontology of human speech for other reasons. There are three specific areas where it would require supplementary justification. First, in the case of speaking in the absence of others, one would have to question whether normativity would do the work Wolterstorff requires. While he makes a convincing argument that one can speak without the success conditions relying upon the hearer, he does not show if it would make sense to speak of normative stances in a situation where this is no other person present. Second, that words are used in thinking requires some sort of explanation. Even if one were not to agree with Farrer that thinking is essentially an inner discourse, that language is used in thinking, where there are no other parties present, does not appear to be explainable in terms of speech and normativity. Third, invective speech appears to defy normativity. If one were to attempt to insult another, the clarifying of rights and obligations conferred becomes complicated. *Should* one be treated as making an insult, or *is* one treated as making an insult? And if one is treated as making an insult, is it because they should be? Normativity makes sense in social relationships, but it becomes less

---

86. Kripke, *Naming and Necessity.*

87. Wolterstorff, *Divine Discourse*, 195–96, 199.

clear in anti-social ones. In either case, a normative view of speech may be insufficient.

Divine Appropriation of Human Speech

Many of the points that Wolterstorff makes with the divine appropriation of human speech are well warranted. Though one may be skeptical as to the extent that such a model can explain the diversity of genres and purposes in biblical literature, he does make a strong case that a text could come about by God using human speech to perform his illocutionary actions. This is not to say that the appropriation model is without difficulty. Speech can be affected in its interpretation and its capacities based on the speaker. For example, children may not be able to perform certain types of speech acts, simply because the cognitive faculties necessary to competently produce locutiones that count as illocutionary acts may not be present. On the other side of the spectrum, even if God uses human speech to perform illocutionary acts, those acts may be radically different based on the divine speaker. Thus, Wolterstorff's claim that divine discourse is "most unusual,"[88] may be an understatement.

Another example may be elucidating. The influence of Searle on Wolterstorff's understanding of speech act theory is apparent in many ways. For that reason, when the latter diverges from the former, the peculiarity deserves attention. While Wolterstorff typically follows the taxonomic distinctions in illocutionary actions outlined by Searle, his work is curiously brief in its treatment of declaratives. It may be that declaratives shade into the other illocutionary actions as Ward says. Whatever the reason, the lack of treatment is fateful in that declaratives display the manner in which speech can change in its relationship to its speaker. Declaratives are unusual in that the "word to world" fit, as Searle puts it, is assured in the activity. In the case of human speech, declaratives typically, if not always, occur with some sort of institutional support.[89] A judge can declare, "not guilty" due to her position within the judicial system, while a pastor can declare, "husband and wife" due to his position within a religious system. However, it appears that God may produce a declarative with or without institutional support, in a manner sharply different from human speech. Humanity in its historical embeddedness and intellectual finitude, will be constrained to declarations such as appropriate to human institutions. God's declarations, however, can be, to some degree, intrinsically supported by the divine self. Whereas an

88. Wolterstorff, "Response," 300.
89. Searle, *Expression and Meaning*, 18–19.

institution can guarantee the word to world fit by binding individuals to a particular normative stance based on the declaration, God can guarantee word to world fit by divine action. The case of declaratives is made even more atypical when one looks at those declarations that have no institutional support and do not have any apparent normative stance. Perhaps the most unusual in the scriptural narrative is God's pronouncement, "Let there be light" (Genesis 1:3). When this is said, light comes to be, and the words and world correspond. Whether or not one believes in the veracity of the creation account in Genesis 1, it does bring up the possibility that God could declare something and instead of taking up a normative stance, he affects reality directly by such an illocutionary act. Thus, Wolterstorff's theory becomes highly unusual when one begins to take into account the character of God and the possibilities afforded to his speech.

Wolterstorff's Calvinistic understanding of God further problematizes his understanding of divine discourse. He believes locutiones are used in speech since illocutionary actions are not "candidates for basic actions."[90] Yet, one might surmise that for God, they could be such candidates. Wolterstorff already mentions the case of revelation posed by Locke, whereby God reveals something directly to an individual without anything like speech taking place.[91] Thus, it would not seem outside of his understanding of the divine that God could assert something without any locutionary act, human or otherwise. One might reply that even if God does not need human locutiones, perhaps he needs human illocutiones to perform his illocutionary actions. Yet, the same type of argument would appear to apply. Locutionary actions aside, it appears possible, at least form Wolterstorff's view, that God could issue a command without needing a human to perform a command which he appropriates. In essence, therefore, he seems to assume an instrumental view of speaking, but holds a theological position that would tend to deny speech's instrumentality in respect to God.

If one in Wolterstorff's position were to deny the necessity of God using human locutionary or illocutionary actions to perform his illocutiones, then it appears prudent to question why God would do so. A traditional answer is that it shows something about God, but this is a strategy that he is hesitant to use. Wolterstorff is clear in his denial of expressive theories of human speech, not because speech cannot express, but because speech can be used in ways that prevents expressivism from being the sole goal of said speech. The presence of "insincerity, deception, and inadvertence"[92] in

90. Wolterstorff, *Divine Discourse*, 86.

91. Wolterstorff, *Divine Discourse*, 27.

92. Wolterstorff, *Divine Discourse*, 76.

speaking prevents understanding it as simply a way of exteriorizing what is interior to a human psyche, soul, mind, etc. Intriguingly, Wolterstorff, does not give expressives a distinct place beside other speech acts, as many speech act theorists do.[93] However, he does believe, like Searle, that every speech act has an accompanying psychological or mental state that must be recognized by the addressee for the speech act to have its intended affect. In this way, every speech act will express something about the speaker. At the bare minimum it will display that which allows for the sincerity condition-als of the illocutionary act to be fulfilled. Thus, if one asserts, then they can be understood not only as making that assertion, but expressing their belief in what is asserted. If one performs a commissive, then one not only makes a promise, but also expresses their intention to perform a future action. It is in this expressive function that may give reason why God would use human speech to perform an illocutionary action. In human speech, the way that Wolterstorff construes it, one can perform an action and display something about oneself in the performance of that action. Thus, if an individual wants to both act and show oneself in activity, then speech appears to be a signifi-cant medium. Consequently, while Wolterstorff wants to downplay expres-sivism, there are cases in which the expressive elements appear to move to the forefront of what is occurring in the speech act, especially when the speech act is, for one reason or another, superfluous.

It should be noticed that this is a traditional way of understanding certain speech acts. The expressive nature of divine speech acts has a sig-nificant hermeneutical implication. If God foreknows or foreordains the failure of a perlocutionary action, both of which are possible from a Calvin-istic perspective,[94] there is some difficulty in interpreting why God would have spoken in the first place. For example, it must be questioned why God would give a command that He knows will not be obeyed or causes not to be obeyed. When God gives the command, through Moses, for the Pharaoh to let the Israelites go, but hardens his heart so he will not obey (Exod 10:20, 27; 11:10), the command seems to serve another purpose besides the acqui-sition of a normative stance, or at least the normative stance that is normally associated with a command. In the case of a speech where there is a failure to attain the success conditions of the perlocutionary part of the speech act, it appears that the expressive nature of that act is the best candidate for why God would have spoken. In the above example, it would mean that God

93. It is likely that Wolterstorff treats expressives as a unique subsection of as-sertives, which simply assert something about the inner state of the utterer.

94. This is a belief to which historical Evangelicalism is sympathetic, especially since the American variety is so heavily influenced by Edwards's brand of Calvinistic theology.

may give the command to Pharaoh not specifically to bring a reaction, but because of how the command expresses something about God. This would be similar to how the Law of God is often understood in the Old Testament within both Jewish and Christian contexts, where it not only provides rules and stipulations concerning personal and corporate conduct, but it also reveals something of the character of God. In other words, though the speech act does not produce the reaction that seems to be its point, it still expresses something about the divine. In this way, there may be times where the authorial discourse interpretation must be supplemented by a focus on divine expression, if not divine revelation.

Wolterstorff, discounts this possibility, arguing that such a "therapeutic" way of understanding speech, where one moves past the speaking to the character or mind of the speaker, is actually degrading.[95] He is, perhaps, correct in arguing that one should not be so quick to surpass what is being said, but probably not right in claiming that trying to know the speaker himself by his speech is offensive. In fact, it appears of necessity in many human relationships. Speaking does not occur in situations without context, but is developed within relationships that have histories. Without these relationships, the normative stance sought by Wolterstorff would be nearly meaningless. In the development and maintenance of relationships, which he would clearly see as important to the Christian tradition, one needs to seek insight into another's selfhood by speech. For example, a child asks his mother for chocolate cake for his birthday. The mother obliges the request, but will also take note of the fact that the child likes chocolate cake, so that she can produce it on other occasions for the pleasure of the child. To gain insight into an individual based on their speech is not unusual and may be a part of the continuity of a relationship over time. Thus, a relationship to God cannot be reduced to speech acts. Moreover, that which allows for the understanding and contextualizing of those speech acts is insight into God based on his speech. In this way, expression plays a significant role in speech, especially if the actions performed through speech could be performed otherwise.

SUMMARY OF ASSESSMENT

Wolterstorff provides a compelling understanding of speech act theory and its uses in attempting to investigate divine discourse. His identification of speech with the illocutionary acts provides the conceptual resources necessary to understand the ways in which individuals can speak for others.

95. Wolterstorff, "Response," 294.

Furthermore, his normative view of speech makes the necessary step beyond previous theories in attempting to delve into the ontology and purpose of speech. This allows him to develop a hermeneutical methodology that is both practicable by the competent language user, and refinable by the scholar. In doing so, he wisely shies away from any attempt to reduce Scripture to a list of assertions,[96] providing a theory that possesses the simplicity of propositionalization while preventing reductiveness through emphasis on the diverse illocutionary postures which a speaker can assume in relation to the noematic content of locutionary acts. In this way, he is able to emphasize a wider sphere than just the cognitive elements of scriptural interpretation, without neglecting those elements.

The difficulties with Wolterstorff's view derive from two areas. The first is the hypothetical nature of his endeavor. He never proposed to give a comprehensive theory of speech and revelation, which is why it has some conspicuous gaps. The second has to do with his lack of in-depth examination of how the being of God can affect speech. Understanding speech instrumentally will not work well within a Calvinistic theological framework, nor will discounting the expressivism inherent in speech. Thus, the unusual nature of God as speaker may require a supplement in the form of revelation for even the appropriation model to work.

---

96. How successful he is in moving away from this is up for some debate, since he appears often to see tropic language as reducible to propositions and illocutionary actions.

EBERHARD JÜNGEL

5

Jüngel's Influences and Methodology

EBERHARD JÜNGEL IS A scholar whose work is difficult for many reasons. Unlike Wolterstorff, whose analytic style focuses more on normal language usage in speech than traditional ways to address the issue, Jüngel's hermeneutical emphasis gives rise to a historical situatedness which makes it necessary to compare and contrast him with his predecessors. His work can be understood, to some degree, as an extension and transformation of the work of previous German theologians and philosophers, in a manner that both draws upon tradition as well as revises it to address issues he believes essential to the relevance of Christian theology. Moreover, his style of writing places strong demands on his reader, in that he assumes a broad knowledge of philosophical and theological work, as well as his own body of writing. He makes no apologies about swift argumentation, nor about leaving parts of his reasoning unsaid on the assumption that his intentions, being based on conversancy with previous thinkers, are clear.[1] Yet, in spite of the numerous obstacles[2] to understanding his thought, such a project is undoubtedly worthwhile, especially from a transdisciplinary perspective. His willingness to address both philosophical and theological concerns,[3] as well as his penetrating insight into the historical issues that are at stake in

---

1. In this way, he has certain similarities to scholastic theologians.

2. One difficulty that almost goes without being said, is the lack of translation of Jüngel's corpus. Consequently, there is a general lack of conversancy with his work, especially in comparison to that of Jürgen Moltmann or Wolfhart Pannenberg.

3. One of the starkest contrasts between Jüngel and Barth is the former's willingness to engage with philosophical discussions and use philosophical categories in explaining and analyzing theological subjects.

understanding God's speech, makes Jüngel a worthy partner in discussion with Evangelical theology.

JÜNGEL'S THEOLOGICAL FOUNDATIONS

German theology has, for 500 years, lived in the shadow of Martin Luther. Jüngel's work is no different. This is not to say that he slavishly follows his forerunner's thinking, nor is he free from other influences that are older.[4] Yet, his work shows marked differences from those who were influenced by the Swiss Reformation, such as Wolterstorff. Calvin's influence on Jüngel can be found, but it is somewhat attenuated by its mediation through Barth. Both Reformers converge and diverge and can, in some ways, be placed on a scale between Catholicism and the more extreme forms of Anabaptism. Luther and Calvin had certain similarities concerning the need for a Magistrate to be involved with ecclesial matters[5] and diverged in their relationship to the Sacraments. Yet, a particular theme comes together between them in the work of Jüngel. Luther's constant desire to preserve a strong distinction between God and humans merges strongly with Barth's Calvinist influenced focus on God as "totally other" (*totaliter aliter*), to provide a basis for Jüngel's constant goal to bridge the apparent gap between a transcendent Divinity and a world-bound humanity. Furthermore, both Reformers had an apparent reliance upon Duns Scotus,[6] whose decision against Aquinas concerning the nature of theology had fateful consequences for the subsequent development of theology on the continent. Whereas Aquinas held that theology was a theoretical science,[7] based on possessing God as content, Scotus saw it as a practical science,[8] owing to its praxis-oriented goal.

4. Though Luther has cast his shadow over Protestantism, Augustine has done so over all of Christendom. Thus, it is not difficult to see his fingerprints on Jüngel's theology.

5. The similarity between Luther and Calvin can be overemphasized in the use of the moniker "Magisterial Reformers" to cover both of them. This appears to be related to the perceived failure of Luther in the Peasant's War and Calvin in the immolation of Michael Servetus. However, the latter's role has probably been overstated, since there has been a failure to show that he had substantial influence on the civil authorities at the time of Servetus's death.

6. Luther's reliance on Scotus is explicit, but Calvin's is implicit. The connection between the scholastic theologian and his Swiss successor has never been founded upon historical evidence, but the conceptual parallel is uncanny. The likely connection is John Major, though nothing clear has been found in Calvin's writings making the association.

7. Aquinas, *Summa* 1.1.4:2–3.

8. Scotus, *Will and Morality*, 127–35.

In doing so, the lines were drawn between the former's focus on the intellect based on an Aristotelian understanding of the rational faculties, and the latter's concentration on divine voluntarism owing to Augustine's introduction of a concept of a will (*voluntas*).[9] Protestantism followed Scotus in focusing on God's will and, consequently, the question of the extent of his sovereign decision presented itself. Though not in perfect agreement as to how this question should be answered, or even approached, both Luther and Calvin agreed that God's will was independent of humanity to the degree that his hand could not be forced by his creation. It was for this reason that they agreed on a belief of election unto salvation.[10] Consequently Jüngel resumes this line of thinking, but is consumed with the question of how God's decision and, indeed, election can reference humans without them being foundational for divine ontology.

Luther's influence on Jüngel, though, exceeds that of Calvin in that his mediation of certain aspects of *via moderna* strongly affects the trajectory of Lutheran theology. Luther's time at Erfuhrt has been characterized variously, with historical theologians taking positions as extreme as it was determinative for his theological development to the idea that it was a passing phase to the Reformer.[11] Though he diverged with his teachers and predecessors at points, especially in his belief concerning their Pelagian tendencies, certain thematic elements can be discerned that continued to influence his theological thinking well into the Reformation. *Via moderna* cannot be simply understood as a reaction to *via antiqua*, since the ideas of Scotus appear to be fundamental to its overall progression. Of significance, was Scotus's reemphasis on the type of theological personalism that would take seriously God's activity in history. This is why Heiko Oberman goes so far as to claim, "This application of the covenantal God-who-acts to the whole realm of action in the world would become a characteristic tenet of the *via moderna*."[12] Scotus's version of realism, being incompatible with the type of nominalism found in Luther's fifteenth-century predecessors, caused his followers to find an unlikely alliance with Thomists. Though their unity was

9. Augustine appears to be one of the first, if not the first, theologian to possess a concept of a will that is a faculty of choice. Prior to this, will was more associated to an actual choice. Thus, the use of θέλημα ("will") in the New Testament appears to be more associated with a divine decision or plan of activity, but not for an intrinsic faculty. See Schrenk, θέλω, θέλημα, θέλησις, 52–59.

10. It is not at all clear whether they agree on the relationship of election to those who will be condemned.

11. For a summary of his time at Erfuhrt, see Brecht, *Martin Luther,* 33–58. For more on his relationship to Gabriel Biel and *via moderna* see Oberman, *Harvest.*

12. Oberman, "Luther and the Via Moderna," 655–56.

more founded on practical concerns than any other, the realism of the *via antiqua* still affected Luther to the degree that he was unwilling to break with the type of realist ontology underlying the two natures Christology of Chalcedonian confession. In this way, Jüngel's work can be seen, as an extension of *via moderna*, but without the strong concerns of Luther with retaining orthodox connections to early creedal theology.

Luther's relationship to the "modern way," with its focus on God's willful activity in history, is further influential on his development of *sola scriptura*, in that unlike many strains of Scholastic theology, he was reluctant to believe that substance metaphysics could rightly analyze God's being. For Luther, God's choice of how he will act in history meant that there was a certain inscrutability concerning who he was prior to his acts of revelation. Thus, Luther saw the hermeneutical locus for understanding God in his will and believed his will could only be understood through how he revealed himself in history. Scripture, as the manner in which God revealed his actions in Christ, then became the primary source for understanding God. In turn, this caused Luther to part ways with those who held to the *via moderna*, since he had a greater skepticism concerning the rational faculty's ability to discern the activity and being of God apart from its representation in the Bible. It is this view that coincides strongly with the Calvinistic tendency to question the ability to know God outside of Scripture, to produce, in Jüngel, a strong belief in the authority of Scripture for the life of Christians, both individually and corporately.

A last mediation of the *via moderna* by Luther, concerns the pietism that is at the heart of how the movement developed. It is without a doubt that the focus on the faculty of the will in the movement was significant, but it has been rightly noticed that it is not just choice or will that is influential to Luther, but the fifteenth-century focus on piety which was appropriated from the Franciscan tradition (especially in Bonaventure).[13] Luther's questioning of the limits of reason, combined with this pietism, gave him a praxis-oriented outlook to theology that finds echoes in Jüngel. As will be explained later, Jüngel's conception of the theological task is heavily determined by his belief that theology is to be to the service of the church and the Christian in their lived faith. In this way he is not unlike Schleiermacher, though filtered through his Lutheranism and resisting the offspring of liberalism. Jüngel agrees with Schleiermacher that theology is a science in its concern for practice and the training of the church.[14] Thus, as Luther sought

---

13. Hamm, *Frömmigkeitstheologie.*

14. For more on Jüngel's use of Schleiermacher in his theological methodology, see DeHart, "Eberhard Jüngel," 55–59.

for exegetical matters to be directed by the needs of the life of piety, Jüngel's theology is, likewise, influenced strongly by the desire to be historically appropriate and useful for the activity of a believer in the present.

Another major area of Luther's influence on Jüngel has to do with the crucicentrism found in both scholars. The centrality of the crucifixion of Christ to theology bears two particular fruit in the work of Luther, which then seeds the thinking of Jüngel. First, the Reformer believed that theology must reckon with the fact that God, in Christ, suffered upon the cross. Unwilling to follow the trend of Catholic theology in emphasizing God's impassibility, Luther conceived of a theology that he believed to make better sense of the hypostatic union as seen in orthodoxy.[15] Second, the Reformer gives the cross a strong place of hermeneutical significance within his theology. The defining theme that draws together the various areas of his systematic theological thinking is the death and resurrection of the Christ. Jüngel, similarly, conceives of theology as revolving around the cross and lets this theme affect his conception of God's being. However, it would be mistaken to lump him in, without distinction, with other theopaschite theologians. He has a lesser tendency to use "negation" talk to refer to the event of the cross and refuses to see the death of God as an irresolvable dialectic. In fact, he wants to see death as being a possibility inherent to God in his divinity.[16] Thus, he writes, "Passion and death are not a metaphysical piece of misfortune which overtook the Son of God who became man. God chose this 'fate.'"[17] Revealed in this quote is not just a use of divine passion, but Jüngel's reluctance to use a "metaphysical" understanding of God. For

15. This movement from a God that has great continuity with the pre-Socratic conception of divinity, to one that has a strong concentration on the work of the man Jesus upon the cross, causes Paul Allen to write, "It is, to put perhaps a bit crudely, a transition from an impersonal to a personal foundation of theological logic" (Allen, *Theological Method*, 123). This is not how Jüngel would conceive of it, since the whole idea of a trinitarian "person" is not, in his view, the best way to conceive of the differentiation in the Godhead. Yet, the idea of a movement where the centrality of the concrete person should define being is probably apropos.

16. For Jüngel's defense against the argument that "death of God" phraseology is not justified exegetically, see Jüngel, *God as the Mystery*, 218–22; *Gott als Geheimnis*, 297–301. Hereafter, "GT" will stand for the German translation.

17. Jüngel and Webster, *God's Being*, 102. For John Webster's summarization of Jüngel's position, see Jüngel and Webster, *God's Being*, xvii. It will be admitted that the interpretive difficulties of understanding Jüngel's position is similar to that of understanding Plato or Kierkegaard. He primarily presents the material as being a reflection of Barth's position, without explicitly providing his endorsement. However, a further reading of his corpus makes it clear that he often agrees with Barth, especially in the areas that *God's Being* addresses. Thus, it will be assumed that Jüngel's explanation of Barth typically includes his agreement, except where explicitly noted.

him, if God is to be conceived as one who can identify[18] with Jesus upon the cross and, consequently, as one who can suffer, then any philosophical perspective that argues for a type of impassibility that prevents such identification is theologically unsustainable. For Jüngel, God's being is not static, but a matter of chosen enactment. Thus, intrinsic to God's divinity is choice, and that choice being definitive of his being. Suffering, though difficult to reconcile with some of the metaphysical perspectives coming out of Greek philosophy, is consistent, from Jüngel's perspective, with a God who can choose to be who he is in a human capable of suffering.

Whereas Luther's association with Jüngel can be seen most acutely in a theology of the cross, Karl Barth's and Rudolf Bultmann's influence can be found in bringing Christological categories together with the question of how humans can speak about God. In fact, Jüngel conceived of his early theological project, in *Paulus und Jesus,* as a mediating between both scholars. He writes, "This book can be seen as a synthesis between New Testament exegesis and dogmatics, or between the thought of Rudolf Bultmann and Karl Barth. It is not a manufactured synthesis, but is based in the common reference to the same Word."[19] To speak about the Word of God, as necessitated by the call to proclamation, means that those within the church (i.e., Christians) must think about the theological foundations for speech about God. In doing so, both believe, in spite of their differences,[20] that there must be a foundation for God-talk in Christ, since he is the Word of God in flesh. Furthermore, both Barth and Bultmann affect the way that Jüngel conceives of the implications of this Christ-centered speech. In terms of Barth, he gains a propensity to use a type of event ontology when understanding the being of God. He does not want to identify God with his activity, since this would prevent the type of separation necessary to keep the Creator distinct from the creation. Thus, he writes, "God's being is not identified with becoming; rather, God's being is ontologically located."[21] Jüngel, when a question of God's being is investigated, proposes that Barth understood this in terms of "becoming," or God's incarnation in Christ. He will, later, move away from

18. It will be admitted that Jüngel's use of "identification" is ambiguous at best, which leads to the necessity of seeking conceptual clarity. This will be sought later in the next chapter.

19. Jüngel, *Paulus und Jesus,* v. Author's translation.

20. A few of the differences that affect Jüngel's overall theological work include differences on the role of historical criticism in theology, variations concerning the method and merits of theological exegesis, and conflicting emphases on those scriptural texts which should illumine the question of the Word of God.

21. Jüngel, *God's Being,* xxv. Furthermore, he writes, "'God's essence and work are not twofold but one.' Yet Barth makes a sharp distinction between the reality of God and the reality which owes its existence to God's work" (Jüngel, *God's Being,* 45).

this terminology to distinguish his own position, but the practice of looking at particular historical events to define the being of God is preserved. Similarly, Bultmann influences Jüngel to move towards an event orientation, by moving away from the "salvation history" perspectives common toward the beginning of the twentieth century, to explanations using the idea of a "salvation event."[22] This event terminology will be parsed out later, but it is mentioned to show the manner in which both of Jüngel's closest theological influences gravitated towards event understandings that becomes indicative of his theology of "coming."

In Barth and Bultmann, Jüngel finds the event orientation by which he will develop a theological ontology. In Gerhard Ebeling and Ernst Fuchs, he is provided with the type of event that would allow for a natural move between a theology of the cross to the being of God. Their hermeneutical style of theology is significant to Jüngel in many ways, a lack of space prohibiting the mention of all but a few. Their focus on the question and answer structure of theological inquiry, which is no doubt influenced by their reading of Heidegger, is significant to Jüngel even when he decided to part ways with the methodology.[23] The culturally situated activity of questioning is never far from Jüngel's focus, who both analyzes the lines of thinking that evolve into contemporary issues and possesses a keen sense of the significance of history to the overall project of understanding God's speech and revelation. Consequently, he claims that "the connection of systematic thinking and historical analysis should express the hermeneutical insight presupposed in this book that the perceiving and understanding reason is thoroughly historical in its depth structure."[24] Moreover, Jüngel gains from Ebeling and Fuchs a propensity to view the believer's entrance and continuance in the

22. For this movement, see Dalferth, "God and the Mystery of Words," 87. For a reiteration of this type of argumentation, see Jüngel, *God as the Mystery*, 189.

23. Jüngel writes: "The scandal which the word of the cross is for the wisdom of the world is not to be found in the fact that it is not reasonable enough. That explains why I regard the question-answer model in which man is asserted to be the question to which talk about God is supposed to answer as inappropriate" (Jüngel, *God as the Mystery*, xiv). It should be noted that the question-answer model that he is attacking appears to have more in common with Tillich's version than that of Fuchs and Ebeling. Yet, his skepticism towards the overall usefulness of the "question-answer model," appears also to be founded on the reluctance of seeing humans as the question to which God is the answer. Knowing how this could lead to anthropological considerations to be the presupposition of theological ones, a practice that gives rise to some of his tension with Bultmann, Jüngel wants to follow Barth in seeing God's "Yes" as preceding any act of questioning.

24. Jüngel, *God as the Mystery*, vii.

Christian form of life as being strongly connected to the power of the gospel to interrupt one's life and thinking.[25]

Yet, it must be recognized that the Ebeling and Fuchs's most significant influence on Jüngel comes in the form of mediating a Heideggerian philosophy of language and ontology that provides the main category through which he analyzes God's identification with Jesus of Nazareth. Heidegger, as in many other ways, had a considerable development in his understanding of speech from *Being and Time* to his later writings. His later work, *Unterwegs zur Sprache*,[26] was especially influential in providing a view of speech as being more substantively related to reality than had previously been admitted. Instead of seeing human speech as merely an attempt to refer to reality, Ebeling and Fuchs viewed it as providing for the manner in which reality could be. Human life is lived in the world, but only done so through language. Thus, though the world is not constructed,[27] one's interaction with the world as real must be mediated through speech. This leads Fuchs to develop the concept "speech event" (*Sprachereignis*)[28] and Ebeling to employ the idea of a "word event" (*Wortgeschehen*),[29] whereby language is not merely an instrument for making statements about reality, but the primary way in which humans can be drawn into reality. In many ways, reality is dependent on speech and not the other way around.[30] Based on this understanding, Jüngel employs the idea of a "speech event" to great effect in providing a Christological understanding of trinitarian being, an idea that will be explained in greater detail later.

Two important side notes based on Jüngel's inclination towards the centrality of speech to the question of reality must be given. First, his understanding of reality as *Wirklichkeit* will lead to an understanding of being in terms of *Sein*, whereby being is not a static essence or substrate for

25. A few examples of this proclivity would include his comparison of the word "God" to "invective" (*Schimpfwort* [Jüngel, *God as the Mystery*, 11]) and his use of "interruption" (*Unterbrechung, unterbrechen*) terminology (Jüngel, *God as the Mystery*, 165, 301).

26. Heidegger, *Unerwegs zur Sprache*.

27. In analyzing Fuchs's thought, Roland Spjuth writes, "At the same time, it needs to be noted that the ontological priority of language does not suggest that Fuchs claims that the world is a human construction. He speaks rather of language coming before the person, so that the address creates the space which makes human living possible" (Spjuth, "Redemption Without Actuality," 507).

28. Fuchs, *Marburger*, 243–5.

29. Ebeling, "Wort Gottes," 319–48.

30. This is what compels Spjuth to write, "From this ontological perspective, Fuchs then affirms the language-event (*Sprachereignis*) as the place where God acts to determine human reality" (Spjuth, "Redemption Without Actuality," 507).

predication, but is what it is in enactment. This, too, is a tribute to Jüngel's Barthian heritage in Barth's mediation of the Hegelian emphasis on action in ontology. Second, the fact that reality is determined by speech does not mean that he is a subjectivist, since he has a tendency not to form a strong theoretical connection between "reality" and "realism." For Jüngel, Christianity is realist at its core, since it believes that both Creator and creation possess an independence with reference to the individual. However, reality is something that is defined through speech, and thus possesses a dependence on speech. In this way, Jüngel combines a dynamic view of reality with an acutely realist bent.

The previous discussion displays the complex manner in which Jüngel is related to multiple theological traditions. His work should not be understood as an *ad hoc* combination of disparate perspectives, but as an attempt to draw together various views that seek to interact with the same thing, i.e., the Word of God. A full discussion of Jüngel's philosophical influences would be impossible and those that are of significance will be mentioned as they present themselves in an analysis of his thought.[31] What is important to note, however, is that Jüngel does have philosophical influences. Barth's cynicism concerning philosophy did not translate to a similar reluctance in his interpreter. It is true that much of the philosophical thinking that pervades Jüngel's work comes theologically mediated, as is especially the case of Hegel, Heidegger, and Kierkegaard. However, this does not blunt the fact that he was not only willing to engage with Athens, but he believed one had to.[32]

JÜNGEL'S PROJECT

As with Wolterstorff and Farrer, the diversity of subject matter found within Jüngel's scholarly writing often prevents any summarization of his overall project. However, as with them, certain themes are present when one limits themselves to work related solely to speech and revelation. From a historical

31. Philosophical influences include, but are not limited to: Kierkegaard's anti-rationalism, focus on personal piety, and reluctance to domesticate God; Hegel's anti-Enlightenment sentiments, strong correlation between God and history, attack on previous metaphysical systems, and reliance upon theopaschite themes; Nietzsche and Feuerbach's critiques of theism, propensity for existential analysis, and tendency to take lines of thinking to their logical end; Heidegger's understanding of ontology and language, concentration on possibility, and investigation of death and finite time.

32. Though Jüngel perceived Barth to be anti-metaphysical and anti-theistic (See Jüngel, *God's Being*, 99–103), he numerous times points to the usefulness of interacting with metaphysics as a Christian theologian. See also Jüngel, *God as the Mystery*, 49, 71.

perspective, Jüngel's work can be seen as an arbitration between Barth and Bultmann, whereby he uses insights of the latter in combination with a radicalization of the former. Whereas Barth appeared to be concerned, at times, to show how his position fell within previous Reformed orthodoxy, Jüngel appears to be much more willing to break with the previous tradition. Furthermore, his work employs hermeneutical terms and practices in the reframing of a Barthian "Word of God" theology. Thus, he is committed to recognizing existential concerns, as well as demonstrating the cultural expression of theological insights.[33]

Theologically, one can discern three significant themes in Jüngel's work on revelation and divine speech. First, he is staunchly committed to retaining the trinitarian nature of Christian theology. He sees the failure to do so as being to the detriment to the Christian faith in general, a concern he shares with Jürgen Moltmann[34] and Karl Rahner. Of this, Rahner writes:

> All of these considerations should not lead us to overlook the fact that, despite their orthodox confession of the Trinity, Christians are, in their practical life, almost mere "monotheists." We must be willing to admit that, should the doctrine of the Trinity have to be dropped as false, the major part of religious literature could well remain virtually unchanged.[35]

This biting criticism is one with which Jüngel wholeheartedly agrees, which is why he is consumed with a trinitarian reframing of traditional areas of systematic theology. For example, in Jüngel's mind, anthropology is not a doctrine of humanity *per se*, but a doctrine of the anthropological implications of the Trinity's work in salvation.[36] As will be seen later, this practice betrays a theological methodology that is only reluctantly phenomenological, and that only occasionally.

The similarity between Jüngel and Moltmann and Rahner does not end there, but leads to the second theme that guides his work. Jüngel believes the distinction between the "immanent" and "economic" Trinity to be an unfortunate error. He agrees with Rahner, whom he quotes, that "*The 'economic' Trinity is the 'immanent' Trinity and the 'immanent' Trinity is the*

---

33. Two notable examples would be his understanding of the debate between theism and atheism (Jüngel, *God as the Mystery*, 43–104) and his explanation of the significance of Hegel concerning the death of God (Jüngel, *God as the Mystery*, 63–99).

34. See Moltmann, *Trinity and the Kingdom*, 1–20. Intriguingly, Moltmann has criticized Jüngel for not consistently applying a trintarian hermeneutic.

35. Rahner, *Trinity*, 10.

36. See Jüngel, *Justification*.

'economic' Trinity."[37] Jüngel makes explicit that *Gottes Sein ist im Werden* is an attempt to explain Barth's unwillingness to separate these concepts.[38] This does not mean that he believes that the two cannot be distinguished, but that they cannot be placed in the type of irreconcilable opposition as they had traditionally been understood. Jüngel sees the economic Trinity as speaking to the concrete activities of God in this world, where the immanent Trinity is the summary of how those concrete activities reveal the being of God. Thus, the immanent Trinity is not an unknowable God behind the knowable activities of the economic Trinity. In contrast, the immanent Trinity is the God who shows himself in historical activity. Such a thematic element has many far-reaching implications for Jüngel's thought. It means that not only is God knowable in himself, but that he is knowable though his activity as interpreted in his speech. Thus, the idea that "God corresponds to himself"[39] will provide the necessary foundation for how He can move between the Word of God, to God himself. Such a move relates to the last thematic element in Jüngel's understanding of speech and revelation.

Third, since God corresponds to himself and he has identified with Jesus of Nazareth, Jüngel develops a theological ontology based on the cross. In contrast to Catholicism and much of Protestantism, he is willing to entertain and even defend the idea that God can be said to suffer and die in Christ. In this way, he may fall in the middle of the spectrum of those theologians of the Lutheran tradition that seek to understand the implications of the cross to divine ontology. He is not so extreme as to dwell on the death of God without trinitarian distinctions and without seeking resolution to the *aporia* contained therein, nor is he going to fully agree with Luther, who in spite of abandoning the impassibility that is characteristic of scholastic perspectives, was unwilling to allow the suffering of God in Christ to lead to the abandonment of immutability. For Jüngel, the significance of God's suffering is such that a failure to recognize this prevents the clear and concrete understanding of who God is, in that he is who he is at the cross. Thus, Jüngel's theopaschite theology relates strongly to his understanding of God's speech and revelation, in such a way that they mutually condition one another, with the outcome being that God is knowable through his speech, but only in such a way that is historically mediated and such that there are implications to the divine ontology. Only in this way can death on the cross

---

37. Rahner quoted in Jüngel, *God as the Mystery*, 370.

38. For an analysis of the dispute between Braun and Gollwitzer as understood by Jüngel, see Webster, *Eberhard Jüngel*, 17–18.

39. Jüngel, *God's Being*, 68.

have universal validity and applicability. Thus, Jüngel finds himself in agreement with Hegel when he claims,

> If the death of Christ, understood as the sacrificial death for our
> sins, should not soon "no longer be true," then the "Good Friday
> which was otherwise historical," the death of Christ, may not
> be understood as though it "did not affect the nature of God.[40]

Jüngel, thus, believes that God can be known, but only at the cross. Such a thematic element will radically affect the manner in which he construes divine speech.

Along with these three themes, a formal concern for Jüngel deserves attention. As a theologian, he believes he must be self-critical in his academic endeavors. This gives rise for a concern for criteria that can be used to assess the validity of a theological position. To do theology requires one to speak and think about God, one of whom it appears impossible to speak and think. Thus, one must responsibly speak about divinity and can do so only with the aid of norms for right speech. Such a view is significant in light of his considerable philosophical and theological backdrop. Jüngel was likely affected by Fuchs's concerns about theological methodology,[41] as well as the anti-instrumental understanding of theology as found in Kierkegaard and Barth.[42] He agreed with Aristotle[43] and Heidegger[44] that subject matter determines method, which is why God becomes the criterion for his own understanding. With the difficulty of knowing God comes the need to be self-critical. This is similar to how Christoph Schwöbel characterizes Barth's *Dogmatics*, writing:

> The systematic structure of the *Church Dogmatics* is the reso-
> lution of the dilemma posed in 1922: as theologians we must
> speak of God, but as human beings we cannot. The resolution
> of this dilemma lies not in a 'third option' that could somehow
> transcend the 'contradiction' between 'must' and 'cannot.' It is

---

40. Jüngel, *God as the Mystery*, 77. Jüngel is quoting excerpts from Hegel, *Lecture on the History of Philosophy*.

41. See Fuchs, *Was Ist Theologie?*

42. Kierkegaard and Barth both appeared to be anti-instrumental in their understanding of theology since both were anti-national in their view of the relationship between the church and the state. Kierkegaard was prompted by perceived complacency in his people, while Barth was compelled by the dangers of the church's role in World Wars. Thus, both came to view the use of theology for other ends as inherently antithetical to theology's role in one's understanding of God.

43. Aristotle, "Metaphysics," 984b.

44. Heidegger, *Being and Time*, 4–7.

to be found in God's free action and can only be expressed in
sentences about God's free action. The *Church Dogmatics* tries
to formulate these propositions, and tries and tries again in the
ever new attempt to start at the beginning.[45]

The difficulty, if not impossibility, of speaking about God means that one
must reflectively return to the start of theology and think it through "anew."[46]
Thus, Jüngel's explanation of Barth in *Gottes Sein* mirrors *Dogmatics* in not
being a systematic argument in tight logical progression. Instead he continues to think the same subject from different perspectives, which is why
Webster sees the themes presented therein as "parallel lines of inquiry."[47]
Consequently, the difficulty of bringing God to thought or speech means
both that God must be his own criterion for understanding and that theology must continue to critically appraise its own activity. Jüngel explains,
"The thought of a God who speaks out of himself does exclude the idea that
the thought which thinks God can be grounded independently of the God
who is to be thought."[48] As God is his own criterion, theology's legitimacy is
demarcated by its relationship to the cross of Christ[49] as attested to in Scripture. Thus, like Barth, Jüngel places strong emphasis on exegetical endeavors in theological method. He writes, "Third, the decision has already been
made in the approach of evangelical theology that this possibility which
guides thought in the task of thinking God as God is steered by the reality
of the biblical texts."[50] Jüngel, for this reason, emphasizes the significance of
Scripture to any attempt at doing theology.

45. Schwöbel, "Theology," 31.

46. Jüngel, *God as the Mystery*, 154; GT, 205.

47. Webster, *God's Being*, xiii.

48. Jüngel, *God as the Mystery*, 158.

49. Jüngel writes, "A theology which is responsive to the gospel, meaning a theology which is responsive to the crucified man Jesus as the true God, knows that it is
fundamentally different from something like philosophical theology in this one thing:
single-mindedly and unswervingly, based on its specific task, it attempts to think God
from the encounter with God, and thus to think thought anew (*neu denken*)" (Jüngel,
God as the Mystery, 154; GT, 205).

50. Jüngel, *God as the Mystery*, 155; GT, 205. See also Jüngel, *God as the Mystery*,
50. From a similar perspective, Muis writes, "*Barth hat aber durchaus Recht, wenn er
nach der Begründung jeder Rede von Gott fragt, und es erscheint mir richtig, diese zuerst
in der Schrift zu suchen, die bleibend gegenüber der Kirche steht*" (Muis, "Die Rede von
Gott," 61).

JÜNGEL'S METHODOLOGY

As with many Christian scholars, Jüngel appears to be an academic caught between two worlds. However, without a doubt, he is a theologian caught between two dialectics. The first dialectical method can be seen in the Kierkegaardian influenced early work of Barth, especially *Der Römerbrief*. Barth was influenced in his dialectic by multiple factors. Similar to Kierkegaard, Barth was opposed to any development of a Christian understanding that could allow an individual believer to make no choice for God, or that would place no obligations on them. In many ways, his decision to focus on the paradoxical nature of faith, carrying similar themes to Luther (e.g., *simul justus et peccator*, freedom and bondage, life and death, etc.), was an attack on the non-committal type of theism that did not take seriously the trinitarian nature of God and manner in which the believer was meant to respond in faith. This is why Jüngel claims, "To the degree that German theology today criticizes theism, it is a theology in the school of "dialectical theology."[51] Thus, with his proclivity towards trinitarian concerns and its attendant conflict with theism, as well as his recognition of the *kerygmatic* necessity of being able to call individuals to faith, Jüngel had an attractive alternative, in Barth's work, to the overly anthropological and naturalistic theologies coming out of the nineteenth century. It becomes evident, within his discussion of Descartes, that the methodological concerns of early modernism were for him indicative of an unwillingness to let God guide inquiry concerning himself.[52] Thus, an alternative method that has a willingness to bear tension in order to allow God to be the criterion of his own understanding appeared preferable. Yet, Jüngel does not end up following the Kierkegaardian line, for the same reason that Barth moved as he evolved into a dogmatician. Though he is unafraid of paradox and, with his predecessor, emphasizes the need for mystery in Christian theology, Jüngel believes that there are times that resolution should be sought. Furthermore, he believes that inconsistency requires resolution.[53] Thus, he would likely agree with John Macquarrie, who stated, "Theology can bear paradox, but not inconsistency."[54]

51. Jüngel, *God as the Mystery*, 43.

52. Jüngel, *God as the Mystery*, 104–26.

53. Jüngel, commenting on Barth, writes, "Over against the assumption of such a dialectical transcendence of God, which must necessarily lead to paradoxical statements about God's being, God's being is to be thought of as free from all dialectic, as 'free event, free act, free life'" (Jüngel, *God's Being*, 79–80).

54. Macquarrie, *Scope of Demythologization*, 26.

The other dialectic that gave Jüngel pause when developing his own methodology was that of Hegel, whose thesis-antithesis-synthesis structure has been often emulated within theology. The Hegelian dialectic had three main draws, each of which would be significant to Jüngel. First, Hegel's method recognized the need for resolution of those dialectical elements that could no longer be seen as being held in tension, but were actually in conflict. Second, Hegelian dialectic made the promise of advancement, such that skeptical sentiments could be assuaged as greater understanding and clarity were possible. Third, if one were to set aside the idea of "absolute knowledge," Hegel's work possessed a type of provisional nature that would complement Jüngel's desire for theology to be more reflective and self-critical.[55] Yet, with all the lure of the Hegelian approach for Jüngel, he is disinclined toward any dialectic perspective where the two individual elements are sublated into a third. For him, the most significant dialectic through which theology must work, is that between God and humans. This dialectic, for obvious reasons, resists synthesis. Jüngel realizes that Hegel's method tends to place the thesis and antithesis on similar ontological footing, which is why he does not agree with his analysis of becoming as the synthesis between being and non-being. Similar to the Augustinian tradition that sees evil as being parasitic on goodness,[56] Jüngel does not want to afford non-being ontological priority along with being.[57] Concerning this he writes, "The becoming in which God's being remains is no μέσον [mean] between non-being and being, participating in both. Rather, God's being in becoming excludes non-being as that which is not willed by God."[58] Thus, resolution must have correct correlates and proceed in such a way that the ontological differentiation between each is retained. Jüngel takes up a concern for consistency and progress from Hegel, without retaining the categorical destruction of the individuality of the elements contained in the thesis and antithesis.

The backdrop for Jüngel's revised dialectical methodology, then, takes dialectical form. On the one hand is the early Barthian concern for retaining the individuality of the elements of the dialectic, even at the cost

---

55. In fact, even if one were to keep Hegel's "absolute knowledge," one might be able to use an eschatological perspective making all historical knowledge provisional and thus retaining a Hegelian sense of both development and lack of historical consummation.

56. Augustine, *Enchiridion*, 11–30.

57. This move is also significant since it prevents Jüngel from falling prey to those objections which plague Heidegger's early work concerning the ontological status of non-being.

58. Jüngel, *God's Being*, 93.

of insuperable tension. On the other is the Hegelian desire for resolution and progress, even at the cost of individuality. Jüngel attempts to come to a method that is faithful to both concerns by providing a dialectical method of investigation that seeks resolution, not in a synthesis, but in a more careful analysis of the thesis. In doing so, Jüngel believes he can show that in spite of the individuality of the elements, the area of opposition is actually a false dialectic.[59] Such a methodology can be seen most clearly in two different applications. First, in Jüngel's analysis of being and becoming, he does not propose a third term, but seeks an analysis of being whereby it is not in opposition to becoming. He comes to the conclusion that, in the case of God, being is to be located in becoming, an idea that will be expounded later. Second, the dialectic of God and man is resolved by arguing that God possesses humanity. In both cases, an analytic of one of the dialectical elements allows for the resolution of the tension without combining them or leading to an "abolishing of every difference" (*einer jede Differenz aufhebenden*).[60]

Jüngel's revised dialectical methodology is, in itself, impractical without supplement. Since the resolution of the dialectic depends on the analysis of the terms in such a way that one can be reconciled to the other based on a careful inquiry into the nature of the other, the question of analysis arises. As was mentioned earlier, Jüngel sees the criterion for theological analysis in God himself, which gives rise to a method of inquiry that is strongly exegetical and Christocentric. His pursuit of a clear understanding and/or definition of the thesis follows the same path. It is illuminating to recognize that Jüngel sees his process of thinking as being in stark contrast to the *remoto deo* manner in which Wolfhart Pannenberg proceeds.[61] One could argue that there are actually strong similarities between his and Pannenberg's methods, but they are obscured by the fact that both scholars begin with opposite sides of the dialectic. It is perhaps similarity in certain substantive perspectives that induces Jüngel to say of his counterpart's practice that it is pursued with "impressive consequentiality."[62] In any case, his pursuit of resolution begins with theological inquiry.

Jüngel is not content to begin with a theological understanding of a thesis without moving towards its ramifications in terms of its antithesis. This relates to Jüngel's overall understanding of the theological task. For

59. Such a method is based on the idea that dialectical relationships are not necessarily absolute, in the sense that all of the aspects of both the thesis and antithesis are in tension.

60. Jüngel, *God as the Mystery*, 288; GT, 394.

61. For Jüngel's criticism of Pannenberg, see Jüngel, *God as the Mystery*, 17n6; GT, 19–20n6.

62. Jüngel, *God as the Mystery*, viii.

him, the theological task is a task of correspondence between the Word of God and human attempts to represent God's Word in human words. Thus, he writes:

> Die Theologie ist insofern weder das erste Wort (das bleibt immer Gottes Wort) noch das letzte Wort (das soll auf Erden der Glaube haben, um *es betend* an Gott zurückzugeben), sondern das Wort zwischen den Wörtern, das die Entsprechung zwischen Gottes Wort und Menschen-Wort wahrende Wort.[63]

The church's *kerygmatic* responsibility leads to the necessity of humans speaking about God to represent the Word of God. Yet, human attempts at doing so are fraught with many difficulties and dangers, which means that proclamations from humanity may not correspond to the Word in Christ such that it can become the Word of God to the believer in the response of faith. Thus, Jüngel sees theology as a science[64] with the task of thinking about human speech concerning the Word and making sure that there is preserved in the former the core that is necessary for the latter to come to the hearer when God bestows faith. Theology seeks to understand the human word about God to make sure that it can be the bearer of the Word of God. In order to do this, the theologian is tasked with understanding the Word, which is Christ, and can only do so from the Bible. Thus, he claims, "Wir werden zwar sagen müssen, daß das Wort Gottes in der Bibel und nur in der Bibel zu *suchen* ist."[65] It is for this reason that Jüngel calls the theological task, "consequent interpretation" (*konsequent Auslegung*).[66] It begins with the Bible, which is, from his view, human testimony concerning the speech event in Christ. Its goal is then to discern from this the Word of God, which becomes the measure of both human speech and activity.

Such a view requires both qualification and extension. The first qualification revolves around the reason why theology necessarily seeks to understand the dialectical task in such a way as to bring the thesis (i.e., God) to bear on the antithesis (i.e., humanity). The simple exegetical reason is that Jüngel believes that Scripture points to the significance of all human life being understood in terms of God, or *coram Deo*. Yet, the theological answer for him is more complicated. Jüngel believes that the legitimacy of the theological task relates to the ability of the theologian to meet those challenges brought against the Christian faith. It is these challenges that

63. Jüngel, "Die Freiheit," 16.

64. For Jüngel's argumentation concerning the inclusion of theology among the sciences, see DeHart, "Jüngel on the Structure of Theology," 51–55.

65. Jüngel, "Die Freiheit," 16.

66. Jüngel, "Die Freiheit," 19.

"provoke" (*herausfordern*) the response of theology and thus provides the boundaries for theology.[67] In the circumscription of those issues with which theology has to reckon, theology finds its essence. The two types of objections which Jüngel recognizes, are those in reference to subject/content (*Sache*) and those in reference to time (*Zeit*).[68] The latter of these, in short, leads to the claim that theology must speak to its time, since it is at the service of the church and concerned with the ability of the Word of God to speak today. In this way, Jüngel is not unlike Hegel, who claimed that "philosophy is *its own time comprehended in thoughts*."[69] Consequently, there is a necessary movement of theology in taking what it understands to be the Word found in the Bible and to give it dogmatic expression in relation to objections as to its *Sache* and to use it for contemporary analysis of human life in order to deal with objections as to its *Zeit*. In this way, the dialectical distinction is retained, while the antithesis is given proper understanding through its relationship to its thesis.

Jüngel's methodology mirrors that of Luther, whose understanding of law and grace allowed for the possibility for something to be philosophically analyzed, but is given treatment under theology when it is brought into relationship to God. Jüngel, for all intents and purposes, is taking Luther's relationship between philosophy and theology, as interpreted theologically in law and grace,[70] and giving it dialectical treatment through the hermeneutical category of the speech event.

Furthermore, the theological task, in its goal of seeking correspondence between human speech about God and the Word of God itself, has effects, in turn, on exegetical activities. The Bible is the human testimony concerning the Word of God and, thereby, contains both *kerygmatic* statements and theological ones. In the first instance, the authors of Scripture sought to proclaim the Word of God, in the second, they attempted to interpret the significance of the Word of God in light of the contemporary setting. For his reason, theologians must be open to the possibility that not all of the statements found in Scripture point to the Word of God, but some are human attempts at understanding it. Thus, the theologian may aid the exegete in the determination of what in the Biblical text is integral to its *kerygmatic* function and what can be determined to be the human theological reflection on the *kerygma*.

---

67. Jüngel, "Die Freiheit," 12.

68. Jüngel, "Die Freiheit," 12.

69. Hegel, *Philosophy of Right*, 21.

70. Dalferth, *Theology and Philosophy*, 76–88.

Since theology has practical functions for the church and Jüngel's theological methodology necessarily moves towards the explanation of the antithesis in terms of the thesis, he continually seeks to bring his understanding to bear on the phenomena of human life, especially speech. For example, in both his understanding of time and in his analysis of love, he does not merely provide a theological perspective, but continues on to deal with the human experience of each. In doing so, Jüngel shows a predilection towards evaluating normal language usage, not unlike the common practice in analytic philosophy. The justification for this procedure can be seen in the following quote:

> But if, conversely, our presupposition is correct, then the 'portion of truth' (*particula veri*) of that conclusion (which as such would be a wrong conclusion) could only be that a God who definitively discloses himself in one man and through this one man to all men ontologically defines with such an act of definitive self-disclosure the human existence of all people so that based on such a revelatory act anthropological phenomena in man would have to become understandable which are indebted to that divine act but which by no means have their reality only in relation to that act.[71]

Jüngel is opposed to any attempts at finding a general anthropological condition for the thinkability of God apart from inquiry into the being of God himself. However, even in opposition to this type of activity he attempts to see a modicum of truth. That modicum resides in his belief that "anthropological phenomena" should be based on, and therefore, be reconciled to the theological presupposition of said phenomena. Yet, those phenomena "by no means have their reality only in relation to that act," such that they possess the possibility of being investigated in a non-theological manner.[72]

The consequence of this perspective is that the theological explanation can be reconciled to phenomena that are distinctly human, but in being human, they can be investigated and understood in certain ways apart from God. Once again, his analysis of love helps elucidate how his method is practically applied. In understanding love, he performs a philosophical analysis of what love means when humans use the term and how it relates to God. He writes:

71. Jüngel, *God as the Mystery*, 155.

72. As will be mentioned later, part of Jüngel's difficulty will be that his theory may not make clear sense of the knowledge found in other fields. If there is a way to bring about a "Jüngelian" perspective on other scholarly pursuits, it may be found in this attempt to allow human phenomena to be pursued apart from theology.

> To think God as love is the task of theology. And in doing so, it must accomplish two things. It must, on the one hand, do justice to the essence of love, which as a predicate of God may not contradict what people experience as love. And on the other hand, it must do justice to the being of God which remains so distinctive from the event of human love that "God" does not become a superfluous word.[73]

Here we see that Jüngel is concerned with understanding love in a manner that both makes sense of the way the word describes a fundamental human "experience" and also one that is related to the "being of God" in such a way that God retains his significance to understanding human love even when he retains his distinction from humans.

In summary, Jüngel's dialectic methodology begins with a thesis which, theologically understood, contains a manner of reconciliation with its antithesis. Yet, that antithesis retains its identity in that it can be understood, in some ways, without reference to the thesis. However, that antithesis may gain new understanding and/or find its transcendental foundation in the thesis. In proceeding this way, Jüngel seeks to allow God to be God and humans to be human. With this in mind, an explanation of Jüngel's actual view of divine speech and revelation will be given in light of this methodology. Paul Dehart provides a succinct description of his goal in writing, "For Jüngel, even the most basic philosophical categories of being and existence must be radically reformulated under the decisive impact of the founding event of Christian faith and its historically mediated linguistic forms."[74]

---

73. Jüngel, *God as the Mystery*, 315.
74. DeHart, "Eberhard Jüngel," 54.

6

Jüngel's View of Divine Speech
and Revelation

CHARACTERIZATION OF DIVINE SPEECH

Jüngel's Understanding of Divine Speech

THAT WOLTERSTORFF AND JÜNGEL'S diverging methodologies lead to different conclusions concerning the nature of divine speech and revelation can be seen just from the order in which their material must be approached. Where the former begins with human speech and then moves on to divine speech and revelation, the latter begins with divine speech and moves toward revelation and human speech. Following his hermeneutical interpretation of Luther's methodology, he does believe that human speech can receive philosophic treatment, but that when it does, it receives theological interpretation by a preceding analysis of the Word. Jüngel's understanding of divine speech is difficult to delineate, for his previously mentioned penchant for assuming that his reader is conversant with all of the theological material[1] upon which he is drawing. Thus, the main category for dealing with divine speech, the "Word of God," is left undefined.

That the phrase "Word of God" is difficult to understand within Jüngel's work can be seen in the unwillingness of John Webster, who is probably his most well-known English language interpreter, to provide anything more than a functional understanding. Consistent with his attempt to

---

1. It is interesting to note that Jüngel is far less likely to make assumptions upon his readers' understandings in the area of philosophy, often producing extended explanations of philosophical ideas.

Christologically define theological ideas, Jüngel follows the classical tradition in seeing the Word of God as being primarily identified with Christ, but proceeds in a manner similar to Barth to draw the implications concerning divine ontology based on this fact. In Christ, one has God's self-interpretation, a self-interpretation that corresponds exactly with himself. This is why Jüngel claims that "God's Word is identical with God Himself,"[2] a sentiment that both he and Barth draw from the larger tradition. However, what separates his position from scholasticism and elements of the early church fathers is that this self-interpretation is solely by divine fiat and is not preceded by God's nature. Significant, though not unprecedented, within his position is the idea that the primary speaker is God himself, with other phenomena of speech being secondary modes. Unlike Wolterstorff, who gave ascendancy to human speaking as the paradigm for how speech is understood in general, Jüngel wants to emphasize God as the first speaker. In speaking, God interprets himself and thereby manifests his being. From this idea arises an exegetical difficulty that will be addressed later, which is the relationship of speech to the being of God. When Jüngel claims that "the being of the speaker expresses itself" ("*Im Wort äußert sich das Sein des Redenden*")[3] in speech, it would appear that he is claiming that God is and then speaks, with the speech being the superfluous act of expressing what his being is statically. However, his quick movement between the Word of God which is his self-interpretation and the word of God which is his manifestation to humans, gives rise to the need to differentiate between the primary act of God speaking and the secondary one. Thus, not unlike Barth's distinction between the Word of God as Christ and the Scripture that can become the word of God as it addresses the individual, Jüngel retains a similar distinction. As it will be argued, within Jüngel's thought the primary speech of God is actually constitutive of, if not influential upon, his being. He then conceives of God's speech to humans in terms of the manifestation, through a secondary event of speech, of the differentiation and unity wrought through the primary event.

The Word of God, therefore, is the primary event of speech that is to be identified with Jesus Christ. In this event is God's self-interpretation, whereby God chooses how he will be, i.e., what his being will be.[4] How

2. Jüngel, *God's Being*, 27.

3. Jüngel, *God as the Mystery*, 176; GT, 238.

4. Jüngel does not seem to be concerned with the idea that God is able to choose, in some way or another, who he is. In this way, he is more in line with the Eastern churches and their preference for the choice of God over being. Why Jüngel proceeds this way is no doubt related to the Barthian mediated Calvinistic emphasis on the sovereignty, freedom, and independence of God.

the Word of God makes God present as God, such that he can be treated in a secondary speech event requires clarification. Jüngel does this by introducing the aforementioned idea of a speech event. Fuchs claimed that "language makes being into an event."[5] Jüngel follows both he and Ebeling in this type of understanding, reflecting a Heideggerian ontology of being. From this perspective, being is something that cannot be actual without speech in that it can only be present[6] through speech. Thus, God can only be through the speech event where he chooses (i.e., elects) who he will be. It is for this reason that Jüngel can make the somewhat nebulous claim that "God is the event of self-determination, God is self-determination taking place."[7] In the speech event, humans may speak about God only because God has already determined to present himself as God to them in Christ. The Word of God, consequently, is the event of God's self-determination through the speech event.

Jüngel's typical nomenclature when speaking of God's self-determination is replete with "event" terminology. There are a few reasons why this is significant. One is that event terminology prevents the static understanding of being typical of metaphysical approaches, whereby one is and then does. In the event terminology, God is who he is in his doing. The other reason for the focus on event is likely in connection with Barth and Bultmann's movement towards event talk as a way to take heed of the existential dimensions of a Christian view of salvation. Jüngel prefers "event" speech since it causes the idea of a speech event to not only focus on the speaker, but also the one who is addressed. This is seen when such terms are brought into contrast with "act" type terms that are preferred in post-Hegelian German ontological thinking. When discussing speech acts, the individual performing the action is clearly in focus, as Wolterstorff clearly demonstrates, since the performance of the act is independent of the receptivity of any hearer. The act gives preference to the actor. Were there to be no hearer, a hearer who ignores, or a hearer who rebels would make little difference.

Speech events, in contradistinction, have both the speaker and hearer in mind as they are both given entrance into the single event. Jüngel does not believe that speech event occurs unless both speaker and hearer are drawn together, which is reminiscent of the Barthian idea that Scripture can become the word of God when it affects the believer. It is for this reason that

5. Fuchs, *Studies in the Historical Jesus*, 253.

6. A clarification of the philosophical and theological issues surrounding the idea of "presence" is outside of the scope of the present paper. For an introduction to the issue, see Dalferth, *Becoming Present*.

7. Jüngel, *God as the Mystery*, 36.

he takes pains to explain the address function of speech.[8] Consequently, this event is fully existential in the sense that it does not solely affect the intellect of the individual hearing. For this reason, Jüngel claims:

> Language does certainly have the function of uniting people with that which is being talked about, uniting them in such a way that not only through the word something penetrates the person's consciousness (*in cogitationem*), but that the entire person is drawn out of himself in the process. Such acts of speaking which permit a person to be drawn out of himself are what we would call *language events*, to borrow from Ernst Fuchs.[9]

It is in the speech event that humans and God can be united such that humans can be addressed by God and redefined in terms of that address. The existentiality of this event means that humans have responsibility to respond, since it, as Ebeling states it, "tolerates no neutrality."[10] It is also in this address, as will be demonstrated later, whereby humans can speak about God.

If the speech event draws speaker and the addressee into the singular event, the natural question arises as to how this occurs in the primary speech event. The secondary event, whereby humans are addressed by God is somewhat transparent. However, how God's being can be constituted in a speech event is much more difficult. Jüngel attempts to surmount this complication in his typically Christological fashion by claiming, "The corresponding hermeneutical study of the problem of the speakability of God is also nourished by the material statement that God has defined himself through identification with the crucified Jesus."[11] What this identification (*Identifikation*) entails is far from clear, but definitely contains a few related elements. First, the identification appears to be related to the sacramental nature of speech. For Jüngel, God does not come to speech from without, but is actually present in the speech event. Just as the sacraments were understood to both symbolize something and actually contain the very presence of that thing, so speech both manifests God and allows God to be present in the speech. In Jüngel's understanding, Jesus is the primary sacrament of God. He claims, "The sacramental priority of the man Jesus consists in the fact that in the existence of this man God is uniquely objective."[12] Thus, God possesses an otherness in being the Word of God, but is also

8. Jüngel, *God as the Mystery*, 9–14.

9. Jüngel, *God as the Mystery*, 11–12.

10. Ebeling, *God and Word*, 31.

11. Jüngel, *God as the Mystery*, x; GT, xiii.

12. Jüngel, *God as the Mystery*, 67.

identical to God in that God is present in him. "Identification" terminology then, is a manner in which Jüngel can express the idea that God is present as God in Christ, without what he believes to be the tautology if Jesus were to be understood in traditional categories concerning a union of divine and human natures. In order for the Word of God to be the self-interpretation of God and not simply God repeated, some differentiation must occur. Of this Jüngel claims, "To identify oneself with another, foreign essence implies the capacity to differentiate oneself."[13] Thus, the Trinity expresses the idea that God is differentiated in his decision to be present in Jesus, who is not God, but comes to be the Word of God. In this way the speech event is God speaking in God (the Word) as God (the Spirit).

Identification, in other words, presents an extension of Luther's idea that God manifests or acts *sub contrario*, in that God's trinitarian being is actually constituted *sub contrario*.[14] Moreover, it presents a radicalization of the *communicatio idiomatum* whereby Luther contains partial agreement with the scholastics. Luther, in defending the ubiquity of Christ's body and blood so as to defend consubstantiation, apparently believed that the human nature could receive attributes (including omnipresence) from his divine nature. However, though he did permit statements concerning the suffering of God, it is less clear if he believed that the humanity of Christ could confer attributes upon his divinity.[15] Jüngel, though spurning the "nature" language that he connects with the metaphysical view of God, essentially defends the view not only that God, as God, can receive human characteristics, but that God somehow becomes human by his identification with Christ. This is the reason, as will be mentioned later, that he is quick to deny immutability. Where Luther defended some sort of *communicatio idiomatum*, Jüngel's "identification" language is much stronger. The divine is divine in its choice to be identical to Christ on the cross.

To summarize: In the speech event, God determines Himself to be the God who reveals himself to humanity as the crucified one. Thus, in the primary speech event, i.e., the Word of God in Jesus Christ, God's being is determined as God being revealed as God in Christ. In fact, it is this idea

13. Jüngel, *God as the Mystery*, 363.

14. Jüngel contrasts his position with previous perspectives in Christendom in writing, "That God became *man* was for the classic trinitarian doctrine not the constitutively determining event for the trinitarian being of God, although it then derived from that event as a further consequence of the basic thought" (Jüngel, *God as the Mystery*, 37).

15. For the argument that Christ's human nature could confer attributes to the divine nature, see Ngien, *Suffering of God*. For the position that the *communicatio idiomatum* only occurs from the divine to the human in Luther's Christology, see Luy, *Dominus Mortis*.

that Jüngel praises as Hegel's "grand theological accomplishment," where he develops "a philosophically conceived theology of the Crucified One as the doctrine of the Triune God."[16]

Role of Divine Speech in Jüngel's Thought

Divine speech plays a more substantive role in Jüngel's thought than in many theologians who have preceded and succeeded him. Where he agrees that speech can manifest being, his Heideggerian ontology of speech and reality views it as a way for being to be being, at least in the case of God. It is in speech that God can interpret himself and thus be differentiated from himself. Thus, speech functions, in some ways, like Barth's view of God's "primal decision"[17] in election, in that it is the way that God chooses to be what he will be. For Barth, God's decision is not primarily concerning humanity, but a decision concerning himself.[18] Yet, God's decision to be a Savior in Christ has obvious implications for humanity, even if they are not the direct goal of the decision. Similarly, Jüngel sees divine speech functioning as God's self-differentiation in that he interprets his own being in identity with Jesus at the cross, with that self-interpretation bearing on the destiny of humans.[19] In divine speech, God can interpret himself, and he interprets himself as *Immanuel* (Isa 7:14; Matt 1:23).

An important implication of Jüngel's view of divine speech is that God's trinitarian nature can no longer be held in abstract, since its foundation is a historical event. In God's identification with Jesus, particularly in his crucifixion, he is differentiated as historical being in a concrete relationship. This has certain similarities to previous theological attempts to understand God's unity in differentiation (or differentiation in unity), while diverging in a startling way. In the concretization of God's relationship at the cross, Jüngel resumes the type of relational ontology that has been often used to explain the economic Trinity. In doing so, he follows a rather traditional explanation of the use of "Father," "Son," and "Holy Spirit" terminology.[20] However, since he equates the economic and immanent Trinity, this relational ontology is not representational. God is, in his decision of identification, actually

---

16. Jüngel, God as the Mystery, 94.

17. Jüngel, *God's Being*, 14, 83.

18. Barth, *CD* 2/2:3. For Jüngel's explanation, see Jüngel, *God's Being*, 84–89.

19. Ironically, Moltmann appears to criticize Jüngel for not having proper trinitarian differentiation when expositing the cross (Moltmann, *Crucified God*, 204). For Jüngel's response to similar criticism, see Jüngel, *God's Being*, 136n24.

20. Jüngel, *God as the Mystery*, 48.

relational. Thus, the event of the cross is not merely a display of who God is, it becomes part of who God is.[21] In this way, God's relationality is not only concrete, but God must be understood as historical being.

Divine speech not only serves to explain the trinitarian differentiation in God's being, a differentiation that is concrete and historical, but it also serves as the transcendental for human existence and speech. In being a speaker, God is capable of addressing humans and through that address constitute them in their being. Since being as meaningful being can only be present through speech, which can make being present in its meaningfulness, human being can only be what it is in the speech event that gives it meaning. Moreover, in the speech event which constitutes the trinitarian distinctions, God makes himself the object of his own speech and thus opens the possibility of him becoming the object of other speech. In coming as the Word of God, he can be understood as meaningful being that can be understood in Jesus Christ. In speaking to humans, he objectifies himself and allows himself to become speakable and thinkable by humans. In doing so, God "brings [human] existence into a definite relationship to his existence,"[22] thus defining humanity through its relationship to him. God's being, as meaningful, becomes the foundation for human being in that humans gain their meaning in concrete relationship to the God who addresses them. This is why Jüngel approves of Rahner's anthropology to some degree, claiming "Both ontically and existentially we are to be 'hearers of the Word.'"[23] Speech, with its divine inception, is such a fundamental aspect of humanity that he claims that man, in a speechless world, would come forth, but "not as man."[24]

Yet, when God constitutes individuals in their humanity through speech, it is a constitution of freedom. This has two significant implications. First, it means that even though humans are primarily addressed by God, they can, as hearers and speakers, address and be addressed by others.[25]

---

21. There are certain difficulties that will remain unaddressed in this particular concept. Foremost of which is the ability for a historical event to be taken up into the divine ontology, even previous to its occurrence in world history. Jüngel give some inklings at a solution in the orientation of the divine Father to the divine Son even previous to the crucifixion, but the issue remains largely unexplained. Though Jüngel wants to distinguish himself from Hegel, who sees world history as necessary to God in the sense that the self-realization of the *Geist* cannot occur otherwise, certain similarities could allow for the conflation of the views, were Jüngel's insistence on divine voluntarism and worldly time's reliance upon God be left aside.

22. Jüngel, *God's Being*, 69.

23. Jüngel, "Humanity in Correspondence," 125. Cf. Rahner, *Hearers of the Word*.

24. Jüngel, *Gott als Geheimnis*, 216. Author's translation.

25. Jüngel, *Gott als Geheimnis*, 155–156.

Thus, God allows, in defining the relationship of humans to himself, a type of free subjectivity in humans that allow them to speak in ways that do not refer to God, or indeed even to speak against him. Second, humans are given the freedom to determine themselves in speech in a limited fashion. In choosing who to address and how to address, individuals make fundamental choices about themselves and define, to some degree,[26] the being they will be. Thus, the divine speech provides the foundation for human existence and freedom. How God's speech grounds human speech will be addressed later, but suffice it to say that the totality of human life is bound up in the divine Word.[27]

CHARACTERIZATION OF DIVINE REVELATION

Jüngel's Understanding of Divine Revelation

When understanding the event of divine revelation, Jüngel concentrates on the unveiling of God Himself. In contrast to Wolterstorff, who defined agent self-revelation in terms of an "aspect or item of knowledge"[28] that is revealed about the agent, Jüngel is thinking of the revelation of the agent himself. This move is not unprecedented, as it can be found in many of the dialectic theologians,[29] following the afore movement of German idealism. Agreeing with the scholastic theologians that "*Scriptura sacra non est dei loquentis persona*,"[30] Jüngel also is clear that he agrees with Barth in claiming that "Revelation is *Dei loquentis persona*."[31] Thus, revelation is intimately related to speech, though not divine speech itself. Jüngel recognizes that the primary speech event (i.e., divine speech) does not necessarily entail that God will speak to humans, since such speech must be a gracious act. Following the Reformed theologians, then, he uses the concept of revelation as a way

26. Though Jüngel does not make it explicit, humans cannot define themselves ultimately, which is likely why he makes the distinction between "self-definition" (*Selbstbestimmung*) and "self-grounding" (*Selbstbegründung*), the latter of which only comes from divine speech. Jüngel, *God as the Mystery*, 164; GT, 220.

27. For a somewhat similar treatment of the anthropological implications of God's Word, see Brunner, *Revelation and Reason*, 54.

28. Wolterstorff, *Divine Discourse*, 25.

29. Barth notwithstanding, Brunner agrees with personal revelation as the primary understanding in theology. He writes, "Divine revelation is not a book or a doctrine; the Revelation is God Himself in His self-manifestation within history" (Brunner, *Revelation and Reason*, 8). Brunner also states, "The real content of revelation in the Bible is not 'something,' but *God Himself*" (Brunner, *Revelation and Reason*, 25).

30. Jüngel, *God as the Mystery*, 157.

31. Jüngel, *God's Being*, 27.

to place the responsibility and credit of God addressing humanity on God alone.[32] Jüngel believes that he is in line with Lombard, against Aquinas, in placing the Trinity at the forefront of theology.[33] In terms of revelation, this pattern is no different. In order, "to keep any idea of synergism far from the Christian concept of revelation . . . all this must be grounded in the being of God."[34] Consequently, Jüngel follows Barth in seeing a trinitarian structure in revelation, whereby God is Revealer, Revealed, and Revealedness.[35] In this way, the unveiling of God's being comes by God alone.

It is a peculiarity of Jüngel's understanding of divine revelation that he, to a large degree, ignores other phenomena that could be understood as revelatory.[36] Whereas Wolterstorff is quick to give many examples and attempt to distill them into a core concept, Jüngel prefers to examine what he considers to be the paradigmatic event. Jüngel takes a theology of the cross and God's gracious freedom as his presuppositions and, therefore, limits his discussion to personal (and indeed self-revelation). This has a few significant consequences. First, Jüngel will be moved toward a Barthian understanding of bibliology that keeps Scripture and revelation separate, through related. To allow the Bible to be called revelation would be, for Jüngel, an attack on the uniqueness of God's revelation in Jesus Christ, as well a display of the ignorance of the gains of historical criticism.[37] He agrees with Barth in seeing Scripture as the testimony to God's revelation in Christ. Yet, the Bible, being the first and normative description of the Christian community's reaction in faith to the Word of God, is held above other testimony and therefore rightly called canonical. Second, this simplifies certain aspects of the relationship between divine speech and human speech, since the revelatory point of contact between the two is singular and simple. Jüngel does not have to draw a relationship between knowing about someone and knowing them, as would be required if there were ways in which revelation

32. It would be a failure of historical research, if one were to not recognize that revelation was also used by Protestants in a polemical manner to divest authority from the Catholic church, since no ecclesiastical authentication is needed to believe that the Scripture could reveal God.

33. Jüngel, *God's Being*, 16n6.

34. Jüngel, *God's Being*, 30.

35. For Jüngel's view of the significance of Barth's structure of revelation, see Jüngel, *God's Being*, 28–37; *God as the Mystery*, 380–9.

36. Some examples might be prophetic utterance, visions, dreams, burning bushes, the *shekinah* (שׁכִינה), etc.

37. It must be admitted, that Jüngel is not nearly as enthusiastic as Bultmann was concerning the significance of historical criticism, though he is more amicable toward the discipline than Barth. For a helpful elucidation of Barth's view, see Smend, "Nachkritische Schriftauslegung."

could encompass learning "items of knowledge" about someone. The reduction of phenomena means that if he is successful in using Christ to mediate between human and divine speech, then there is no more work to be done.

The concentration of the responsibility of the revelatory act upon God himself means that the presentation of the divine being in Christ must be a self-interpreting Word. Whereas understanding an item of knowledge revealed concerning someone would require a particular interpretive horizon against which to understand that item, an interpretive horizon that may include the identity of the individual to whom that article of knowledge refers, personal revelation in Jesus Christ is peculiar in providing the interpretive horizon along with the person being known. Since, as will be explored later, Jüngel does not allow for the separation of form and content in the act of revelation, then God's identification with Jesus means that God himself is presented along with the interpretive framework, which is the act of Jesus Christ going to the cross. Thus, the Easter confession of the risen Christ is a confession that God himself is present as God in the event of Jesus' death and resurrection, such that that event shows God as the one who reveals himself in love. Consequently, God's personal revelation in Christ is a bestowal of the divine presence in such a way as he can be recognized as God through the interpretive framework of the crucifixion.

The Relationship Between Divine Speech and Revelation

At first glance, Jüngel's understanding of revelation appears to be an artifact of Barthian neo-orthodoxy, due to the expanded role he gives divine speech. Yet, though its function is admittedly different, it has a significant conceptual role in providing a bridge between God and humanity. That God's trinitarian being is conceived in the speech event of his identifying with Jesus, it already implies a relational ontology, as well as the possibility of address. In that God chooses the cross in his self-definition, which is to the benefit of humanity, as well as his decision to identify with the human Jesus at the cross, he displays an orientation towards humanity that expresses a desire to take humanity into the divine being. In this way, the Trinity itself already displays a desire for God to approach humans. This is similar to Barth's seeing the Trinity as the "anticipatory form"[38] of God's self-giving in revelation. Thus, revelation is the logical consequence of divine speech, as it is the manner of God's approach.

The significance of revelation, as the manner in which God approaches humanity, can be appreciated in light of Jüngel's revised dialectic. In the

38. Jüngel, God's Being, 42.

dialectical relationship between divine and human speech,[39] revelation is a third term. Yet, in light of Jüngel's attempt to refrain from amalgamated mediations, contra Hegel, revelation must be subsumed under one term in a manner that allows for resolution of the thesis and antithesis. In this case, revelation is clearly placed under divine speech in a way that allows the divine Word to come to human words. God's Word, in being a "going out"[40] that is receptive to humanity, is already in anticipation of revelation. Revelation, in being the trinitarian activity of God coming to humans, is based on the divine Word, which gives it purpose and structure.

Though there are formal similarities between Barth and Jüngel concerning the idea of revelation, it performs somewhat different functions based on the manner in which they diverge concerning the function of divine speech. Whereas early in Jüngel's career, he approvingly comments on Barth's understanding of God's eternal will to love as determining God's essence,[41] he later begins to move emphasis to God's decision to identify with the man Jesus as being constitutive of being. Where he understands Barth as seeing the incarnation as "an event which presupposes a self-distinction in God,"[42] such that the economic Trinity is reflective of the immanent Trinity, Jüngel sees the event of identification with Jesus at the cross as that which brings about said self-distinction. Thus, where both would agree with Rahner's equating of the economic and immanent Trinity, he does so with a different locus of equation. In other words, for him, not only is God "the event, the 'werden,' of this interpreting,"[43] but he is this event at the cross. It must be admitted that Jüngel makes certain statements where he appears to interpret Barth as holding essentially the same view as him,[44] but it is likely that Jüngel overstates the similarity between the positions. It is true that

39. That God and humans are in dialectic is unquestionable within Jüngel's work. However, this does not mean that every activity or quality of God and humans are also in dialectic. However, since speech in the speech event is constitutive of both divine and human being, then it appears the dialectic of God and humans carries over to speech.

40. Jüngel writes, "But if faith does participate in God himself, without penetrating God in such a way that it forces itself between God and God, then God's being must be thought as a being which allows that it be participated in, that is, a being which turns outward what it is inwardly" (Jüngel, *God as the Mystery*, 176).

41. Jüngel, *God's Being*, 6.

42. Jüngel, *God's Being*, 30.

43. Braaten and Jenson, "Trinitarian Theology," 182.

44. For many statements toward this end, see Jüngel, *God's Being*, 81–95. One example would be his claim, "For Barth, this relatedness without which *historia praeveniens* would not be *gratia praeveniens* [prevenient grace] is given in the fact that, in the being of Jesus Christ who is in the beginning with God, that is, in that primal history, God determines himself to be God as man" (Jüngel, *God's Being*, 91–92).

Barth moved on later in his career to address the "humanity of God,"[45] recognizing the failure in his polemical work to do justice to the God-human relationship in his emphasis on the Divine as "wholly other." Moreover, he does believe that at "no level of time can we have to do with God without having also to do with this [Jesus]."[46] Yet, for his position to be truly the same as Jüngel's, there would have to be an equating of God's self-election in the incarnation of Christ and God's identification with the man Jesus in the crucifixion, which does not seem to be the case.[47] In fact, Jüngel's discussion of the *logos* in Barth's thinking,[48] as well as his use of "prototype"[49] terminology, would appear to militate such equation. It is true that Barth does not want to speak of the second person of the Godhead without recognizing that that person is Jesus Christ, but it must also be recognized that in doing so that Barth frames that decision and its structure in terms of election such that the historical nature is not given the same strength of emphasis as in Jüngel, whereby that event of the cross is constitutive of the divine nature.

Whereas it appears that Barth wants to argue that God is trinitarian in structure, which allows for the self-interpretation in the word and the repetition seen in revelation, Jüngel wants to argue that the speech event is the way in which God is who He is. Thus, the speech event where God identifies with Christ is not just a choice reflecting God's trinitarian being, but part of God's being itself.[50] Jüngel's view, in this way, appears to be more indicative of an extension of Lutheran thought,[51] whereas, Barth's appears to be an extension of Calvin. As Christopher Holmes has noted, Reformed influences on Barth gave rise to a use of the immanent Trinity to defend the aseity of God.[52] Yet, for Jüngel, identification of God with Jesus at the cross already precludes this as a possibility. Hence, Barth's incarnational focused trinitarian doctrine allowed him to defend God's independence, while Jüngel's Lutheran theopaschite focus prevents him from doing so. Along with aseity, other traditional attributes of God are dismissed. He writes:

45. Barth, *Humanity of God*; *Die Menschlichkeit Gottes*.

46. Barth, *CD* 4/2:33.

47. For an expanded treatment of the difference between Barth and Jüngel in this area, see Malysz, *Trinity, Freedom, and Love*, 61–116.

48. Jüngel, *God's Being*, 94–98.

49. Jüngel, *God's Being*, 36.

50. Malysz makes a similar point in differentiating between God's "self-interpretation" in Christ, in which Barth believes, and God's "self-definition" at the cross, in which Jüngel believes. See Malysz, *Trinity, Freedom, and Love*, 74.

51. It appears that Jüngel would also characterize his work this way. See Jüngel, *God as the Mystery*, 37.

52. Holmes, "Eberhard Jüngel's," 103.

By orienting this distinction between God and God to the Crucified One, we have significantly corrected the classical doctrine of God. For this distinction between God and God based on the cross of Jesus Christ has destroyed the axiom of absoluteness, the axiom of apathy, and the axiom of immutability which are unsuitable axioms for the Christian concept of God.[53]

It is significant to note that while Jüngel is clearly differentiated from Barth in this area, he is, in many ways, carrying on the project that his predecessor started. Barth was never shy about critiquing "metaphysical" views of God, such as one that is seen in a bare theism that does not account for the Trinity. He believed these were largely a carryover from Greek philosophical speculation, but they hardly did justice to the God of the Bible. Yet, in his tie to Reformed theology, these metaphysical perspectives appear to continue to have influence on Barth. Thus, Jüngel's crucicentric understanding of the being of God requires a purge of any of the metaphysical presuppositions that he believed plagued Reformed (and indeed Catholic) scholasticism. This means ceasing to defend the immutability of God.[54] In doing so, Jüngel does provide a locus for how one should interpret God. In that God is defined at the cross, then he must be understood as self-giving love. Hence, for Jüngel, there is a contrariness towards the traditionally conceived metaphysical view of God and the loving God of the cross. Or, in other words,

The dominant concepts of traditional thinking about God, the concepts of divine dominion, omnipotence, and supremacy over the world, are radically subordinated to the definition of God as love, a definition which expresses the divine essence more stringently.[55]

Though Jüngel's idea of revelation plays a similar structural role in his theology to that of Karl Barth, there is a difference in that the latter's desire to retain a connection to past orthodoxy, caused him to still give precedence of the idea of being over becoming. Further than this, his desire to retain divine immutability means that the actuality of being is given precedence

---

53. Jüngel, *God as the Mystery*, 373.

54. For the distinction that Jüngel sees between his view and that of "Reformed orthodoxy," see Jüngel, *God as the Mystery*, 184. Colin Gunton argues that Jüngel is still attempting to retain some sort of immutability in his work (Gunton, "Being," 7–22), but this only appears to be a statement possible with a substantial redefinition of immutability. Moltmann appears to take the same direction as Jüngel's work, but to an even greater degree. See Moltmann, *Trinity and the Kingdom*, 64, 94–96, 159.

55. Jüngel, *God as the Mystery*, 260.

over the possibility of being. In essence, questions of being are answered in the incarnation (i.e., the "becoming"), but one must recognize that there is a pointed difference between God's being and his choice to become incarnate. The actuality of his being is, for Barth, his self-election to be savior, while this allows the possibility of coming in incarnation. Thus, revelation draws the connection between the immanent and economic Trinity, while retaining the differentiation necessary to give the primacy to the actuality of being Barth desires in his defense of divine aseity. Even though, for Barth, there is no difference between God *pro nobis* and *pro se*, revelation allows the historicity of the Christ to open up an understanding of who God is.

For Jüngel, in contrast, revelation has a different role since he equates the immanent and economic Trinity more radically. If God is who he is at the cross, then one does not need revelation to tie God's decision (i.e., possibility of being) with who he is (i.e., actuality of being). His self-differentiated trinitarian nature is constituted in the event, not simply manifested within it. Thus, God does not possess actual being and then possibilities, but God is his possibilities. In this way, Jüngel is able to retain the primacy of possibility over actuality,[56] through which he can equate the economic and immanent trinities in such a way that the they refer to the ultimate possibility, which is God's decision to be who he is (immanently) in his identification with Christ (economically). Thus, there is no move from economic to the immanent Trinity.

This appears to be at least part of the reason for his evolution to "coming" terminology from "becoming." Though the use of "coming" differentiates Jüngel's position from that of Barth in multiple ways, one is particularly noteworthy. With "coming," an eschatological focus is clearly in view, as the language mirrors typical speech in Scripture and in German theology concerning the eschaton.[57] Yet it is different from Barth's emphasis on eschatology, since God has defined himself in terms of the future-oriented event of the cross. Jüngel writes, "The word "come" is taken seriously here to the extent that it interprets God's being as an event from God to God, an event in which God is not only his own derivation but also his future."[58] Where Barth's eschatological understanding starts with God's derivation and attempts to show its applicability in the contemporary setting, Jüngel, not

56. For Jüngel's understanding of possible and actual, see his discussion of "more than necessary" (Jüngel, *God as Mystery*, 24–35) and his explicit treatment in Jüngel, "World as Possibility," 95–123.

57. This can be seen in Bultmann, Moltmann, and Pannenberg. Moltmann writes, "God's Being is in his coming, not in his becoming. If it were in his becoming, then it would also be in his passing away" (Moltmann, *Coming of God*, 23).

58. Jüngel, *God as the Mystery*, 36.

unlike the idea of the "futurity of God" presented by Moltmann,[59] wants to focus on the directionality of God's *telos*. Thus, it is not that God is the God who acts eschatologically in Christ's death and resurrection, but that God's eschatological being is what it is in those events. For Barth, to perhaps simplify too much, God acts eschatologically. For Jüngel, God is eschatological.

To summarize, Jüngel's resolution to the dialectic of human and divine speech is found in using revelation to reconcile the thesis and antithesis. However, this is done not by a mediation between the two, but by subsuming revelation under divine speech in a way that relates it to human speech. In doing so, Jüngel's understanding of the revelatory event both extends Barth's work and also differs from it. The metaphysical criticism is continued, such that the speech event prevents an understanding of God in the way traditionally seen in Reformed theology. Moreover, revelation takes a more substantial role in that it does not perform the task of bringing together the immanent and economic Trinity, but actually functions to define the divine ontology. Consequently, to fully develop the relationship of divine and human requires revelation as the dialectic resolution, but in a way that does so in favor of the former.

CHARACTERIZATION OF HUMAN SPEECH

In the course of the twentieth century, referential views of speech came under strong criticism in the West. With phenomenological influence on the continent, and Wittgenstein's influence in analytic philosophy, human speech was recognized as an activity that was neither monolithic, nor simple to investigate. This complicating of speech has led to a reevaluation of how it relates to theology. Thus, the "linguistic turn" in philosophy was followed, with surprisingly little lapse in time, by a linguistic turn in theology. Jüngel, being a very philosophic theologian, is significantly influenced by these developments. Though primarily Heideggerian in his understanding of language, he shows some conversancy with other traditions, even the speech act theory[60] that is at the core of Wolterstorff's work. Not unlike philosophers of language during his time, he downplays the sign function of words. However, he does so in a way that is somewhat moderate, not willing to eject reference altogether. He wants to view speech not in terms of communication of ideas,[61] but in terms of an existential event that involves the

---

59. Jüngel, *Coming of God*, 20–23.
60. See Jüngel, *God as the Mystery*, 10–11.
61. Jüngel, *God as the Mystery*, 6, 171.

whole of the human person. Elucidation of how this is the case will serve to provide the backdrop for how human and divine speech relate.

As was mentioned earlier, Jüngel's view of speech could be described as sacramental. In order to develop the implications of his perspective, a significant passage in *God as the Mystery of the World* will be examined. Jüngel writes:

> Under certain circumstances, words can allow something to happen which is present in the words or with them or through them. The sign function of the word would be in such an instance only one and possibly not even the decisive function of language. When the judge utters a judgment, then while he speaks the event happens which the language expresses. . . . The act of speaking does not result in something different from itself; instead, its effect consists of the fact that the person addressed and the result of what is said are both drawn into the act of speaking.[62]

Jüngel distinguishes his view from referential perspectives by using terminology similar to that which is used to explain the Lutheran understanding of the Lord's Supper. He explains that something happens "in," "with," and "through" words. In this event, the semiotic function of words is not suspended, but loses its place of supremacy to that which occurs through the words. Thus, language functions similar to the declarative speech act in that what is said affects reality such that the relationship between the speaker and addressee is changed through the words. Intriguingly, then, Jüngel has a similar understanding to Wolterstorff's normative theory of language. When God approaches a human in the speech event, God is actually present as he and the addressee are drawn into the event. Though God is not the words, his presence is mediated through them. Thus, Jüngel approvingly states:

> The indirectness of our participation in the truth of God consists in the fact that "God gives Himself to be known . . . in an objectivity different from His own, in a creaturely objectivity." For Barth, the fact that in his work God gives himself to be known *sub contraria specie* [under the opposite species] is a sacramental matter.[63]

In that God comes in a worldly manner, means that he always comes as a mediated presence. Though speculative, it is worthy to note that Heidegger's

62. Jüngel, *God as the Mystery*, 10.
63. Jüngel, *God's Being*, 65.

understanding of finite time holds that *Dasein* can only be understood as "being-in-the world." It becomes clear that at least some of what prevents Heidegger from completing *Being and Time* is his difficulty with theology.[64] Thus, Jüngel might be interpreted as an attempt to reconcile Heidegger's view of worldly being with a God who is, initially, other-worldly in his existence. This reconciliation, then, is that God chooses to enact his being in the world in a way that mirrors (or perhaps assumes!) the way that humanity (or more accurately *Dasein*) is essentially "being-in-the-world." God's mediated presence occurred at the incarnation in the Word of God and also can occur through the *kerygmatic* function of the gospel. This marks a development from his earlier work, where he focused on how the words came to the hearer, to a more sustained emphasis on how speech can bring about the speech event of God's presence.[65]

Not only is God's being differentiated through the speech event, but God's being as revealed to humanity also occurs through the speech event. This is significant in that this brings together the interpretive function of language with the manner in which it can mediate presence. In the primary speech event, God determines himself to be who he is in identification with Jesus on the cross. This determination is essentially God's self-interpretation. God chooses who he will be, and he is the one who is present at the cross. Thus, speech is inherently interpretive[66] and in interpretation it can be determinative. In human speech, the speech event can occur whereby God's presence is mediated, but it is presence that is interpreted. In this way, human speech and divine speech share a sacramental nature, which occurs through interpretation.

THE RELATIONSHIP BETWEEN DIVINE SPEECH, REVELATION, AND HUMAN SPEECH

Revelation, then, in the work of Jüngel, is the bridge between divine speech and human speech. In divine speech, God differentiates himself in the speech event. The speech event, in being an orientation towards humanity as God interprets himself in Jesus, necessitates a way in which God can come before humanity. Thus, revelation is the act whereby God is present as God to humans through the Word. Yet, in order for that Word of God to approach humans, who were not present at the cross, human speech interprets

---

64. Heidegger, "Phenomenology and Theology."

65. For Jüngel's own assessment of his development, see Jüngel, *God as the Mystery*, 295.

66. Jüngel, *God's Being*, 24.

the revelation of God. Thus, Jüngel claims: "Thus *the revelation of God itself is that which makes the interpretation of revelation possible. This is because* 'revelation is the self-interpretation of God.' But as the *self-interpretation of God,* revelation is the root of the doctrine of the Trinity."[67] How revelation makes human interpretation possible is that revelation allows God to become the object of human speech, which is why Jüngel holds that "God's being-as-object is his being-revealed" (*"Gottes Gegenständlich-Sein ist sein Offenbar-Sein"*).[68] The phrases are also reminiscent of Heidegger's terminology in *Being and Time,* especially his use of *"in-der-Welt-sein."* Jüngel uses the language to stress that God's being is inseparable from revelation, since intrinsic to his being is the revelatory act. Hence, the way that he deals with the difficulty of objectifying talk about God is to hold that God objectifies himself in revelation. He becomes speakable in that he is concrete historical being in Jesus at the cross.[69] Thus, since God possesses humanity (i.e., orientation towards humanity), he can come to human speech.

Not only can human speech, based on God's revelatory act, interpret God's self-interpretation, but through the speech event the human's self-understanding is affected. The secondary speech event can occur whereby God's presence is present with the words such that in being addressed, individuals are called before God. In this, the relationship is defined whereby the addressee's experiences, beliefs, and activities are called into question. This is why Jüngel claims, "The "word of God" is to be understood as the abbreviated formulation of the entire fact that God addresses us about himself and thus about ourselves."[70] In essence, the speech event allows them to recognize that they live life *coram Deo,* such that everything about them is re-defined. The speech event causes the individual to come to a new self-interpretation, which is in light of God's eternal Word. By recognizing themselves before God, one addressed by the Word recognizes possibilities that they did not see before. In this way, God's speech event to humans is interruptive.[71] It breaks them free from slavery to the actual (i.e., their history) and frees them toward their possibilities (i.e., new being).

---

67. Jüngel, *God's Being,* 27.

68. Jüngel, *God's Being,* 57. For the German version, see Jüngel, *Gottes Sein,* 57.

69. More than this, God becomes thinkable since, from Jüngel's perspective, speakability is foundational for thinkability. See Jüngel, *God as the Mystery,* 12–14, 105–225.

70. Jüngel, *God as the Mystery,* 174.

71. This idea is similar to Heidegger's understanding of how particular events, such as language or art, can cause disruption such that one is called out of inauthenticity toward a conscious recognition of an event. See Heidegger, "Origin," 139–212. This mirrors understanding of tool use in Heidegger, *Being and Time,* 69–70.

SUMMARY OF JÜNGEL'S DIVINE VIEW OF SPEECH AND REVELATION

To grasp Jüngel's perspective on speech and revelation is complex in many ways. One must not only understand his nuanced theory, but can only do so when understanding his extensive list of influences. As the confluence of many theological and philosophical traditions, he is both an expert synthesizer and the object of endless interpretation. The core of his theory begins with an understanding of the trinitarian nature of God and how it relates to humanity. God is self-differentiated in the speech event, which is his interpretation of himself at the cross. By identifying himself with the death of Jesus, he both displays himself as love and as the one who possesses humanity. In both of these manifestations, God in eternity was already a being towards humanity such that it assured his activity in coming to humans. This activity is the event of revelation. In revelation, God comes as Jesus Christ so that he can become the object of interpretive human speech and thus provide the possibility of the speech event whereby the Word of God comes to humans. By coming as object, God's self-interpretation can be interpreted and open humans to their existential possibilities.

7

An Assessment of Jüngel's Perspective

BENEFITS OF JÜNGEL'S POSITION

Defense of the Speakability of God

THE BENEFITS OF JÜNGEL'S view are many, with a few being highlighted here for the purpose of further discussion. There has been a tendency in Christianity to elevate the transcendence of God such that God becomes his transcendence. Jüngel demonstrates that this can be seen in two ways, one philosophical and one theological. Philosophically, the separation between existence and essence in God allows one to conceive of God's activity apart from his being. For Jüngel, one, though not the only, perpetrator of this type of schism is Descartes,[1] whose methodological doubt allowed one to speak of the existence of God apart from who he is.[2] On the theological side, Jüngel sees such tendency in the desire to split the economic and immanent Trinity. In both of these cases, speech about God appears to be nearly impossible. His criticism of analogy in Aquinas has some merit, though he perhaps overstates the faults and does not recognize when he falls into the same practice.[3] What is significant, though, is his attempt both to

1. Jüngel, *God as the Mystery*, 111–22.

2. One could, perhaps, proffer a defense of Descartes in that he offers an ontological argument for God's existence, such that existence and essence are tied together. However, such an answer would likely be insufficient for Jüngel since Descartes develops his view independently of God's trinitarian nature.

3. Jüngel appears to, at times, speak of God aside from his theological definition at the cross. Moreover, he speaks about theological terms by asking how they are normally used. If I. M. Crombie is correct in his interpretation of Aquinas's Five Ways,

defend the speakability of God and to preserve a strongly trinitarian understanding of speech and revelation, while taking heed of the criticisms and aporias inherent in the opposing view.[4] Speakability must be preserved for a few reasons. First, the missiological nature of the church would be all but impossible if God were not speakable, since Scripture not only speaks of God coming to Christians, but Christians going out into the world. Thus, the missional nature inherent within the *kerygmatic* activity of the church would purely be a mystical endeavor if it could not use the mediation of human speech. Evangelicalism, with its emphasis on evangelism in ecclesiological contexts, requires the speakability of God and thus finds significant support in Jüngel's argumentation.

Second, that there exists speech that is appropriate to God prevents God from speaking through anything. It would seem that if God appeared everywhere, then he would appear nowhere. For God being semiotically present in all things would evoke a type of pantheism that would be difficult to reconcile with Jüngel's understanding of God's independence from the world,[5] as well as the uniqueness of the cross event. Moreover, that God can be made the object of speech will naturally invoke the question of what speech is appropriate. For Jüngel, this is where the work of both Barth and Bultmann converge. He notices that,

> If we understand Bultmann's programme as the concern for appropriate speech about God (and so about humanity), and if we see this concern fulfilled in not objectifying God or letting him be objectified as an It or He, but in bringing him to speech as Thou, and so speaking of him appropriately, then we shall not overlook a striking parallel to the significance which Barth attributes (and gives) to the doctrine of the Trinity.[6]

It should be recognized that this idea has more difficult consequences for Bultmann than Barth due to his relationship with historical criticism. For

---

then there appears to be some similarity between Jüngel and his Scholastic dialogue partner. This is further supported by certain formal similarities between Jüngel's view of metaphor and Aquinas use of analogy.

4. One example can be seen in Jüngel's claim, "The hermeneutic of the unspeakability of God appears to preserve the essence of God as a mystery" (Jüngel, *God as the Mystery*, 245).

5. If one were to hold a process perspective, then this difficulty would take a different note, since the idea that God could be mediated through anything would not be troublesome. However, from this perspective, it would be hard to conceive of the function of God-talk at all. Panentheism would appear to have an easier time with this difficulty in preserving something of God that is not identified with the world.

6. Jüngel, *God's Being*, 34.

Bultmann, historical critical work is, in many ways, how one secures appropriate speech by using it to prevent mythological talk about God. Yet, in using it in this way, one might wonder why it could not be argued that the gospel of Christ, the cross, etc., should be understood as mythological. Thus, Macquarrie notices that Bultmann is forced to choose where demythologization must end, and it does so at the cross.[7] For Barth and Jüngel, this difficulty is seen to a lesser extent, since the former largely ignores historical criticism, while the latter limits its role. In any case, Jüngel's defense of the possibility of speech allows for the development of a grammar of appropriate speech.[8] It is in this area that theology draws upon the normative nature of the Biblical text to provide criteria for the ways in which God should and should not receive objectification in the speaking of believers. It is this possibility of speech that can prove to be foundational for the dogmatic function of Scripture that Evangelicalism holds to be significant.

Third, defending speakability, as Jüngel suggests, allows for God's thinkability. He believes that the modern debate between theism and atheism is largely an offspring of the difficulty of thinking about God which arose out of the difficulty of speaking about him.[9] Since God became unspeakable in terms of common metaphysical presuppositions, atheism arose. Jüngel believes, though, that a bare theism, without trinitarian concreteness, was an unsatisfactory solution which did not give proper attention to the aporia of divine speech from whence atheism came. When one recognizes that one can speak about God since he spoke first, then the Word becomes the "place of the conceivability of God."[10] In this, God can be the subject of theology, but only as theology comes to grips with the Word.

Employment of Event Speech

Jüngel's employment of the speech event is significant in his theology, because it hedges against some of the failed attempts to conceive of how God can come to speech. The speech event, in a significant way, keeps a close

7. For a detailed treatment of this difficulty, see Macquarrie, *Scope of Demythologization*.

8. How this grammar should be developed is not itself an unproblematic endeavor. The extremes of this case, within Protestantism, would be evangelicalism on one side and liberalism on the other. In the former case, Scripture itself would provide the grammar for appropriate speech about God since it would be considered God's speech itself, while in the latter, various tools of a psychological, sociological, scientific, or philosophic perspective would be employed.

9. Jüngel, *God as the Mystery*, 49–150.

10. Jüngel, *God as the Mystery*, 150.

connection between the form and content of what is being said, a concern that he gains from Barth.[11] When employed in an exegetical context, this prevents the type of propositionalizing of the text that reduces Scripture to doctrinal assertions with two significant outcomes. It would keep the text from being understood as solely engaging the intellect. Thus, the existential dimensions of the text are preserved. Jüngel would agree with Luther that text is not simply about what Christians are to know and with, surprisingly, Jonathan Edwards, who believed that the Christian life was inconceivable without the affections.[12] The speech event, which can happen in the scriptural text, is not meant simply to be a purveyance of information. Thus, Jüngel notes:

> The event character of this event, its *dynamis* (power), is shared with the speech which speaks of it. In communicating this content, not just information about it is being passed along. The content shares itself in such a way that a distinction between it and talk about it can be made only through an abstraction. What is expressed in the "word of the cross" is thus itself the full relation of language.[13]

Preventing this type of propositionalizing of the text also allows certain genres and devices of human language to once again speak for God. The strong tradition of emphasis on assertions of the text, or the prose genre, has often led to viewing tropic speech as mere "rhetorical ornamentation."[14] Yet, Jüngel argues that these alternative ways of speaking, such as metaphor, parable, and analogy, may be more appropriate when attempting to speak about God. In this way, Scripture is not reduced to textbook of information, but remains a living narrative of God's loving work in salvation. By defending the diverse manners in which the text operates, it can retain the foundation for the type of piety that is central to Evangelicalism.

The employment of speech event also has the significant benefit of averting the depersonalization of God speaking. When speech is simply a mode of communication, then what approaches one in the act of speaking is a something (i.e., informative content) and not a someone. However, the speech event draws the speaker and the addressee into the event such

---

11. "However, for Barth the being of God does not come to speech only as the content of revelation. Revelation is, indeed, God's self-interpretation, and so an event that does not allow itself to be separated into form and content" (Jüngel, *God's Being*, 27–28).

12. Edwards, *Treatise on Religious Affections*.

13. Jüngel, *God as the Mystery*, 287.

14. For Jüngel's criticism of this view, see Jüngel, "Metaphorical Truth," 21–26.

that the speaker does not fade from view. In this way, the speech event can be a place of encounter of God and not just a place to learn about God. Where the Word of God is mediated through the text, God comes as God in the event. Furthermore, the consistent maintenance of the speaker's role has important theological implications. In the speech event, God's role as speaker is emphasized in such a way that it prevents him from possessing being that is so transcendent and static, that it is a mere caricature of the God of Christianity. In the speech event, God's real presence is mediated, and thus the God who is over the world is, sacramentally, within the world. Moreover, the type of static ontology of being that permitted not only no development of God, but no activity in the world, is precluded. In the speech event, he enacts his being as one who speaks. Thus, he cannot possess the type of detachment which borders on deism that has been promoted at various points in the history of Christian theology.

Finally, the speech event provides the mechanism whereby two types of differentiation can be sustained. The first differentiation is within the trinitarian being of God himself. In that God interprets himself in the Word, a revelatory tautology is avoided.[15] Humans are not to know that "God is God," which is trivial, but they are to know that "God is his Word." The second differentiation is that between God and humans. In that the divine speech event is the basis of revelation, it also is the basis of a significant mode of distinction between the revealer and those to whom he reveals himself. Jüngel, similar to his dialectical predecessors, realizes that if humans, in their subjectivity, are responsible for their knowledge of God, then God loses his distinctiveness as Lord. Revelation remedies this in that the whole of revelation is concentrated in the Trinity. Thus, in the act of God coming to humans, God is distinguished from them. In the speech event, the question of how the divine can be the object of speech without the type of objectification that treats him like things in the world is answered. In revelation, God can become the subject of the speech event, such that he is speakable. This objectivity is sanctioned by God as reflective of his externalizing nature in the primary speech event. Yet, as a secondary speech event based on revelation, God's sovereignty is preserved in that he makes himself the meaningful object of human interpretation.

---

15. Jüngel writes, "God's reiteration is not, however, tautological identity, but indeed self-interpretation" (Jüngel, *God's Being*, 110).

A Consistently Applied Theology of the Cross

Jüngel has a tendency to find a thematic element that he believes can provide the necessary foundation for explaining diverse phenomena, analyzing that element, and then showing how it relates to the phenomena. In developing a theological anthropology, he uses justification. In understanding Christ's teaching, he uses parables.[16] In understanding the being of God, he uses a theology of the cross. This methodology is not unusual to him, since Barth and Moltmann similarly choose a Christological entrance into the question of the Trinity and revelation. However, whereas Barth focuses on incarnation and Moltmann focuses on eschatological being, Jüngel's sights are set squarely on the cross. Whether this is a valid central theme, or even a valid methodology, he does not really address. Instead, he throws his support for what he believes to be the central Lutheran concern.[17] If one agrees with this concern, then Jüngel provides a compelling vision of what the cross means concerning the being of a God who reveals.

One of the most noteworthy advantages of Jüngel's theology of the cross has to do with the relationship of God to history. When delving into the issue of divine speech and revelation, the question of how it relates to the historical lives of humans naturally arises. As was mentioned earlier, this is one of the benefits, as well as the detriments, to Wolterstorff's theory. Jüngel, likely due to his Hegelian influence, is concerned strongly with history and the way that it can problematize any divine-human interaction. He shies away from some of the traditional attempts to reconcile divinity to human history, believing them to be based on a mistaken view of God's transcendence[18] or a misunderstanding of where the locus of the question lies. Instead, he reconciles it, not unlike other areas of his dialectic, toward the divine thesis. In that God is defined at the cross, then God is already a historical being in that he is oriented toward a historical event whereby he

16. For Webster's criticism of this practice, see Webster, *Eberhard Jüngel*, 14. This difficulty will be resumed later in the chapter.

17. Why he does this is not explained with any length. A few possibilities are likely. Jüngel clearly believes that Luther's work was a necessary corrective to the overly speculative and metaphysical theology of scholasticism. His attraction to the work of Barth, who has similar themes, would appear to make Jüngel's support of a theology of the cross, at least partly, a matter of choosing an alternative to what he clearly believed to be mistaken. Moreover, Jüngel likely realizes that there are exegetical reasons for taking the crucifixion as a central aspect of Christian theology. Finally, he is constantly concerned with what makes a Christian theology uniquely Christian. Thus, the cross of Christ, which is a "folly to those who are perishing" (1 Cor 1:18) appears significant in developing a distinctly Christian understanding of God.

18. One example of this type of theory would be Paul Helm, who argues that God does not have "temporal relations" with humanity. See Helm, "What is Divine Eternity?"

desires a shared history with humankind. Concerning this, Jüngel claims, "Where the economic doctrine of the Trinity speaks of God's history with man, the immanent doctrine of the Trinity must speak of God's historicity. God's history is his coming to man. God's historicity is God's being as it comes (being in coming)."[19] In that God is historical being, the difficulty of human historicity is somewhat dissipated. God can speak to humans in history, because he is historical as one who has taken up humanity into his being. Thus, God has defined himself in terms of his historical relationship with humans, a relationship that is established and differentiated through the speech event. Consequently, in Jüngel, there is a natural way to reconcile God and humanity through history and the speech event. Evangelicalism, possessing both a concern with history and a relatively unformed theology of history, finds fertile grounds for the development and purification of an understanding of God's historical activity.

Furthermore, Jüngel's theology of the cross has the benefit of answering another significant question concerning divine (and human) speech. As theological issues concerning revelation arise, especially as they relate to the Bible, the subject of historical criticism is not far behind. He refrains from extremes, not wanting to dismiss it completely, nor to embrace it excessively. The difficulty with Bultmann's project of demythologization is that he does not have enough of an argument concerning where the practice of historical criticism in general should end. Should the cross be ejected if historians deemed it to lack historical veracity? Jüngel, however, has a natural answer to the questions, which is that the cross is the beginning and end of historical criticism. It is the beginning in that God's decision to be identified with the cross of Christ opens him up to historical inquiry. Yet, since God has "given us time,"[20] so that individuals "have time for him,"[21] the cross is the place of this givenness. At the cross, whereby God is distinguished in the speech event, he has oriented himself to humankind such that he will reveal to them. That revelation is an event and thus requires time and history. Therefore, in the revelatory event of the cross, humans are granted time and given history. For this reason, the cross of Christ as the place of the speech event whereby history is given its essence and God's love and holiness are revealed, itself cannot be questioned by historical criticism, owing to its transcendental nature. In this way, interior to Jüngel's crucicentric understanding of divine speech and being, it is given both the possibility and limit of historical criticism. In this way, Evangelicalism finds support

19. Jüngel, *God as the Mystery*, 347.

20. Barth, *CD* 2/1:62.

21. Jüngel, *God's Being*, 69.

for its concern with historical inquiry, as well as its reluctance towards critical methodologies.

Attending to the Text

The last area where Jüngel's work on speech and revelation has significant benefits to the debate in the field at large is on the existential dimensions of the Christian faith. The strain of Kierkegaard that comes through Barth is apparent in his attempt to take seriously that Christianity is not just a subject to be thought, but is a life to be lived. This is reinforced by the Lutheran continuance of the pietist tradition that has roots in the Franciscan concerns presented in Scotus. Thus, though consumed with highly theoretical matters, the implications of his theory to the practical life of the believer are never far from view. This can be seen in his focus on the *kerygma*, his attempt to explain experience in light of the speech event, and his account of faith. As was shown earlier, Jüngel believes that the speech event is a more fully existential theory than the previously used referential views of language, with significant repercussion in the area of the scriptural text.

Yet, it is not just his view of language, but his view of God's being, that supports a change in the focal point of scriptural understanding. As has been mentioned Jüngel believes that the philosophically influenced metaphysical understanding of God has largely obfuscated the reality of God's relationship to the world. Divinity conceived in terms of absolute presence and, therefore, actuality, does not do justice to the type of contingency necessary to make sense of God's interaction with the world, as well as his gracious decision to be identified with Jesus on the cross. God must be understood as present in his absence (i.e., "*als Abwesender anwesend*"),[22] and therefore not just existent in actuality, but also in possibility. This has far-reaching implications, not of the least of which is the need to revise the understanding of reality to include the possible.[23] Thus, Jüngel claims:

> Theologically it cannot be maintained that only that which is necessary is essential. Accidence also has its essence, and the contingent is also essential. That which happens contingently must not necessarily be less than necessary, or become capriciousness, merely because it is not necessary, it can also be *more than necessary*.[24]

22. Jüngel, *God as the Mystery*, 166; GT, 222.

23. See Jüngel, "Die Welt," 417–42. For a more extended treatment and extension of this idea, see Dalferth, *Die Wirklichkeit des Möglichen*.

24. Jüngel, *God as the Mystery*, 24; GT, 30.

He realizes the idea that "more than necessary" ("*mehr als notwendig*")[25] is somewhat problematic, but it appears to be his way of recognizing that God is essentially, but not necessarily, gracious. Though he does not mention the word in this context, it could be argued that Jüngel is trying to develop an ontology of grace. Were God to be necessarily gracious, then the idea would lose the type of contingency that prevents his activity from being the remunerating of wages.[26] God does not have to give of himself, but that must be a possibility. Thus, God possesses a quality that is essential, but not necessary, in that he is gracious. Hence, reality cannot just be reduced to what is actual, but it must include the possible.[27]

The ontology of grace which gives a higher premium to possibility in divine being, coupled with the existential nature of the speech event, causes Jüngel to remove the previously held stress on scriptural prose. He appears to believe that such types of speech focus on the actual to the detriment of possibility. Thus, Jüngel elevates the significance of analogy, metaphor, and parable in his understanding of scriptural language. His view of parable appears comparable to that of Paul Ricoeur, who understands fiction and poetry "to intend being, not under the modality of being-given, but under the modality of power to be."[28]

Though Jüngel would not be as prone to using fiction in such a fashion, he does believe that the modality of possibility is momentous for speech expressing an understanding of God. In doing so, he understands metaphor not merely as a didactic tool for the relay of ideas, but as a way of opening one up to possibilities. For this reason, Jüngel's view is not altogether different from Heidegger's aesthetic theory.[29] Unlike Wolterstorff, Jüngel does not want to understand metaphor as indirect speech, but direct in a different way. He admits that it does not have the same type of directness that the indicative statement does, but believes that it is even more direct in that it focuses on the concrete.[30] Whereas the indicative focuses on propositional content, which can be abstracting, he believes that thinking and truth

---

25. Jüngel possesses a rhetorical style that likes to make statements that appear bombastic and then explain them in such a way as they are not as extreme as they first appear. "More than necessary" is Jüngel's way of speaking of God's worldly non-necessity because he is not just defined by necessity, but by possibility.

26. This type of contrast is present in Romans 6:23.

27. Noteworthy in this view of reality is that Jüngel does not allow such a position to degrade into any of the more extreme forms of subjectivism.

28. Ricoeur, *Hermeneutics*, 142. For different analyses, see Black, *Models and Metaphors*; Martinich, "Theory of Metaphor," 485–96.

29. See Heidegger, "Origin of the Work of Art."

30. Jüngel, *God as the Mystery*, 292.

require more.[31] If one were to use Heideggerian terms, one might say that Jüngel believed that metaphor reveals a more primordial relationship in its disruptive nature than indicative language, since the latter has a tendency to reduce entities and activities to "presence-at-hand" (*Vorhandenheit*) or objective presence.[32]

In analogy, metaphor, and parable, language gains new meaning by being brought into a new context.[33] Thus, metaphor opens up possibilities by providing novel meaning to previously held signs. In this type of semiotic renewal, metaphor has a considerable role in mediating understanding of a God who is defined at the cross by his gracious contingency. Events, which are signs[34] that already have previous interpretations, can be interpreted anew in light of divine presence. The upshot of Jüngel's view of divine being and possibility is that genres of biblical literature that were downplayed or, at times, outrightly rejected, are once again given a position of importance. Thus, his view is a needed corrective of previously reductive positions in biblical hermeneutics,[35] ones that Evangelicalism have alternately been guilty of and also criticized.

A CRITIQUE OF JÜNGEL'S POSITION

The Phenomena of Speech and Revelation

From a methodological perspective, the most glaring difficulty in the work of Eberhard Jüngel is the manner in which he simplifies speech and revelation. Webster is correct in this type of criticism, but not for the reason that he holds. He argues: "[Jüngel's] manner could very loosely be termed 'monist.' That is to say, he tends to adhere very closely to one intellectual strategy to the exclusion of others, and tends to emphasize the coherent,

---

31. Jüngel, *Metaphorical Truth*, 26–27.

32. Heidegger writes: "We can abstract from nature's kind of being as handiness; we can discover and define it in its pure objective presence" (Heidegger, *Being and Time*, 66).

33. For comparable views, see Black, *Models and Metaphors*, 39; Riceour, "Metaphor and Reference," 215–56.

34. In this, Jüngel follows the long tradition that traces back to Augustine, whereby all things are signs with the potential of pointing one to God. See Augustine, *On Christian Teaching*, bks. 1–3.

35. A few examples of this would include critical methodologies that only allow authority to the recognized sayings of Jesus, liberal methodologies that privilege particular passages while denying the significance of others, and the Evangelical privileging of propositional content without the recognition of literary form.

unitary nature of his material."[36] In defense of Jüngel, the focus on one strategy is only incorrect if other strategies are necessary, which Webster does
not argue. Furthermore, to argue that his work is weaker for its emphasis on
the "unitary nature of his material" would be a criticism that could be lev-
eled against most dogmaticians and systematic theologians. That Jüngel is
reductive is not necessarily an inherent weakness, unless a critic can be successful in one of two endeavors: 1) Produce criteria for proper or improper
reduction and show where his theory is defective. 2) Show that there are
issues that he addresses inadequately, either by his claiming that his theory
is comprehensive enough to cover an area that it cannot, or by the failure of
his theory to correctly make sense of a topic, concerning which he claims
it can. Both of these need explanations before they can be further applied.

A philosophical argument that makes no distinctions between positions is typically unhelpful, since the purpose of the making such an argument is to distinguish between views one should hold and those that one
should not. Thus, to produce a criticism that can be applied to all positions rarely produces advancement in the understanding of a topic.[37] That
Jüngel's work is reductive is not a detriment to his theory, per se, since all
type of thinking is going to be reductive. Humans, in any thought process,
necessarily simplify the activity of thinking since the finite mind cannot
entertain all possibilities and relationships between ideas. Thus, as Dalferth
argues, there are ways in which we orient ourselves that systematically ignore certain information and experiences that are deemed unimportant
for what is being contemplated.[38] In this way, reduction, though often used
to malign theories, is a necessary way of human life. For this reason, to
criticize Jüngel's work as being reductive would need to provide criteria for
how his thought displays the negative type of reduction that will lead to a
fundamental misunderstanding of the issue at hand. Unfortunately, such an
understanding will cut against his theory later, with his preference for tropic
types of speech in reference to God.

What Webster comes closer to doing (under 2 above), is showing that
Jüngel's understanding of speech and revelation does not cover the domain
of phenomena, which it purports to explain. Webster writes:

---

36. Webster, *Eberhard Jüngel*, 5.

37. "Rarely" is used since a philosophical argument that applies to all known positions could be helpful in the sense that it forces individuals to seek answers elsewhere.
However, a philosophical argument that applies to not just all actual positions, but to
all possible ones, serves no practical purpose.

38. Dalferth, *Theology and Philosophy*, 7–8.

For his work tends to elevate metaphor, parable and analogy to a position where they become the only appropriate modes of Christian speech. In effect, this suppresses the multi-level, pluriform character of Christian religious language, failing to catch the range of its possibilities, and replacing an under-emphasis on tropic language by an over-emphasis.[39]

This accusation of reductionism is much more substantiated. Jüngel, though preventing the type of oversimplification that removes metaphor, parable, and analogy from appropriate speech about God, is guilty of the same type of oversimplification in both questioning the appropriateness of assertorial speech as well as failing to show how scriptural assertions should be understood in relation to metaphor, etc. In doing this, he follows the liberal tendency to focus on the sayings or parables of Jesus,[40] while downplaying the other types of texts. This is ironic, since his dissertation investigates the work of Paul and his theological anthropology emphasizes the Pauline doctrine of justification.[41]

Jüngel's attempt to retain a strong significance for metaphorical language, then, is strained for more than one reason. At the very least, his view may itself simplify metaphor to the point of not being able to cover many scriptural assertions. Intriguingly, though Jesus's role as speaker is significant in parabolic activity, Jüngel is much less apt to extol his role as interpreter. In the Parable of the Sower, Jesus provides a metaphorical story which includes seeds sown on four different soils and the ensuing consequences. When asked by his disciples why he speaks in parables, Jesus answers:

> To you it has been given to know the secrets of the kingdom of heaven, but to them it has not been given. For to him who has will more be given, and he will have abundance; but from him who has not, even what he has will be taken away. (Matt 13:11–12)

When asked for the reason why he would speak in parables, there is no hint of the sacramental nature of language. That is not to deny that this could be a possibility, since we have already seen the fruit that could be born from the speech event understanding. However, language can, and apparently is, used in other ways in the gospel. Jesus's answer is difficult for Jüngel in two ways. First, Jüngel claims that "it is an hermeneutical error of grave consequences when parables and metaphors are understood as a kind of veiling

---

39. Webster, "Eberhard Jüngel," 50.

40. Jüngel, *God as the Mystery*, 157.

41. See Jüngel, *Paulus und Jesus*; *Justification*.

which is supposed to make something "more mysterious" than it already is."[42] Yet, this appears to be exactly what is occurring. In order to prevent those whose "heart has grown dull" (ἐπαχύνθη . . . ἡ καρδία) (Matt 13:15) from understanding, while still speaking to the disciples and others who are receptive, he speaks parabolically. Second, though Jüngel wants to see the parables as irreducible speech events,[43] Jesus provides a very specific interpretation of his own parable (Matt 13:18–23). Thus, even though Jüngel understands metaphors and parables as being the most appropriate speech concerning God and his activity in the Kingdom, Jesus uses propositional language when speaking to his disciples, providing an, if not the, interpretation of the soils.

Metaphor is, consequently, significant to the understanding of God, but must be understood within the grander context of different ways of speaking about God. Jüngel would be better served to speak of the fact that metaphor is not always reducible, or not reducible without some loss. Yet, even if there is loss, this may just be a necessary reflection of the truth that speaking about God will necessarily be reductive in some manner. In calling for speech about himself, God must sanction simplification. Thus, conceptual reconstruction, the use of assertorial language, etc., may be one of the ways in which speaking about divinity, though reductive, may be appropriate. Moreover, the interrelated nature between metaphor and non-metaphorical speech is more complex than Jüngel appears to admit. If one were to come to those narratives in the New Testament where Jesus does not, unlike in the parable of the soils, preface his teaching by claiming it is a parable, one would wonder why they are categorized as such. To take parabolic utterance and elevate it, is not to realize that it is embedded in other types of linguistic structures that allow for the possibility of recognizing it as metaphor. If not, one might be able take the parable of the Good Samaritan (Luke 10:30–35) and simply understand it as a historical report. Yet, it is intertwined with questions, assertions, narrations, etc., which make it clear that it is not only a parable but also a parable with a point that can be referenced apart from the parable itself.[44]

Two other arguments deserve note, as to the significance of a wider domain of appropriate speech concerning God. First, Jüngel's preference for metaphor has to do with his understanding of its relationship to possibility. In reacting, as a good dialectical theologian, against the focus on actual

---

42. Jüngel, *God as the Mystery*, 292.

43. In this, Jüngel is likely influenced by both Fuchs and Barth. For an analysis of this relationship, see Webster, *Eberhard Jüngel*, 10.

44. i.e., "Who . . . proved neighbor . . . ?" (Luke 10:37)

presence in metaphysically influenced perspectives on God, he gives strong preference to the possible. He believes this is more in line with divine freedom as assumed in Scripture, as well as the eschatological nature of Jesus life and Kingdom proclamation. Yet, it is possible to argue that such an emphasis can fail to recognize the inseparability of the possible from the actual. One can discern a similar argument in Ricoeur's claim that the temporal ecstasies are both indivisible and indissoluble.[45] Each requires the others, and each permeates the others. Moreover, Heidegger promotes a similar understanding in that what are called past, present, and future, in the natural sciences, are really the inseparable unity for *Dasein* of being "thrown," having "projects" and enacting one's life.[46] Therefore, though Jüngel is correct, along with Dalferth, to give a greater emphasis on possibility for human understanding of reality, his emphasis appears come with the less desirable deprecation of the actual. Language, though needing the idea of possibility inherent within metaphor, especially in its ability to innovate and extend meaning, it also requires the constancy of non-metaphorical speech. Metaphor appears to require non-metaphorical language to identify metaphors as metaphors, and to provide the narrative backdrop for the metaphor to do what it is meant to do.[47] Referential language can be understood as reified metaphors that provide stability necessary for speech to be used in relationships that are historical. Since relationships are interactive over time, if only metaphor was used, with its constant innovation, meaning would gain a type of plasticity that not only allows extension, which is important, but also prevents two individuals from ever knowing if they are speaking about the same world. Referential views of language, though much maligned, are rightly declared to be oversimplifications, but wrongly declared to be dispensable. This may be the reason that even when emphasizing the speech event nature of speaking, Jüngel does not want to remove semiotic and referential functions.[48] Where the Evangelical must hold to a significant place for assertions in the revelation of knowledge, which may be significant for theology as well as the interpretation of God's self-revelation in Christ, she does not necessarily require Scripture to be reduced to assertorial or literal language. This does not mean that such reduction does not occur. Evangelicalism shares with Jüngel a propensity to elevate specific (though

---

45. Ricoeur, *Time and Narrative*, 207–40.

46. See Heidegger, *Being and Time*, 126–29, 135–41

47. For Jüngel's view of the narrative involved in metaphor, see Jüngel, "Metaphorical Truth," 61–63.

48. Jüngel, *God as the Mystery*, 6–9.

admittedly different) ways of speaking about God, when neither position requires that this be so.

Second, there is a practical necessity to assertorial language, as well as reductive speech. Missiologically, it is difficult to know whether the church could fulfill its *kerygmatic* function if only metaphorical language is appropriate. Jüngel realizes that the story of Jesus is, as proclamation in nature "does not simply address one privately but rather in such a way that it can be passed on as something addressing everyone."[49] Yet, translation or preaching will both require some linguistic movement from the base story. For example, Peter's theological explication of the gospel of the resurrected Christ in Acts 2 is not given in primarily metaphorical terms. Part of the significance of the role of the apostles in foundation of the church after the ascension of Christ, had to do with their interpretation of the life of Jesus. When they did so, they did use metaphors to speak of his life and work, but also simply made referential statements and narrated literally. Didactically, there is a practically necessity for non-metaphorical language. Humans often seek the proposition of what is said for memory's sake. For example, Jesus's hearers could not be expected to memorize his parables when he spoke them. Hence, the proposition, not unlike had been claimed in analytic philosophy, allows the parable to move beyond its temporality. This is done not in a Platonic way, but simply in the continuity of enactment of the person as a historical individual. For the parable to remain alive in the mind of the hearers, a reduction of the parable may be required. Related to this, is the fact that since the Kingdom of God does not just require a reaction at a particular time, but a life that is reoriented before God, the need for the parables to have a manner of continuity is significant. The sacramental nature of the speech events appears to allow for some impact in the parables that requires little interpretation, which is significant to missiology. However, the conceptualizable nature of the parables allows for the impact to continue as assertions about God are used for continued application, which has soteriological and ecclesiological significance. Similarly, it appears that appropriate speech about God cannot be reduced to metaphor and parables, since non-metaphorical language is necessary at various levels.

It should be noted that though Jüngel's position on metaphor may be untenable from an exegetical perspective, he has a much stronger argument concerning his understanding of the metaphorical nature of God becoming present in the Word of God. The rupture structure of God's coming, as well as the manner in which that coming is in identification with another, points to a metaphorical activity. It is the theological understanding that is most

49. Jüngel, *God as the Mystery*, 306.

tenable, but not without criticism. In chapters 11–12, amidst an outline of the manner in which a consistent understanding of speech and revelation can be sought in conversation with Jüngel, Wolterstorff, and Farrer, it will be argued that Jüngel is only able to provide a partial picture of significance of the Word event by using the category of metaphor. It will parallel the reasons given here concerning human speech testifying to God, specifically that there is a need for understanding God coming in identification with Jesus Christ in a non-metaphorical manner to bring consistency and continuity between that event and the history of humanity. In other words, even if metaphors are foundational for language, literal language's reification of metaphor may mirror God's identification with a historical event that, in its constancy, gives rise to the ability to speak and think about God directly. Thus, the Evangelical's continuance of a two natures Christology is not only justified, but there even remains the possibility that such a view could have points of contact to appropriate certain aspects of Jüngel's trinitarian ontology.[50]

Not only is Jüngel's view of speech unnecessarily reductive, but so is his understanding of revelation. The revelatory event, within the Barthian tradition, is typically understood in terms of Christ. Though correct that this is the most significant revelatory act, overemphasis of this point often leads to a dismissal of other events of revelation. In many ways, the term "revelation" becomes a technical term for a token event and not a type of event.[51] Thus, happenings such as a burning bush, a prophetic utterance, a dream or vision, etc., cannot be understood to be revelatory. For Jüngel, this is, at least practically, the outcome of his perspective. Whereas Wolterstorff consciously sets aside the incarnation, while claiming its importance to a full idea of revelation, Jüngel sets aside all but the incarnation. Though revelation may be at its most significant in terms of personal self-revelation, this does not negate the possibility that something else can also be revelatory, such as a statement. Moreover, there appear to be times where revelation of "items of knowledge" may be important to personal revelation. This seems to be an implication of Augustine's relating of knowledge and love

50. Only parts could be assumed, as is obvious, since "identification" itself would not be able to function within an Evangelical system. However, the idea that God's self-interpretation is metaphorical in structure could be used, as long as it is understood that the Word becomes reified and continuous in the constancy of the trinitarian life. Thus, Christ not only possesses the immutability that Evangelicalism would defend, but also possesses the constancy necessary to argue that God's eschatological presence in Christ is both real and continuous.

51. In order to defend the uniqueness and paradigmatic nature of God's self-revelation in Christ, Jüngel appears to deny that revelation is an event type, but is only the token event of God's concrete identification with the man Jesus at the cross.

in *De Trinitate.*[52] The Bishop of Hippo recognized the difficulty in relating to God in that it appears one would need to know him to love him, but that one could not really know him without loving him. Similarly, it is difficult to know if one could be revealed in person without any accompanying knowledge being revealed about the person. Though Jüngel is correct in his emphasis on revelation in the Trinity, a substantial task in understanding the idea is to relate the revelation of God in himself to other forms of revelation. It must be recognized that he is not ignorant of this difficulty and that one's agreement with the strength of his overall understanding of revelation will, in many ways, rise or fall with one's assessment of whether Scripture can legitimately be explained solely in terms of testimony. If not, then the Evangelical perspective on inspiration provides a compelling alternative.

Methodology and Metaphysics

Methodology in theology is a difficult issue in that methodological considerations are often used to dismiss legitimate concerns or downplay the difference between God and humans. For example, in Descartes's case, methodology was more for the purpose of providing certainty, than for the development of faith. Whereas faith is understood in terms of trust, to believe that right method could lead to perfect certainty is to attempt to do away with trust. Yet, methodological concerns can be legitimate when they are not an attempt to be dismissive of theological understanding, but reflective of it. In this way, Jüngel's methodology has both benefits and weaknesses. The most significant benefit is that he, in his dialectic methodology, both looks at the theological understanding of a particular idea, as well as its phenomenological presentation in everyday life. When examining love, he performs an analysis of it in terms of how it presents itself within normal contexts. He then seeks to reconcile this with a theologically defined view of love.[53] This method is significant since it provides the natural bridge between normal language usage, and the way in which language can be transformed in theological contexts, without losing connection to said mundane uses. Such methodology is found in his predecessor, Ebeling, who uses something similar in understanding the term "God."[54] This bridge is important if one wants to be able to connect theology to other fields of

---

52. Augustine, *Trinity*, 247–50.

53. Jüngel, *God as the Mystery*, 317–30.

54. Ebeling believes that this type of method is not unlike that of Aquinas's in the early part of the *Summa*. See Ebeling, *God and Word*, 26.

study, such that speech in one can relate to speech in the other.[55] Moreover, this methodology is supportive of Evangelicalism's attempt to show that the understanding of Scripture is related to all areas of life, without giving up the supremacy of Scripture in the development of an a manner of interpreting those areas.

Within Jüngel's methodology, two difficulties are apparent. First, he appears to be inconsistent in its application. Whereas love is given treatment both theologically and non-theologically, speech is not afforded the same luxury. His assumption of a Heideggerian account of language and being prevents the type of in-depth examination of speech that would allow him to recognize its more multifarious usage. Second, the actual bridge between theological and non-theological accounts of phenomena is never explicated clearly. His relationship between both appears to be *ad hoc* at times. Ironically, it appears that Jüngel is in need of a metaphysical perspective, or at least some principle of unity, to bring harmony between both types of speech. Without this, there is no strong justification for a dialectical consideration of divine and human speech. Though Jüngel appears to need a metaphysic, he is reluctant to develop one. Recognizing some of the difficulties that have been wrought from a metaphysical perspective of God, he is rightly cautious. Yet, his caution leads to paralysis, which further leads to his commendation to "simply leaving [metaphysics] to itself."[56] It will be argued, later, that metaphysics, when rightly understood, will not be antagonistic to Jüngel's hermeneutical backdrop or dialectical methodology.

The Being of God and Hermeneutics

Jüngel takes the, not unusual, position of placing love in a position of hermeneutical supremacy when understanding the being of God. He claims,

> The corresponding hermeneutical study of the problem of the speakability of God is also nourished by the material statement that God has defined himself through identification with the crucified Jesus. . . . For then we can say that God is love. As love he is the mystery of the world.[57]

---

55. Unfortunately, Jüngel does not pursue an understanding of how the different fields relate. This is especially problematic in light of the perceived antithetical nature of science and revelation. See Brunner, *Revelation and Reason*, 294–309. For a criticism of this failure, see Dalferth, *Mystery of Words*, 98.

56. Jüngel, *God as the Mystery*, 49.

57. Jüngel, *God as the Mystery*, x.

For Jüngel, God's definition through identification has a very particular interpretation. The God who is identified with the crucified Jesus must be understood primarily *and* paradigmatically as love.[58] In this way, any purported understanding of God must find its legitimacy in relationship to the manner in which it relates to God's love. An example can be seen in Jüngel's treatment of divine power. Though there are times that God's power has been interpreted as antithetical to his love, Jüngel claims that power must be understood in terms of love. Thus, he writes, "There is, however, only one phenomenon in which power and weakness do not contradict each other, in which rather power can perfect itself as weakness. This phenomenon is the event of love."[59]

The legitimacy of the practice of making love the interpretive locus of the being of God, based on the event of the cross, requires justification in a few areas. Jüngel does not provide much exegetical support for the exercise, deriving his support externally. He recognizes that the supremacy of love has strong traditional support. Moreover, he believes it is the legitimate outcome of his theopaschite presupposition. For Jüngel, if the being of God is defined at the cross, then it is defined as love. It should be noted that this move is relatively rapid and has great significance in terms of scriptural exegesis. In many ways, God's self-definition as love provides a criterion for which texts matter in understanding divine being, as well as how texts should be interpreted. Jüngel, perhaps because he never wrote significantly in the area of commentaries, is willing to be selective in his exegesis. This, however, is a problematic practice for a myriad of reasons. Augustine's argument against the admission of errancy of Scripture appears to be analogous. The Bishop writes:

> For if you once admit into such a high sanctuary of authority one false statement as made in the way of duty, there will not be left a single sentence of those books which, if appearing to any one difficult in practice or hard to believe, may not by the same fatal rule be explained away, as a statement in which, intentionally, and under a sense of duty, the author declared what was not true.[60]

Regardless of what one believes concerning the errancy of Scripture, his argument appears applicable. Augustine believed that if one allowed an individual to declare a portion of the text to be false, then individuals will begin to disregard other parts simply because they were difficult to interpret

58. Jüngel, *God as the Mystery*, 316.

59. Jüngel, *God as the Mystery*, 206.

60. Augustine, *Letters*, 28.3:252.

or difficult to live. Similarly, Jüngel's willingness towards selectivity in scriptural interpretation appears to be prone to a similar danger. When texts appear to be in contradiction to his understanding of love, they can be dismissed or reinterpreted. For example, he dismisses the possibility of God being jealous,[61] without serious attempts at finding a mechanism of reconciliation.[62] This is not contradictory to his theological methodology, since he believes the word of theology is meant to seek understanding of the Word of God such that Jesus Christ can be the criterion for significance of Scripture.

Since texts can be *kerygmatic* or a reflection of the author's human situatedness in theological reflection, Jüngel believes theology helps determine which texts rightly reflect the Word of God. Yet, if his initial selection of texts and their interpretation, on which he builds his theological exegesis, is prone to criticism, then his later selectivity based on his understanding of the Word may not be consistent. The two outcomes, then are as follows: First, a failure at interpretation initially may provide Jüngel with an insufficient understanding of God's self-interpretation in the Word, which could cause him to be incorrectly selective concerning the significance of other Biblical texts. Jüngel is right to not pretend that all texts point with the same specificity and concreteness to the Word of God. Yet, his ability to use Jesus to draw distinctions between how texts can variously succeed and fail to testify to God's self-interpretation in the Word event will only be as convincing as his initial interpretation of the cross. Second, the rapidity by which Jüngel moves from his understanding of the Word to how Scripture can be the norm for Christian thought may prevent the type of disruptive nature that Jüngel wants to retain. Instead of Scripture providing norms which can mold one's understanding, Scripture is prevented from interruption of one's preconceived understanding of love. In other words, his willingness to disregard texts may prevent the Word from the disruption necessary to display God's presence.

Not only does Jüngel not provide enough exegetical and theological justification for the idea that God is to be understood primarily as love, but there are actually exegetical and theological reasons that may argue differently, or at least give one cause to proceed cautiously. Brunner argues that a theology of the cross must understand love as being in dialectic with holiness. He writes that love stands in "dialectical relation to holiness, without

61. Jüngel, *God as the Mystery*, 261.

62. One possibility would be the understanding of love in terms of the particularity of love, such that if one is in a love relationship, they would desire fidelity. In this case, love and jealousy would not be antithetical even if the prior is held as being more central.

any analogy."[63] Brunner does not deny that there is unity between them,[64] but does want to resist the sublating of one into the other. The question must be asked whether he has a reasonable argument. Exegetically, terms for holiness or its cognates (ἅγιος, ἁγιασμός, ἁγιάζω, etc.) are used nearly as much in the New Testament as terms for love (ἀγαπάω, φιλέω, etc.). Theologically, the cross is an event that stresses the dialectic. It is the passing from the Old into the New, the place of life and death, the unity of God and man (in Jüngel's view), etc. Thus, the interpretation of the cross as love, without reference to holiness, too easily resolves the tension that is meant to be represented in the crucified Jesus. Overall, Dalferth's criticism of hermeneutical theology appears to be correct, in that he writes, "often the christological proposals are more prescriptive in character than descriptive because the constructive conceptual task of theology is not sufficiently clearly distinguished from the expressive language of faith."[65] Jüngel appears to fail to do justice to the scriptural norms concerning how one should speak about God and his activity, with the outcome that theology makes declarations that have exegetical deficiencies. Evangelicalism attempts, though not always successfully, at retaining this dialectic since the love of God is often understood in terms of holiness, and vice versa. Thus, where Jüngel has the proclivity towards making God's love the criterion for exegetical significance in Scripture, based on his understanding of the cross, the Evangelical will want to retain the complexity and tension inherent in the dialectic of love and holiness.

The last criticism of Jüngel's understanding of the relationship between God's being and hermeneutics, has to do with the somewhat diminished role of the Holy Spirit.[66] In *God as the Mystery of the World*, the Spirit is not addressed until the end of the book, and then, only tangentially. Emphasizing a particular member of the Trinity is not unusual. It might be argued that Pannenberg, Moltmann, and Jüngel variously emphasize the Father, Son, and Holy Spirit. This, as a practice, does not provide intrinsically difficult. However, when you claim that a full trinitarian understanding of revelation is necessary, as the latter does, then it appears incumbent to provide a more developed pneumatology.[67] Such an oversight seems problematic

---

63. Brunner, *Revelation and Reason*, 45–46.

64. Brunner, *Revelation and Reason*, 46.

65. Jüngel, *God as the Mystery*, 95. It must be admitted that Dalferth tends to agree with Jüngel's understanding of the cross.

66. This is a common criticism of Jüngel. See Wainwright, "Church and Sacrament(s)," 95; Webster, *Eberhard Jüngel*, 76.

67. For a brief explanation of their differences in understanding the Holy Spirit, see Milbank, "Second Difference," 222–25.

for two, previously, mentioned reasons. First, without the Holy Spirit, the complications of sin to a doctrine of revelation may be insurmountable.[68] Second, the eschatological nature of God's revelation in Christ makes the Spirit a significant factor in the speech event. Evangelicalism, with its claims to the importance of "conversionism," will require a more developed pneumatological understanding such that "new birth" is given proper theological elucidation.

SUMMARY OF ASSESSMENT

Jüngel's understanding of divine speech and revelation is complex and nuanced. His revision of his predecessor's dialectical methodology allows for greater success at bringing together human and divine speech. Moreover, his employment of speech events, though somewhat overly reductive, is helpful in understanding what is occurring in speech. His Barthian view of revelation is also significant, as is his explication of the significance of the revelatory act in mediating between primary and secondary speech events. Furthermore, his theology of the cross is consistently applied and allows him to defend the speakability and thinkability of God. He also defends Scripture from the type of reductionism that sets aside tropic ways of speaking.

Yet, Jüngel's view is, itself, reductionist in another way in downplaying the role of assertorial speech, as well as leaving underdeveloped the relationship between metaphorical and non-metaphorical texts. Though many of his criticisms of metaphysics are warranted, he appears in want of a metaphysic that would allow unity to theological and non-theological types of speaking. Furthermore, his concentration of the hermeneutical primacy of love may be inconsistent with the exegetical evidence, while his interpretation of the material statement concerning the identification of God and the cross of Jesus may lead to a loss of the significance of divine holiness. It would appear to be more consistent to hold holiness and love in a dialectic at the cross.

---

68. This is often the view in a Calvinist influenced understanding of revelation.

AUSTIN FARRER

8

Farrer's Influences and Methodology

AUSTIN FARRER IS A fascinating philosophical and theological figure in that he is both a creature of tradition, as well as, an innovator and a nonconformist. Though converted to Anglicanism and schooled in High Church piety, his Baptist roots can be observed in his inquiry into Reformed themes against a Catholic backdrop.[1] Thus, though Thomas looms large over his thought, he is by no means a Thomist. He gains a penchant to rational theology from the Church of England and its mediation of scholasticism, while tempering it with pietism and a focus on God's revelatory activity that is more characteristic of his upbringing. It is this combination that both makes Farrer an intriguing subject, especially when his work is investigated in conjunction with Jüngel's Lutheran background and Wolterstorff's version of Calvinism, and also makes his work difficult to analyze. It might be an understatement to call his work eclectic, both in influences and in subject matter. Moreover, Farrer's style, often poetic and intentional, along with his propensity to use theologians and philosophers without explicit mention of their work, complicates interpretation. These complexities compelled Robert MacSwain, a scholar who is undoubtedly sympathetic to his work, to claim, "Cultural and academic trends have in many ways made Farrer seem old-fashioned or irrelevant, but Farrer's idiosyncrasies and difficulties have not helped his reputation."[2] In light of the intricacy of his thought

1. Concerning this, Robert MacSwain writes, "His conviction is built on two principles: (1) his Catholic belief in the reality of apostolic succession and consequent role of the sacraments, and (2) his Reformed belief that Scripture is the touchstone of doctrine" (MacSwain, "Above, Beside, Within," 42).

2. MacSwain, "Above, Beside, Within," 36.

and the obstacles to a correct representation of theology and philosophy, any proposal as to how to understand his overall project must be tentative and constantly open to qualifications. With this in mind, it could be argued that Farrer's work should be understood as a personalistic/voluntaristic recasting of scholastic metaphysics. Thus, his terminology and categories are influenced by Scholastic Aristotelianism even as he attempts to "purge out the Old Aristotelian leaven from the voluntarist metaphysics [he] sketched so many years ago in *Finite and Infinite*."[3] His view of divine speech and revelation, then, can be understood in terms of how his Reformed influences cause him to both converge upon and diverge with Catholic scholasticism. In this, he can give voice to concerns that correspond to Evangelicalism's own desire to continue many aspects of orthodoxy without the indiscriminate acceptance of previous theological traditions.

FARRER'S THEOLOGICAL AND PHILOSOPHICAL FOUNDATIONS[4]

Due to his lack of citations, Farrer's influences often have to be reconstructed by ideological similarities and biographical connections.[5] Unfortunately, this will be somewhat speculative and require one to often speak in probabilities. The least tentative connection, however, can be seen in Farrer's appropriation of Thomism. That is not to say that he has no other connections to Catholicism, since he frequently mentioned the mystical and spiritual writings of the tradition in his sermons.[6] Yet, Aquinas's influence is the most pronounced, even if only a catalyst for Farrer's reactionary movement. For this reason, it is prudent to inquire into the main ways in which the former affected the latter.

---

3. Farrer, *Faith and Speculation*, v.

4. Space will not permit an examination of Farrer's literary influences, which often shade into his philosophical and theological thought. His obvious fellowship with the Metaphysicals, as well as his oft-recognized parallels with Coleridge, warrant a type of scrutiny which the present book cannot do justice. For some of these connections, see Platten, "Diaphanous Thought," 30–50; Mitchell, "Introduction," 1–13; Hedley, "Austin Farrer's Shaping," 106–34; McGrade, "Reason," 115–30.

5. An example of the latter would be his well-documented interaction with Neo-Orthodoxy in his attendance of lectures by Bultmann. Though he is rarely explicit about his reaction to or resumption of German theology, his interest is often coupled with theological comparisons and contrasts to argue for an influence that is at least tangential.

6. For a few examples, see Platten, "Diaphanous Thought," 34.

Drawing a clear picture of the relationship of Farrer to Aquinas is complicated by the development in Farrer's own thought, as typified by the difference between his early work *Finite and Infinite* and his later *Faith and Speculation*.[7] *Finite and Infinite* is often considered a classic of metaphysics, and was a rarity in the Anglo-American world in the twentieth century, especially since it came during a time where the field was still reeling from the attacks launched by positivists in the 30's and 40's. At the time of its writing, Farrer admitted that he was "possessed by the Thomist vision."[8] In it, he attempted to defend the possibility of rational theology, especially in terms of the possibility of the mind's assent to an understanding of God. Yet, like his Catholic counterpart, he was skeptical that one could move beyond a bare theism without something like revelation. In his defense of metaphysics and the possibility of coming to rational knowledge of God aside from revelatory activity, he follows many Thomist and Aristotelian themes. These would include the use of substance as basis for analogical talk about God, a strong relationship between substance and essence,[9] and a confidence in the capacity of reason to examine the world and draw conclusions concerning God. Farrer does not slavishly follow Aquinas, even at this early point in his corpus. Though activity is a significant factor in the Thomist conception of Divine nature, it plays a larger role in Farrer in that substance is intimately tied to action as the "unifying principle"[10] which allows the singularity of substance in spite of a manifold of characteristics and habits that something may express.

By the time of *Faith and Speculation*, Farrer was much more reticent to use categories such as form and substance in metaphysics. Yet, he never fully rejected his rational project, nor metaphysics as a significant factor in philosophical thinking. He continued to defend the possibility of cosmological inference to the nature of God and his activities, but did so giving a primacy to faith. Since God is unique among objects of thought,[11] Farrer believed that only by a stance of faith could one begin to understand him. If God was to be known, he was to be known as a person; a conclusion he draws from the confluence of multiple lines of reasoning. Since God is to be known in the world, there must be some sort of empirical possibility of understanding him. Yet, knowing that he should not be treated as a physical entity, he proposes a restructuring of the empirical principle, claiming, "We

7. See Farrer, *Finite and Infinite; Faith and Speculation.*

8. Farrer, *Finite and Infinite*, ix.

9. Farrer, *Finite and Infinite*, 37–40.

10. Farrer, *Finite and Infinite*, 79.

11. Farrer, *Faith and Speculation*, 10.

can think about no reality, about which we can do nothing but think."[12] Thus, there must be some way to interact with God personally and, from the Christian perspective, this can occur in Jesus Christ. Consequently, Farrer moves in *Faith and Speculation*, towards a primacy in faith in the understanding of God, including his existence. It is this movement that has caused Farrer's work to receive such varied interpretations as seen in the Catholic-influenced Hebblethwaite and the more Protestant leaning Diogenes Allen.[13] Regardless of who is closer to Farrer's work, his later perspective is undoubtedly more removed from his Thomist roots.

Aquinas was representative of scholastic thought in his willingness to examine secular thinkers to see if they could be appropriated by Christian theology. It is this willingness that is often caricaturized as a blind submission to Greek philosophy. There can be no doubt that he was heavily reliant on Aristotle and Plato and at times appears to offer them the benefit of the doubt in the face of criticism, but this type of argumentation neglects the question of whether he had good exegetical or theological reasons to believe similarly to previous philosophers. For Aquinas, it appears that he saw natural similarities between the manner in which Aristotle conceived of reality and what he believed to be portrayed by the writers of Scripture. Thus, part of his project was an answering of how such correspondence could exist if the only clear knowledge of reality, including God and the true nature of the world, could be had from revelatory sources. It appears that Aquinas surmises the possibility of natural theology from his belief that it was actually occurring. It is this belief that finds a certain parallel in the early thought of Farrer. It is true that his relationship to Aristotle became increasingly strained as he realized that Aristotle's categories of causation and understanding of being would not be able to fully bear the theological personalism that he grew to hold quite stringently. He claimed, "It remains that if we talk theology at all we are committed to 'personality' language. It is the very substance of our discourse, and we must suspect of a watery sophistication any theological statement which tends to dilute it."[14] Yet, the belief that natural theology is possible appears to never evaporate entirely from his thought. To be sure, his manner of doing natural theology was decidedly different from Aquinas, focusing less on inferential arguments[15] about the world and more on the created subject's recognition of dependence upon

---

12. Farrer, *Faith and Speculation*, 22, 172.

13. See Hebblethwaite, *Philosphical Theology*, 27–40.

14. Farrer, "Revelation," 96.

15. For Farrer's beliefs concerning the possibility of proving the existence of God *a posteriori*, see Farrer, *Finite and Infinite*, 1–13.

the creator,[16] but he initially held out the prospect of a natural understanding of God. Whereas the division of labor in thinking within the scholastic mindset was between reason and revelation,[17] Farrer writes:

> 'Reason and Revelation' is a current description, but a bad description, for the antithesis we have to discuss. We ought to say 'Natural Reason and Supernatural Revelation,' and we ought to throw the emphasis on the adjectives rather than upon the nouns. We have not to distinguish between God's action and ours, but between two phases of God's action—his supernatural action, and his action by way of nature.[18]

In this, he is similar to Aquinas in attempting to emphasize the grace of even the "natural" act of thinking of God apart from revelation.[19] For both, God's act in creating humans, endowing them with rational faculties, and providing them with an ordered world is enough to prevent humans from claiming credit for knowing God through nature.[20] It is also due to this common consideration why they can believe that a philosopher can come to natural knowledge of God whereby a Christian can see parallels between the beliefs of faith and the beliefs derived from a posteriori knowledge. Therefore, he is initially in agreement with his scholastic precursor that natural theology is possible, even if it is limited in nature.

As Farrer continues in his career, the limitations on natural theology become more pronounced until he makes a break from Aquinas in seeing cosmological inference requiring a previous acquaintance with God. Farrer, in the more Thomist phase of his thinking, seemed to believe that natural knowledge of God could be had, because it had actually been possessed by those who were not Christian. Thus, he felt compelled to explain this possibility, eventually coming to the conclusion that "There is nothing supernatural

---

16. The role of this dependence is debated. Dalferth holds that such dependence comes from the previous experience of grace that occurs in the life of the believer, while Hebblethwaite argues that Farrer's claim that awareness of "existential insufficiency" only "comes through faith" is an exaggerated concession and not indicative of his overall project. In either case, natural theology may have a role, but scholars differ on what Farrer recognized in its possibilities. See Dalferth, "Esse Est Operari," 183–84; Hebblethwaite, *Philosophical Theology*, 39–40.

17. For an explanation of this view, especially in comparison to other attempts to investigate the relationship between theological and philosophical knowledge, see Dalferth, *Theology and Philosophy*, 61–148.

18. Farrer, *Glass of Vision*, 3.

19. See Aquinas, *Faith, Reason, and Theology*, 13–18.

20. Aquinas, *Faith, Reason, and Theology*, 99.

about Aristotle's enlightenment."[21] As he progresses in an anti-Aristotelian manner, he appears to come closer to the view of Calvin which finds parallel in the *Westminster Confession of Faith*, whereby natural knowledge of God is theoretically possible "if Adam had remained upright,"[22] but not possible in the fallen current state of the world.[23] This is similar to the manner in which *Westminster* also describes an individual's reaction to Scripture.[24] Likewise, Farrer appears to become more skeptical whether an individual in their natural, post-lapsarian, state, could actually come to any understanding of God apart from faith. It should be noted that, unlike some strains of theology, especially from the Barthian tradition,[25] Farrer agrees with Thomism that creation will reflect the Creator in some way that is discernible by reason. Yet, towards the end of his academic career, such understanding would have to be preceded by a relationship with God.

Aquinas's influence on Farrer not only extends to natural theology, but also, as was mentioned previously, to metaphysics. Farrer's introduction to metaphysical thinking occurs relatively early and is significant throughout his career. However, his thoughts on the matter are not monolithic nor unchanging. Though his introduction to metaphysics likely occurs through scholasticism, he progressively moves away from an Aristotelian substance view, since he has difficulty reconciling it with the personal nature of the trinitarian God he believed to be depicted in Scripture. For the scholastics, substances could make choices, which is necessary such that God could choose. However, such choice is not definitive of being, in a way that Farrer believes necessary for a truly personalistic understanding of divine ontology. In spite of this difference, conceptually, his metaphysical understanding had certain parallels to Thomist thinking. Theologically, his version of a substance metaphysics appeared to provide a certain type of stability he needed to prevent his focus on divine voluntarism from shifting too far in the direction of a process understanding, a view from which he was quick to distinguish himself.[26]

21. Farrer, *Glass of Vision*, 5.

22. Calvin, *Institutes*, 1.1:40.

23. For a concise summary of Calvin's view of natural knowledge of God, see Steinmetz, *Calvin in Context*, 23–39.

24. Hodge, *Confession*, 1.5:35.

25. This is not to say that every neo-Barthian sees no such reflection. However, the emphasis on the necessity of divine revelation has driven some in Neo-Orthodoxy to be reluctant to see any such reflection that might provide a naturalistic alternative to God's direct activity.

26. Farrer, *Finite and Infinite*, 299–300; *Faith and Speculation*, 142–55.

In order to see how Farrer separates himself from process thought, a cursory look at his view of voluntarism is necessary. For him, God is to be conceived as "free, absolute, or sovereign Will."[27] Such a perspective has a few implications for his philosophical and theological understanding. First, Farrer believes that God's voluntary decision is a decision for community. Thus, God is not only supposed to be understood in terms of divine Will, but in terms of divine personhood. Thus, he makes the, not unusual, move of understanding the Trinity as fundamentally a doctrine that describes God's relational nature.[28] In this way, divine voluntarism is inseparable from theological personalism, which means that Farrer will always attempt to defend the possibility of God relating personally to humanity. Second, his view of voluntarism also means that a view of God as Absolute Mind will be downplayed in favor of God's free choice.[29] This is not to say that such a perspective is absent, but when he thinks of the manner in which understanding of God can be approached analogically, the human faculty of the will is his typical starting point. Lastly, Farrer's view of divine voluntarism has far-reaching systematic importance to him in areas such as double agency, the practical nature of theology, and his theological anthropology. Thus, his perspective is not limited to outcomes in terms of theology proper.

Farrer is attracted to certain aspects of process philosophy, especially as he follows the path of many twentieth-century Catholics in embracing a developmental view of humanity as supported by evolutionary biology. He agrees with process philosophers that metaphysics is necessary, but must be reframed to deal with what they see to be the overly static nature of Aristotelian substance perspectives. Moreover, Farrer's concern with the complicated nature of the world, the significance of the sciences, and the interface between faith and other disciplines, also gives rise to interaction with process philosophy. Yet, he has two major, interrelated concerns that cause him to reject the overall project of process philosophers. First, in his attempt to understand the complex manner in which the different constituents[30] of the world interact, he finds that their sheer diversity prevents the

---

27. Farrer, *Faith and Speculation*, 173.

28. It should be recognized that his view of the Trinity has strong affinities, as has been noticed by Hebblethwaite, with Augustine's conception. He conceives of the Trinity as a community of two: The Father and the Son, with the Spirit being understood in terms of inspiration. See Farrer, *Saving Belief*, 128–29.

29. Throughout Farrer's writing, he makes allusions to God as Mind, but they tend to be sublimated to a view of God as Will. For a few allusions, see Farrer, *Finite and Infinite*, 102; *Faith and Speculation*, 175.

30. This would include physical entities, processes, actions, non-physical accompaniments to actions such as choices, etc.

type of unity that he believes is necessary for understanding the world and also precludes a consistent metaphysic that can provide such unity. In the face of the strong connection between God's activities and that of humans,[31] as well as Farrer's postulation that God primarily acts through history, it would appear natural for him to move to a type of immanentalism that sees some sort of identification of the world with God. Yet, the unity that God provides, for Farrer, means that "God can be the Universal Mind only by transcending that multiplicity which the Universe is."[32] Second, Farrer's type of voluntarism, requires a personalism that he believes to be absent from most types of process thought. Consequently, he believes that Christianity does not cohere well with those types of ideologies. This stance is further supported by exegetical and theological concerns, especially as they relate to Christianity's conception of the specific actions of God. He writes that "neither providence nor grace is excluded by the scheme of rational theology, as they would be excluded by a consistent pantheism, for instance."[33] Farrer's combination of a Christian perspective on the activities of God with the divine voluntarism he derives from rational theology, prevents pantheistic[34] styles of process philosophy from holding sway over his perspective.

In many ways, Farrer is also influenced from a movement that is at the other end of the metaphysical and philosophical spectrum of process thought, that movement being logical positivism. Though he is attracted to the linguistic concerns of positivism, as well as its strong emphasis on empiricism and logic, he is reluctant to agree with them not only due to his obviously theistic view, but also because he believed that the anti-metaphysical stance of the movement was its largest deficiency. Agreeing with process thought, Farrer saw metaphysics as significant to the logical consistency of science and believed it could be, as it will be demonstrated shortly, a hermeneutical tool by which to understand the progress and discoveries of science. This is why John Glass claims, "His assertion that 'inert substance is indeed completely meaningless' seems to involve an interaction between his response to logical positivism and his response to process thought."[35] In

31. For an explanation of this aspect of Farrer's view, see Hebblethwaite, *Philosophical Theology*, 41–53.

32. Farrer, *Faith and Speculation*, 175.

33. Farrer, *Finite and Infinite*, 299.

34. It should be noted that some of his reasons for rejecting process philosophy are blunted by the types of panentheism that has been common after Charles Hartshorne's polar understanding of God. He is more concerned with theology seeing God as the soul of the world since it does not allow for the transcendence necessary for metaphysics. See Farrer, *Faith and Speculation*, 175.

35. Glasse, "Doing Theology Metaphysically," 329.

reaction to positivism, he recognizes the benefits of a voluntarism that does not capitulate to a completely a posteriori view of the world. In reaction to process thought, he retained an idea of substance, but largely redefines it so as to distinguish it from the Aristotelian sense found in scholastic philosophy. Consequently, he defines *esse* in terms of *operari*[36] to bring the theological dynamism of the latter to the philosophical stability of the former.

Metaphysics, for Farrer, also has the effect of providing a unity that will be foundational to his analogical thinking as well as his understanding of interpretation. In the case of the former, Farrer appears to agree with Aquinas that metaphysics is indispensable to the manner in which God can be understood such that one can predicate characteristics and activities of him. The Scholastic's view has received much examination and elucidation, though his own thoughts on analogy are primarily an attempt to mediate between equivocal and univocal language. Aquinas rightly saw the dangers of equivocal language in the impossibility of speaking or thinking about God, while univocal language did not allow the type of distance necessary to prevent speaking of divinity from occurring in purely human terms. Thus, he wanted to retain the possibility of speech inherent in univocity, with the ontological distance of equivocation. A proper understanding of analogy, thought Aquinas, would relate God's causal activity in the world to language, such that language could provide an understanding of divine being through analysis of that which possesses some similarity to it, while containing the negation necessary to preclude the immanence of God in the mind's activity from conflating Creator and creation. Farrer, in seeking the unity of thought, similar to univocity that allows for the speakability of God, is attracted to metaphysics for the same effect he sees in Aquinas's analogical understanding of predication.

However, more distinctive of the Anglican philosopher is his shift to focus on the hermeneutical role of metaphysical thinking, as an offspring of his difference from Aquinas concerning the nature of theology. As mentioned earlier, Aquinas clearly believed that theology was a theoretical science,[37] but was opposed by John Duns Scotus, whose Aristotelian and Franciscan influences gave rise to his understanding it as an issue of praxis. Farrer sided with the Reformers in following the Scotian line in seeing the Christian life as centrally one of lived piety, a concern he shares with both Jüngel and Wolterstorff.[38] Thus, even as early as *Finite and Infinite*, he

36. Farrer, *Finite and Infinite*, 28. For examinations of this idea, see Glasse, "Doing Theology," 329–34; Dalferth, "*Esse est Operari*."

37. Aquinas, *Summa*, 1.1.4:2–3.

38. This is likely why Farrer continued to hold ministerial positions throughout his lifetime.

attempted to look at the practical implications of metaphysics.[39] This led
to the aforementioned restructuring of the empirical principle, and also a
hermeneutical interest in metaphysical thinking. Consequently, he writes:

> Let it be granted, then, that nothing properly to be called meta-
> physics appears until we have system and comprehensiveness.
> Yet, if we are not to be simply the slaves of a system, if we are to
> be able to criticize and reform it, or even to remind ourselves
> that reality is something more various and vital than the system
> can express, then we must step outside the conventions of the
> system and have recourse to free existential description, that is,
> to the description of each mystery in any analogical terms which
> may appear expressive.[40]

Farrer recognizes that the significance of metaphysics, but also believes
that it must be revisable in relationship to phenomena which do not fall
within its system. For him, this means that metaphysics has a significant
interpretational function, but such a function also requires the possibility of
refining that would allow it to deal with the hermeneutical crisis of claiming
"comprehensiveness," while being unable to interpret (at least in theory) all
possible elements over which it claims explanatory power. Furthermore, the
hermeneutical function of metaphysics may mean that it requires a type of
pluralism that is unseen in a scholastic construal. If metaphysics is necessary
for the description of "mysteries" as Farrer claims[41] and such descriptions
can occur in different ways, then there will be different metaphysical ways
of dealing with particular phenomena. Thus, he asserts, "But the metaphysi-
cian must not predetermine his choice of conceptual instrument: he must
be willing to use such terms as his object appears to demand."[42] Consequently, Farrer believes that Aquinas provides a compelling metaphysical
vision, but moves emphasis from metaphysics as a singular comprehensive
and unchanging system for investigating all things, to a system of overlap-
ping hermeneutical aids that will correspond to the entities it is seeking
to explain.[43] In recognizing this, it is important to note that Farrer never
moves towards relativism of the sorts found in the postmodern movements

---

39. By understanding substance in terms of action and what is necessary for action,
Farrer takes an acutely practical orientation to his understanding of metaphysics.

40. Farrer, *Glass of Vision*, 73.

41. Farrer, *Glass of Vision*, 63.

42. Farrer, *Glass of Vision*, 68.

43. For more on the convergences and divergences of Farrer's work with that of
Aquinas, see Eaton, *Logic of Theism*, 1–72.

starting in the middle of the twentieth century.[44] Yet, he is unwilling to claim that one metaphysical perspective can give a picture of all things to the degree that no other grammar of explanation is necessary.

Farrer is undoubtedly influenced by Aquinas in other areas, such as his sacramental theology, use of analogy, and ecclesiological concerns. Yet, whereas Thomistic thinking is foundational to his scholarship, other philosophical thinkers and movements have a tendency to reinforce his scholastic thinking or give him impetus to drift away from it. Three examples will suffice to show how the multifarious nature of Farrer's thought can, in many ways, be traced to his uncanny talent for synthesizing perceptibly disparate perspectives. The first is the work of Baruch Spinoza, who, first and foremost, reinforces his proclivity towards rational theology. Whereas Neo-Orthodoxy had begun to persuade scholars to question the relationship of theology to philosophy, Farrer never fully abandoned a scholastic confidence concerning the intellect's natural capacity to understand the things of God and the world.[45] In this, the modernity of Spinoza reinforced such confidence and even began to provide him with a method of justifying such rationalism in the face of his emphasis on revelation. In *Glass of Vision*, Farrer explains how his attempts to reconcile how God could reveal personally, without something like the voice of God being present, were at an "impasse" from which Spinoza freed him.[46] Farrer, though recognizing he was using a decidedly Christian reading of the modern philosopher,[47] credited a Spinozan view of God's activity with allowing him to understand revelation in terms of primary and secondary causation, without resorting to any sort of direct miraculous intervention. Thus, when he moves into investigating Scripture, which he considers to be revelatory, he trends towards naturalism and begins to seek analogy between poetic inspiration and the inspiration of the writers of the Bible. In Spinoza, Farrer begins to see the way in which his focus on double agency can touch his theory of revelation in a way that can be investigated in a rational theology.

44. "Here he anticipates and rejects the typically postmodernist claim that philosophical viewpoints are culture-bound in the sense that they would only have developed within a given culture and that their meaning and truth-claims are bound up with the basic presuppositions of that culture" (Mitchell, "Introduction," 5).

45. "By the time these factors began to be operative in Oxford, Farrer had already become used to philosophical speculation unrestricted by the narrow boundaries that positivism imposed and to employing reason in theology to an extent and in a manner that neo-orthodoxy forbade" (Mitchell, "Introduction," 3).

46. Farrer, *Glass of Vision*, 7.

47. "Undoubtedly I misunderstood Spinoza, in somewhat the same fashion as (to quote a high example) St. Augustine misunderstood Plotinus, turning him to Christian uses" (Farrer, *Glass of Vision*, 7–8).

There are two other influences apparent in Farrer's thought, though one should be held in a tentative fashion since he does not appear to make the connection explicit: the previously mentioned logical positivism and existentialism. Farrer was definitely dealing with the former in *Finite and Infinite*, with Glasse believing A.J. Ayer's *Language, Truth, and Logic* to be his direct dialogue partner.[48] Intriguingly, though he was attempting to discredit its skepticism towards metaphysical thinking, he still sought ways in which he could appropriate certain facets of positivism into his perspective. In a manner that foreshadows the eschatological verification of his pupil John Hick,[49] Farrer believed that verification of religious belief could be had, but in a place where logical positivists would not seek. He believed that one could verify the truth of God's existence and activity by experience, but only by that experience which can occur interior to the life of faith.[50] Thus, Hebblethwaite remarks that Farrer believed that the life of faith can produce "present verficatory results."[51] In this way, he did not deny all tenets of positivism's use of verification, but simply believed that the reason the positivist could not verify the Christian faith was that one could only do so by abandoning the positivist position. As Dalferth notices in comparing Farrer to Luther, "They operate with a description of God, but God is a unique being which has to be known by acquaintance not by description."[52]

The last influence, existentialism, is difficult to discern in that it rarely has unambiguous mention. Yet, there appears to be areas of both mediated and unmediated pressure on Farrer's work. His relationship with his theological contemporaries, many of whom were wrestling with the Kierkegaardian reaction to late modern rationalism, provides some impetus for him to think in terms of the human condition. Moreover, he takes serious Aquinas's claims that "*omne quod recipitur in aliquo, recipitur in eo per modum recipientis*,"[53] and brings this into conversation with the existentialism coming out of the late nineteenth century to make the human condition and experience stand out in his theology in a way that exceeds his scholastic predecessors. Farrer goes so far as to claim, "There is no one constant thing which man throughout his history has experienced, except himself; and what he has experienced of himself has been the historic alteration."[54]

48. Glasse, *Doing Theology Metaphorically*, 323.

49. Hick, "Theology and Verification."

50. See Farrer, *Faith and Speculation*, 16–35; *Saving Belief*, 11–36.

51. Hebblethwaite, *Philosophical Theology*, 15.

52. Dalferth, "Esse Est Operari," 195.

53. Aquinas, *Summa*, 1.75.5:367.

54. Farrer, "Revelation," 91.

Perhaps encouraged by his Baptist piety, Farrer is ultimately concerned with existential issues and brings together various sources to begin to address them.[55]

FARRER'S PROJECT

Since Farrer's thinking is broad, his project resists any simplified treatment. However, in line with his religious and intellectual background, two lines can be discerned. The first has to do with his desire to continue in the activity of rational theology, even when it requires him to largely refine and redefine historically orthodox positions. Basil Mitchell, who was considerably influenced by Farrer, claims of his associate:

> This Christian language had for him been largely formed by Aquinas, but Farrer was never formally a Thomist, as his friend and colleague, Eric Mascall, was. His project was to take Christian belief as he found it and seek to render it as clear and coherent as he could make it, and relate it intelligibly to whatever else we could claim to know.[56]

The prospect of rational theology is closely related to his decision to defend and extend metaphysical theology, not so much to provide an overarching theory of all things, but to provide one with an interpretational aid in examining two disparate realities together (i.e., the Creator and the creation). Thus, his rational theology comes with an attendant metaphysical leaning, which is revised to bring it in line with the divine voluntarism that he believes to be the best model for the interaction between God and humanity. Though he had attended lectures by Bultmann and read Barth, he refrained from moving towards the self-authenticating Word of the latter or the demythologizing tendencies of the former. Instead, a rational theology that reckoned with the theological concerns of German dialectical theology would be one with a new metaphysic.

Seeking a rational theology further provides some of the distinctive features of Farrer's theology. In attempting to delve into the manner in which Christian thinking has an inherent rationality, he is pushed to look for the foundation for theology, as well as the manner in which theology relates to other disciplines. In terms of the former, Farrer's skepticism concerning

55. Douglas Hedley sees this type of concern as the unifying similarity between the work of Farrer and Basil Mitchell. See Hedley, "Austin Farrer's Shaping," 113.

56. Mitchell, "Introduction," 8. Furthermore, Mitchell makes the argument that "Farrer in all his writings remains an out-and-out rationalist" (Mitchell, "Introduction," 5).

arguments for the existence of God meant that he looked for a foundation for rational inquiry in a non-discursive apprehension of God, but one that is mediated.[57] It is for this reason that David Brown claims that Farrer believed that "God is not an inference from other experience, but an already existing experience in search of a deeper foundation."[58] Thus, the rational theology of the type that Farrer seeks to perform, was not the scholastic natural theology in which observation led to arguments and arguments to an (partial) understanding of God. It was one of experience which led to the revelatory activity of God, which provided a rational framework for the interpretation of all aspects of reality, even those where God's activity does not appear immediately present. Thus, Hefling is correct in characterizing Farrer's work as follows, "And this is where rational theology begins, for its task as Farrer understands it is to clarify those reasons that believers entertain."[59] In terms of relating theology to other disciplines, Farrer is never reluctant about referencing psychology, sociology, biology, physics, and various areas of the humanities in an effort to show the consistency and coherence of Christian truth. Though he believes that Christianity requires one to take a stance within the community in order to verify its claims, he does not believe that it can only be understood in terms of an internal rationality that may not be accessible to modes of inquiry that are outside of its own religious concerns. It is this that differentiates him from Wittgensteinian philosophers of religion from the Swansea school.[60] However, in relating theological thinking to other disciplines, he is clear on the supremacy of the Christian religious perspective. In doing so, he begins to insulate Christianity from attacks in historical and philosophical areas, even when believing in their necessary relationship.

A second significant aspect of Farrer's project can be seen in his attempt to relate doctrine to faith. Since revelation takes a high place in his theological understanding, he is always quick to coordinate the mode of receptivity of the Christian with their understanding of God through revelatory activity. In doing so, he makes certain connections that distinguish him from Wolterstorff and Jüngel. Whereas Wolterstorff believes that revelation can be set aside, to some degree, in the discussion of Scripture, Farrer believes that revelation is the foundation for any sort of divine speech. Thus, if God can speak through the Bible, then revelation is unavoidable.

57. For his theological epistemology, see Henderson, "Valuing in Knowing God."

58. Brown, "Role of Images," 97.

59. Hefling, Jacob's Ladder, 19.

60. For some comparisons of these types of thought, see Henderson, "Austin Farrer and D. Z. Phillips," 223–43.

Furthermore, he is different from Jüngel in that he does not use the category of God's self-attesting Word. Hence, where the hermeneutical theologian focuses on Jesus Christ as the revelatory act of God, Farrer wants to expand revelation to include not only Christ's personal representation of God, but also his and the apostles' interpretation of that representation. Therefore, doctrine is significant since one's faith in respect to Christ will be shaped by the interpretive framework that it provides. Where Jüngel sees the Word of God in Jesus Christ as the test for theology, Farrer emphasizes the Word of God as interpreted by Christ and the writers of the New Testament, such that it can be used as the criterion for theological thinking.

Moreover, this increased emphasis placed on the text of the New Testament gives Farrer a strong concern for exegetical issues. Thus, he begins to delve into hermeneutics to the degree that he can relate the theological aspects of Scripture to its literary form. Where Dalferth is correct in arguing that Farrer should not be read as a proponent of strictly literary style of interpretation,[61] in line with structuralism, he perhaps is overcorrecting in placing literary and theological styles in contradistinction. For Farrer, literary hermeneutics and theological interpretation are not as easily separated since poetic imagination and inspiration are not so simply distinguished. It is the theological concerns, as seen in the imaginative usage and restructuring of divine images, that drives the authors of Scripture. Thus, if "Theology is the analysis and criticism of the revealed images"[62] and those images are presented textually by the apostles and their kin, it will remain difficult to give Farrer's hermeneutics a strictly theological reading. It might be said that for him, doing theology was a literary activity. On Dalferth's behalf, it must be conceded that Farrer's overall hermeneutical conception begins with a theological understanding that forms his method of interpretation. Thus, Farrer must be understood not as simply practicing a theological hermeneutic, but should be understood as having a literary hermeneutic that is formed under strongly theological considerations. Consequently, the pointed focus that Farrer places on relating faith and doctrine begins to particularize his theology and starts to differentiate it from previous Anglican thought. For this reason, he should not be seen as exaggerating when he asserts that "Prayer and dogma are inseparable. They alone can explain each other. Either without the other is meaningless and dead."[63]

61. Dalferth, "Stuff of Revelation," 151.

62. Farrer, *Glass of Vision*, 44.

63. Farrer, *Lord I Believe*, 9. For an examination of how Farrer relates doctrine and practice, see MacSwain, "Above, Beside, Within," 45–46.

FARRER'S METHODOLOGY

Whereas Jüngel's methodology is strongly theological and Wolterstorff's is analytic, Farrer draws from both philosophy and theology in his understanding of divine speech and revelation. There are ways in which his perspective mirrors Jüngel's view of theology as consequent exegesis. For Farrer, theology criticizes and clarifies the meaning of those images used to reveal the character and intentions of God. Thus, his work begins with exegesis and moves on towards dogmatization. Yet, in order for theology to perform such criticism, it requires the unity that metaphysics allows. For this reason, Farrer does not have any difficulty drawing upon the resources of philosophical thinking and terminology to begin to analyze a theological understanding of revelation. Whereas Jüngel sees the Word of God as the criterion for the legitimacy of theological thinking, his Anglican counterpart is more willing to use philosophic concerns as a principle for separating legitimate from illegitimate doctrinal representations of exegetical evidence. For both Jüngel and Farrer, their disposition not to treat Scripture holistically, in contrast to the early church fathers, scholastics, and early Reformers, when determining doctrine, will cause them both to be willing to break from orthodox positions when they believe it is conflict with their chosen loci of interpretation.[64] Hebblethwaite suggests, "Farrer was prepared, on rational grounds, to modify the received tradition."[65]

Farrer's methodological rationalism leads to a particular difficulty, in his early work, that has a long history within Christian thought, namely, the ability to speak of a God. The scriptural and philosophical understanding of the divine could be seen as suggesting that he is too transcendent to be brought to speech in terms similar to those describing things in the world. Though willing to claim the ability to think and speak concerning God, in *Finite and Infinite*, Farrer sides with Aquinas against Scotus on the significance of analogical language in theological thought. This also differentiates his methodology from Jüngel and Wolterstorff. Wolterstorff sees analogy as a tool for analyzing that which is difficult to conceive, similar to Locke, without rejecting the possibility of univocal language. Jüngel's "analogy of advent"[66] is a modification of the Lutheran view of analogy whereby God's

---

64. A few quick examples will suffice to prove this point. Jüngel's willingness to reject divine immutability, though it had typically been the understanding of the church in the first sixteen centuries of Christendom, displays his willingness to break with orthodoxy. Similarly, Farrer was quick to break with any conception of a personal Satan, as well as unwilling to exclude the possibility of soteriological universalism.

65. Hebblethwaite, *Philosophical Theology*, 9.

66. Jüngel, *God as the Mystery*, 285.

primary speech finds analogy, secondarily, in human speech. In essence, God's taking up of humanity allows him to be addressed in human terms, which are analogically related to God's self-interpretation in divine speech. Farrer, in distinction from Wolterstorff, sees analogy as more than a tool, since it is the only way of dealing linguistically and conceptually with God. However, unlike Jüngel, he sees the directionality of the analogical movement to be from human terms to the reality which is in God. Thus, it will be central to the way he examines theological issues and though he reframes scholastic metaphysics he does not similarly reframe their understanding of analogical talk. This creates some tension, which gives way to his subsequent view, found in both *Glass of Vision* and *Faith and Speculation*, as well as his exegetical works, whereby analogy is given a more attenuated role in comparison to the use of inspired images, given by poetic imagination. This perspective, which will be explained later, still can see analogical representation as involved, but uses the concept of "image" in order to move away from a one-to-one conceptual correspondence. Thus, when the idea of "King" is used in relationship to God, it is meant to carry more meaning than the single point of contact often seen in analogies. Moreover, the exegesis of images will require a more complex method, in that poetic imagination is impossible to simply characterize. Furthermore, images are capable of development, as the image is interpreted, combined with other images, and applied in new situations.[67] Thus, images may be polysemic, can evolve, and require an interpretation style that uses literary clues to give one insight necessary to reconstruct the imaginative process of the authors of the text.

As has been demonstrated, Farrer was a thinker of diverse influences and similarly diverse concerns. Though varied in his thinking, he shows a surprising amount of consistency, due to the high premium he places on reason in the investigation of God. He attempted to draw from scholasticism in a way that critically reformed it to deal with what he believed to be legitimate concerns regarding Aristotelian substance metaphysics, concerns that came both from theological sources that emphasized divine voluntarism and exegetical sources that believe Catholicism had caricaturized the God of Scripture. Neither unwilling to completely reject orthodoxy, nor to completely begin to reconstruct metaphysics from the ground up, he continued his dialogue with Thomism even as he took a decidedly Scotian route. With this in mind, his understanding of revelation and divine speech will continually touch upon scholastic themes, while diverging in those areas that he believes will not allow God to be seen as the agent of his own activity.

---

67. Farrer, *Glass of Vision*, 52–56.

9

Farrer's View of Divine Speech and Revelation

CHARACTERIZATION OF DIVINE REVELATION

WHEREAS FOR JÜNGEL REVELATION is primary and in Wolterstorff speech is, Farrer has focused his energies on both at different times in his academic career. At times he concentrated on speech as he analyzed the way in which analogy allows one to speak about God, while at others, he gives primacy to revelation whereby God coming to speech is given its transcendental possibility, as well as its teleology. For the purpose of this chapter, revelation will be addressed first, since it is given longer discussion in Farrer and it appears to have a conceptual primacy that will facilitate the explanation of its relationship with divine and human speech.

As was alluded to earlier, Farrer had an expanded understanding of revelation, especially when compared to Jüngel. He had assessed two common conceptions of revelatory activity and found them lacking. The first is the emphasis, which he connects with Catholic theology, of focusing on revelation as propositional knowledge given by God to believers.[1] His belief

---

1. This connection, though, is admittedly a characterization of the Evangelical perspective. In fact, Evangelicalism would be more closely tied to this type of deficiency, as Aquinas himself recognized that personal understanding of God is superior to doctrinal exposition. Furthermore, Evangelicals would use a similar tactic to respond to such charges, which is to emphasize the significance of a relational understanding of God, while not so easily separating and/or simplifying the propositional content of Christian beliefs. For a summary of Aquinas's position on personal knowledge, see Stump, "Eternity, Simplicity, and Presence," 42–46.

in theological personalism makes this insufficient, since knowledge about an individual is not enough for one to know that individual. Thus, the intimacy of relationship that he believes to be depicted in Scripture, precludes reducing revelation to propositional content that is presented linguistically. The second conception is the belief that revelation occurs solely through historical event, which Farrer criticizes since such events still require interpretation for them to possess any meaning. Consequently, he writes, "It does not seem as though the theory of revelation by divine events alone is any more satisfactory than the theory of dictated propositions."[2] In his criticism of the prevailing views, Farrer begins to develop a theological understanding of revelation that includes both events where God's action is displayed, along with the interpretation of those events. Again, Dalferth is instructive, writing:

> But, just as revelation cannot be identified with scriptural propositions, so it cannot come in events by themselves without interpretation: Bare historical events are not revelation, but neither is revelation a mere interpretation of events. Rather, Farrer argues, it is the interplay between a particular event and a particular interpretation: Namely, Jesus's life and death and the apostolic interpretation of these events.[3]

Thus, revelation is both event and interpretation, with neither being dispensable, even if the event retains primacy.

Unlike his scholastic precursors, Farrer followed the early twentieth-century practice of drawing a strong distinction[4] between personal revelation and the idea of revelation in general. With his view that event and interpretation are both involved, the question naturally arises as to what personal revelation is to Farrer and how does it fit with his overall concept of revelatory activity. Not unlike his Neo-Orthodox contemporaries, he clearly believes that "primary revelation is Jesus Christ himself."[5] It is only through this revelation that one can have a personal relationship with God

2. Farrer, *Glass of Vision*, 38.

3. Dalferth, "Stuff," 152.

4. This is not to say that this distinction has not occurred previously, but it was not until the Reformation that revelation became an emphasized theological topic and it was not until late-nineteenth-century and early-twentieth-century reactions to existentialism that personal revelation is given extended distinct treatment. There had, previous to the nineteenth century, been a long tradition of mysticism, as well as many claims of direct revelation from God. Yet, even in the debates concerning the legitimacy of these purported forms of revelation, there was not quite the sustained treatments found in dialectical theology and subsequent movements.

5. Farrer, *Glass of Vision*, 39.

and even have the possibility of clearly talking about God at all. Holding to the orthodox formulation of Christ's personhood, Farrer believed that Christ was only one person within the Godhead, but he retained a place of primacy in revelation not because, as in the case of Barth, it was in him God chose how he would be, but because it was in Christ that God was made accessible. Thus, he does not see God's act in Christ as definitive of God's being, as is the case of Jüngel, but as an act necessary for disclosure of God's being which was already defined in God's self. Farrer does not want to, unlike his counterpart, so quickly give up on God's immutability. Hence, Jesus cannot be the event of God's trinitarian being, but He must be the way in which God's trinitarian being can be made known to those of great ontological difference to the divine.[6] He claims, "Unless God has gathered himself out of his immensity and come to me as man, I do not even know that he is God."[7] In this way, Farrer's view of God's personal self-revelation has affinities with Barth without moving in the direction of divine self-definition through election in Christ. Though seeing God's being as residing in his action, in distinction from Aquinas, he does not ever appear to take this to mean that God can wholly decide who he is in voluntary decision directed toward Christ. Instead, Christ reveals the trinitarian activity in his relationship to the Father and provides the accessibility conditions for a believer to enter into understanding of that revelation.[8] In fact, Farrer's movement of revising metaphysics to be consistent with voluntarism has a deeply theological root. For him:

> The self-incarnation of God gives the highest reality to 'personal' language about God, but that is not to say that we can work out a

---

6. For a more in-depth discussion of this idea, see Farrer, *Saving Belief*, 49–52. For an analysis see MacSwain, "Above, Beside, Within," 51–55.

7. Farrer, *Celebration of Faith*, 88.

8. Farrer, like Jüngel, appears to mirror Augustine in focusing the social aspects of the Trinity on the Father and Son, with the Holy Spirit's personhood deriving from the relationship between the other two. MacSwain believes this may create a certain tension with orthodoxy and with other instances of Farrer's own formulation of the Trinity (MacSwain, "Above, Beside, Within," 52). However, he may be underestimating the manner in which Farrer presents the Spirit's personhood, not recognizing that it is necessary for a proper trinitarian understanding that each member of the Godhead expresses their personhood differently in relationship. If the Spirit were to express his personhood to the Father similarly to the Son, the Trinity would breakdown both in its exegetical presentation and its conceptual formulation. For a view of the Trinity that places greater emphasis on dissimilarity of personhood between the members of the Godhead, see Volf, *After our Likeness*, as well as the trinitarian works of his *doktorvater*, Jürgen Moltmann.

priori from the verbal notion 'a personal God' the consequence
'self-disclosed in the mode of incarnation.'[9]

It is the incarnation that gives impetus to speaking of a personal God and
not personal language giving cause to believe in incarnation.

Platten gives a brief summary of the manner in which personal revelation fits within Farrer's rational theology, arguing that:

> Farrer's point is, as we noted earlier, that God is there present
> in us. It is for us to identify his presence, and the incarnation is
> central to this process. It is through Jesus that the coinherence of
> God and man has been made explicit. Bare theism without the
> person of Jesus is not enough.[10]

It should be noted, that in addressing the personal revelation of God in
Christ, Farrer follows the not unusual practice of speaking of this revelation in two manners. The first manner is the objective way in which he is
the revelation of God, regardless of human reaction to that revelation. In
this way, he follows a distinction similar to Wolterstorff's use of the ides
of "intransitive revelation." For Farrer, calling Christ the revelation of God
aside from reference to the believer is his way of speaking of the necessity of
recognizing revelation as occurring in Christ, for revelation to actually occur. In essence, the person and work of Jesus Christ is the necessary, though
not sufficient condition for the revelation of God to be actualized. The other
way in which Farrer speaks of revelation is the actual event of revelation
in Christ coming to the individual believer in the act of faith. Revelation
only occurs, in its most full sense, when the actual unveiling occurs in the
presence of another. Thus, he claims, "So the sheer occurrence of Christ's
existence is the perfection of revelation to Man, but it is not yet the perfection, or even the beginning of revelation to us, unless we are enabled
to apprehend the fathomless mystery which his manhood is."[11] This can
occur, in Farrer's view through Scripture. In Scripture, the events of Christ's
life are given inspired interpretation that allows for revelation to be, as was
mentioned before, the combination of events and their interpretation.

To understand how personal revelation relates to revelation through
Scripture, one must first examine Farrer's view of history and then understand how this relates to inspiration. His perspective, in essence, separates
two different ways of speaking of an event being historical. One is of the
event having actually occurred, while the other is that the event is significant

9. Farrer, "Revelation," 96.
10. Platten, "Diaphanous Thought," 37.
11. Farrer, *Glass of Vision*, 40.

in some fashion to history. Farrer is concerned with whether revelation, since it is based on events that are historical in the first sense, can be exhausted by understanding it as history in the latter. In other words, does revelation of God through history, which he strongly affirms, mean that revelation is simply another type of historical interpretation. While Farrer argues for the interpretive nature of both historical writings and revelation itself, he answers in the negative. His reasoning first looks at the nature of history as a field and what it means to write a history. He notes that simply recording all of the events occurring with all the individuals involved within a period of time would not be a historical writing in the relevant sense. It only becomes a history when a historian, through the use of "diagrammatic fictions," interprets the significance of the events according to their specified criteria. These fictions tend to be conceptual[12] and allow for the selection of events that are significant to the period and/or community involved, as well as providing an interpretive framework for understanding the events therein. Revelation, though interpreting historical events, cannot be simply reduced to history since one is attempting to see the being of God, i.e., God's activity, through it. Since God's actions are, by nature, transcendent in their inception and irreducible to natural occurrences, they are not a part of history proper. Thus, even though God works through history, revelation and theology cannot be resolved "into the succession or interplay of human acts."[13] Farrer, though believing that human activities are the result of double agency, with both God and humans being involved, does not believe that one can easily resolve the way in which God and human wills are involved in free choice. One cannot explain the "causal joint,"[14] but recognizes that it happens and thus every human action is also divine. In relation to history, this means that any human event can be revelatory, since God is active. However, they can only be revelatory when divine intention is seen in them. Since the understanding of this intention is not through historical channels,[15] revelation cannot be subsumed under history.

Since history must be interpreted to become revelation, but the interpretation is not through typical historical patterns, the question arises as to how any individual can thereby understand events in such a way as to recognize God's revelatory activity in them. For Farrer, inspiration becomes

12. Farrer, in fact, often uses "diagrammatic fiction" and "diagrammatic concept" interchangeably. See Farrer, *Faith and Speculation*, 86–103.

13. Farrer, *Faith and Speculation*, 93.

14. Farrer, *Faith and Speculation*, 65, 172, 174–75.

15. Farrer illustrates this by speaking of a spiritual interpretation of Augustine, which would not be considered historical since it did not come through "historical channels" (Farrer, *Faith and Speculation*, 92).

key to this movement from the appearance of natural events, to the divine activity in them. The prophets, as well as the apostles, where inspired by God such that they could recognize God working in the world. In this way, Farrer's viewpoint is not unlike the Calvinist tradition, which places emphasis both on inspiration and double agency in the revelatory act. However, the Anglican differentiates himself from his Reformed precursors by the peculiar way in which he sees divine influence in the interpretation of history. Related to his understanding of the mode of God's activity in the human sphere, Farrer understands the work of inspiration not as a divinely imbued ability that is unrelated to the capacities of humanity. Instead, he sees the supernatural nature of inspiration in the extension of natural human abilities to where they can perceive God's work. Farrer, in a Thomist move, applies the hierarchy of being to human faculties and recognizes the mind to be the "luminous apex"[16] which defines humanity. Yet, in doing so, he is quick to prevent the mind from being simplified to strictly reason. He argues that imagination must be placed alongside reason as the powers indicative of humanity, since the latter could not occur without the former.[17] Thus, Farrer relates inspiration to poetic imagination.[18] In the same way that the poet employs their imagination in describing their singular experience of the world, the apostles use their divinely supernaturalized imagination to describe the way in which God is active in the world.

Farrer's view of inspiration, in its relationship to his understanding of history and poetry, is what allows personal revelation in Jesus Christ to become revelation in the sense of event and interpretation. In relating revelation to history, he needs some sort of criteria by which the historical events can be interpreted, mirroring the "diagrammatic fictions" of historical interpretation. For this Farrer speaks of the "mythological fictions,"[19] which serve the purpose of focusing the interpretation of historical events on the activity of God. He writes,

> But God's speaking from heaven is a myth. God revealed himself in former times, as he does now, by things done on earth. If we read a self-disclosure of God to us in the sacred history behind us, we must surely allow that the characters in the story we look back upon read the will of God in the history which lay behind them or about them.[20]

16. Farrer, *Glass of Vision*, 22.

17. Farrer, *Interpretation and Belief*, 39–55.

18. See Farrer, *Interpretation and Belief*, 39–55; *Glass of Vision*, 35–56,

19. Farrer, *Faith and Speculation*, 95–103.

20. Farrer, *Faith and Speculation*, 97.

These mythic fictions, then, are human ways of conceiving God in such a way that his activity can be interpreted as occurring in human events. Though Farrer does not draw the direct connection between these and the "images" which the writers of Scripture use to describe God, it appears that they are nearly identical. In words such as "king" or "lord," the divine activity is given voice through human images to which believers can relate.

Divinely inspired imagination relates to these images, or mythic fictions, in three interrelated ways. First, imagination begins to draw the connections of how these images describe God's work. Second, imagination allows for these images to "enter into fresh combinations, to elaborate themselves, to beget new applications."[21] And finally, imagination is what fills in the gaps, which these images leave by only describing God partially. Farrer uses the illustration of a matchbox to depict the manner in which imaginative construction is required for a holistic picture of something. When one sees a matchbox, he believes that the mind imagines the other three sides to bring unity to one's perception.[22] Similarly, imagination can take images, which like diagrammatic fictions are ultimately simplifying, and begin to fill out a broader picture of divine being. These images can have analogical components in that there is conceptual elements of similarity, but they are not strict analogies in that there is neither one simple relationship between analogues, nor is there a simple way of seeing the similarities between analogues. For Farrer, in his later outlook, understanding God's activity is not a logical and metaphysical project of finding analogical understanding, but is a literary activity of seeking the poetic inspiration behind the apostle's imaginative reconstruction of the divine work in the world.

One could, then, summarize the manner in which personal revelation in Christ can be related to the revelatory activity in the Apostolic interpretation of the events of Christ's life as follows: In the same way that events require interpretation to be historical, Christ's life requires interpretation to be revelatory. The apostles are able to do this by the inspiration of the Holy Spirit, whereby their natural imagination is extended beyond their normal capacities. This allows them to take the divinely sanctioned images and imaginatively begin to apply them to the being of God, combining and evolving these images to relate to the contemporary audience, and to fill in the understanding of divine actions to which these images relate but do not directly refer. It should be noted that this perspective, similar to many strains of Protestant theology, is strongly trinitarian in nature. For Farrer,

21. Farrer, *Glass of Vision*, 54.
22. Farrer, *Interpretation and Belief*, 39.

the Father reveals himself in Jesus Christ, whose life can only be revelatory by the inspiration of the Holy Spirit.

Since revelation can only be perfected "to us" through the apprehension of said revelation, it brings correlative ideas forward to fill out Farrer's view of personal revelation. Revelation in the fullest sense can only occur when Christ's life is recognized and received by faith. It is only in the proper stance in relationship to God that one can recognize that Christ "enacts deity,"[23] thus separating him from any form of rationalism that removes the significance of passive trust to Christian belief. Yet, this does not mean that he trends towards fideism, since his rationalist roots calls for evidence even in the act of faith. It appears, then, that for Farrer faith is what allows one to be in the proper epistemic conditions to understand Christ as the revelation of God and with that revelation to recognize evidence of God's character and activity in creation. Thus, as mentioned earlier, Farrer develops a faith-based verificationism that seeks a middle way between rationalism and fideism.[24] It is also in this way that he is able to emphasize, especially as one can see in Calvinist strains of Reformation theology, the role of the Holy Spirit in the recognition of revelation in Christ. Whereas the Spirit is necessary in inspiration to work on the imaginative faculties of the Scripture writers, he is also necessary in the individual believer to prevent sinfulness from causing one to be unable to recognize the interpretation of God's acts in history. In this way, he has certain similarities with both Wolterstorff and Jüngel (though perhaps more with the latter), drawing strict differences in the roles within the revelatory act of the members of the Godhead.

Another result of the significance of apprehension to revelation, for Farrer, is the further emphasis of the importance of Scripture to the revealing of God. Scholastic and early Protestant theologians had no qualms about calling the Bible "revelation," though the practice became much less frequent as the twentieth century began. This reaction had multiple motivations, including the existential backdrop for revelation (i.e., its transitive nature), the belief that scholasticism and early Protestantism focused too much on propositional knowledge, and the questioning of whether such revelation could square with a strong Christology. Farrer sided with early and medieval Christendom in believing Scripture to be revelatory, though

23. Farrer, *Glass of Vision*, 39.

24. For an extended treatment of this idea, see Allen, "Faith and Recognition," 197–210. See also MacSwain, "Above, Beside, Within," 50. Dalferth also alludes to it in claiming that Farrer "did not hold God's creation and government of nature to be truths received by way of revelation and otherwise uncertified. But he was convinced that we cannot progress very far in our attempts to understand these rational truths about God if we ignore the truth which 'God himself has revealed'" (Dalferth, "Stuff," 149).

he appeared to take Barthian criticisms to heart with his previously mentioned emphasis on revelation in Christ. He did believe that there was a way to naturally apprehend God in the world, an area of dispute between he and Luther,[25] but such apprehension was insufficient since to love God required one to love Him in Christ. Thus, not only is Christ necessary to revelation, but Christ is necessary for the believer's reaction in faith. Thus, he asserts,

> The supernatural act of love is not merely directed upon God, for in that case a natural apprehension of God might suffice, without revelation. It is directed upon God revealed in the act of his incarnation. Our supernatural act is precisely the love of a God revealed: and so the veil is done away, for we cannot love him unless we know him.[26]

Two important points about this quote will help to continue to bear out the connection between personal and scriptural revelation in Farrer. First, the Christian life is not merely an intellectual endeavor, but the totality of one's life directed toward God in love. Thus, Scripture cannot simply be a bearer of propositional knowledge upon which one can build doctrines, since it would not mirror the manner in which the believer is supposed to react. Second, though Scripture cannot simply be the bearer of propositions, it must include knowledge in that the love of God must be particularized such that one can identify the God whom one loves. Knowledge about God is not sufficient to respond to God in faith, but it is a necessary condition of the event. Thus, Scripture allows one to have an understanding of Christ, whereby one can, by the divine activity of the Holy Spirit, begin to recognize that Christ is the revelation of God in redeeming love.

With such a perspective, Farrer's view of Scripture seems to split the difference between the Barthian view which does not see the Bible as revelatory[27] and the view found in certain strains of Protestantism (including Evangelicalism, at times) that sees the Bible as primarily a case of revealed propositional knowledge. For Farrer, Scripture does reveal knowledge concerning God, but primarily acts as the authoritative interpretation of God's self-revelation in Christ. Thus, for God to reveal to believers, it requires not only the incarnation, but the understanding of the incarnation necessary

25. For Luther, apprehension of God was always Christologically mediated. For the differences between Farrer and Luther in this area, see Dalferth, *"Esse Est Operari,"* 195–98.

26. Farrer, *Glass of Vision,* 61.

27. It might be argued that Barth sees Scripture as revelatory since he believes that it is the "word of God" in a secondary sense. Yet, this would not explain the manner in which he sees revelation as the triune act of God to which Scripture is a testimony.

to recognize that Christ, as the Son of God, is the manifestation of divine love. This understanding, recorded in Scripture, starts with Christ's speech concerning himself, but also includes the Apostolic interpretation of his life. Whereas the theological liberalism of the nineteenth century and many different theological movements in the twentieth century focused upon the gospels' presentation of Jesus so much that epistolary literature of the New Testament was largely undermined, Farrer reemphasized their importance as being in continuity with the revelation found in the gospels. More than this, his view also militated against the historical critical views that saw theological inquiry as beginning with historical questions. If the revelatory act is more than just a question of Jesus Christ and his time on earth, but includes the interpretation of his life, then a mere historical examination of his words and deeds will be insufficient to get at the theological meaning of the incarnation. Since the theological understanding is not going to proceed by historical means, as was previously elucidated, then practices such as historical criticism will be of limited use.

Similar to Barth, as well as many others in broader Christendom, Farrer was concerned with the manner in which historical criticism had affected Christian thought and praxis. Also parallel to the dialectical theologian, Farrer reacted to liberal theology by relegating some of its tools to, at the most, a reduced usage. Consequently, he believed that critical methodologies, even if helpful in answering historical questions, was not sufficient to give one insight into Christ's mission or the being of God. Moreover, he believed, as Jüngel and Wolterstorff do, that God could use the writings of Scripture even if they had errors and/or biases. At the most, historical criticism could adjudicate when an author of Scripture made a mistake about a historical event, but it could not affect the interpretations, produced by inspired imagination, concerning the life and actions of Christ. Thus, for Farrer, the revelatory act is not just in Christ, but in the events of Christ's life and their interpretation (by him and by the apostles), both of which require Scripturally revealed knowledge.

CHARACTERIZATION OF DIVINE AND HUMAN SPEECH

Though revelation played a large conceptual role in Farrer's theology, his understanding of divine and human speech was more functional in nature. He assumed that God and humans do speak and began to relate these to revelation, but apparently felt no compulsion to define or explain the phenomena. Therefore, any explication of how he understands them will be fraught with danger. Yet, such a characterization is necessary and for this reason, where wisdom might dictate caution, comprehensiveness and precision promote boldness.

In terms of divine speech, Farrer is distinct from both Wolterstorff and Jüngel in that he does not follow speech act theory or any of the Continental influenced understandings of discourse. He does not see speech as a way of doing things or as a way of being, but is primarily committed to a communicative theory. Though not holding to an Aristotelian substance metaphysic, he still holds to immutability with the attendant traditional belief that the Creator's being must be understood as definable apart from creation. Thus, God's trinitarian being is established prior to any activity in the world. With this being the case, divine speech cannot be constitutive of being or merely instrumental, but is a way in which God can communicate to his creation knowledge concerning himself. Moreover, since this is the way that God communicates understanding of the divine being through the interpretation of the events of Christ's life, language becomes the basis for thinking. Farrer argued:

> We must take it that mind or will comes before all. But not solitary mind. It is a mere superstition to suppose that we know of such a thing as mind in isolation. Mind is a social reality. The characteristic act of mind is to discourse. Real discourse between persons comes first; the mimic dialogue of solitary thought is secondary; the thinker, by a fiction, represents the other in his own mind and talks to himself.[28]

Farrer believed that interaction and relationship with others is what spurred on language, which then became the mode of thinking as it allowed one to have an inner dialogue. Thus, thought is based on language, and language is based on God's desire to interpret his being in the life, death, and resurrection of Christ.

The communicative element of divine speech is always (at least in cases which Farrer mentions) mediated, which is somewhat due to the role of Spinoza in his thinking.[29] Instead of seeing God's speech as primarily a divine voice coming to an individual, he saw it as primarily mediated through natural entities. The naturalist bent of Spinoza, combined with divine intentionality, allows for the possibility of things in the created world bearing divine truth. Parallel to this, is the ability of human words to bear God's interpretation as presented by the imaginative constructions of the apostles. Thus, when discussing revelation in Scripture, he characterizes it

28. Farrer, *Saving Belief*, 63.

29. Farrer, *Glass of Vision*, 9.

as "the verbal declaration of divine truth."[30] For Farrer, to think about the relationship between divine and human speech is to delve into how God's truth is mediated through the authors of the Bible.

Human speech, as far as Farrer is concerned, is also a matter of communication. However, when investigating it, he does not attempt to draw connections to divine speech.[31] Instead, he looks at human language in a manner similar to the analytic methodology of many Anglo-American philosophers. Mitchell is right in writing:

> Indeed in an important respect Farrer was an analytical philosopher. He did not approach philosophical problems with a pre-existing metaphysical theory which he sought to vindicate against rival theories. In a sense he was also an ordinary language philosopher who simply felt entitled to take as his subject matter ordinary Christian language in its doctrinal and devotional use.[32]

It is this propensity to look at language in its usage within the Christian community that gave rise to his recognition of the diverse manners in which words were used. Though concerned with the reduction of human speech to propositions, he did not necessarily dismiss this as a possibility. Yet, his literary background and preoccupation with poetic language[33] caused him to think of speech in its diversity. Thus, even though human speaking is for communication, it can perform that function in multiple different ways. Farrer, then, in recognizing the multifarious nature of discourse sought the most appropriate language for speaking about God. The confluence of his influences and personal beliefs brought analogy to the forefront, in his early writings, as the most natural way to speak about divine truth. His belief in the hermeneutical significance of metaphysics,[34] the theological necessity of keeping Creator and creature distinct,[35] as well as his investigation of how Christians speak about God in a devotional setting, gives him motivation to agree with Aquinas on the importance of analogical speech. Hence, where human speech can be used many different ways, he believed that the most

---

30. Farrer, *Glass of Vision*, 59.

31. In this way, Farrer is similar to Jüngel, who has a robust theory of divine speech, but does not attempt to draw connections to human speech. Instead, he treats human speaking by itself and resorts to philosophical perspectives to delve into everyday speech.

32. Mitchell, "Introduction," 7–8.

33. Farrer, *Glass of Vision*, ix.

34. Glasse, "Doing Theology," 335–38.

35. Farrer, *Finite and Infinite*, 7.

appropriate way with divine realities is analogy. As his career developed, he deviated from the centrality of analogy to the use of images. Thus, human discourse, in theological contexts, speaks in terms of linguistic and conceptual images,[36] which indirectly, but consistently, describe God and his activities.

THE RELATIONSHIP BETWEEN SPEECH AND REVELATION

For Farrer, speech and revelation have an intimate connection. The purpose of divine speech is to communicate divine truth to humanity. As Farrer writes, "[God] is not unwilling to be known, but only (if so) unwilling that, knowing him, we should attribute the achievement to ourselves."[37] God can only be known if he is able convey something about Himself, since personal knowing requires knowledge of the person. However, in order for that to occur as gracious activity, it cannot be attributed to human effort. Thus, not unlike the early Protestant theologians, revelation plays the role in Farrer of attributing to God the credit for his disclosure.

Farrer's expanded understanding of revelation means that human speech will play a larger role for him than for Jüngel or Wolterstorff. Since the revelatory act cannot occur without both divine acts and their interpretation, then God must both carry out events and speak as to the significance of those events. Yet, as was mentioned earlier, God's speaking to humanity is, for Farrer, a mediated act. Thus, God's interpretation of his own work must come through natural means and, as has been argued in the case of Scripture, this means the possibility of divine speech coming through human words. This has two significant implications. First, this means that Farrer believes not only that Scripture can be revelatory, but that in order for revelation to occur, it is essential. Scripture is not simply the testimony concerning Christ, as in Jüngel, or the way that God performs speech acts, as in Wolterstorff. Instead, Scripture is the way in which God's disclosure can become revelation in the fullest sense as the events of Christ's life and death are brought into interaction with Christ's and the apostles' interpretation of those events. Second, for the apostles to be able to interpret Christ's life, without it being attributed to them, they must be able to think beyond the natural and moved to extend their natural thinking to a non-natural object. Thus, the apostolic interpretation, in order to reference God, requires

36. For a discussion of the linguistic nature of images in Farrer, see Brown, "Role of Images," 86.

37. Farrer, *Glass of Vision*, 5.

supernatural thinking and the ability to speak in poetic images. It is this capacity that gives another distinctive facet to Farrer's perspective, especially in contradistinction from Jüngel and Wolterstorff, which is his emphasis on inspiration. To guard revelation's focus on God's grace and to allow for the possibility of human speech carrying a divine message, he employs a non-traditional idea of inspiration. As a result, though he does not agree with fundamentalist perspectives on Scripture, he does elevate its role and authority since it is integral to revelation.[38]

SUMMARY OF FARRER'S VIEW OF DIVINE SPEECH AND REVELATION

Farrer's view of revelation as including both event and interpretation requires a strong view of inspiration and a view of human speech as capable of analogical depiction of God's being. However, this only answers the question of what is occurring in revelation. Farrer himself recognizes that this is only part of the issue. He claims:

> Christians suppose such mysteries to be communicated to them through the scriptures. In particular, we believe that in the New Testament we can as it were over hear men doing supernatural thinking of a privileged order, with pens in their hands. I wish to make a fresh examination of this phenomenon. For I am not content simply to believe that supernatural thinking takes place, nor simply to accept and contemplate what it reveals, according to my own capacity. I desire to know something more in particular about the form and nature of that supernatural thinking.[39]

Farrer's overall theory is not only novel because of his characterization of what revelation is, but also because of how he believes it to occur in human speaking. Since he sees inspiration as an extension of normal human capacities, he relates poetic activity in the usage of images and inspiration in speaking with linguistic representation. Where the poet uses their imagination to produce images, God gives images to Christ and the apostles in inspiration, whereby they imaginatively combine and modify them to interpret the acts of God in Christ. He writes:

> Man cannot conceive it except in images: and these images must be divinely given to him, if he is to know a supernatural divine act. The images began to be given by Jesus Christ; the work

---

38. See Farrer, "Revelation," 89; Farrer, Glass of Vision, 38.

39. Farrer, Glass of Vision, 35.

was continued by the Spirit of Christ moving the minds of the Apostles.[40]

These images are not created by humans, but are given to humans as appropriate ways of human speech indirectly representing the divine though the product of human creativity.

In a discussion of speech and revelation in Farrer, one more idea is noteworthy, which concerns the relationship of metaphysics and theology to inspired images. For Farrer, not all images are the same in significance or centrality. Employing a hierarchy of being, Farrer makes important distinctions between different human acts,[41] as well as between the function of the mind and body.[42] He also applies the idea to revelatory images to provide a differentiation, in terms of importance to Christian belief, between different linguistic representations of God. Theology, then, is Farrer's way of criticizing images to determine their placement in the hierarchy of representation. The criteria of what in Scripture is central to the Christian faith and what is ancillary are theological, but in order to perform such criticism, the tools of philosophy are employed. Thus, Farrer uses metaphysics to provide theology with a way of distinguishing between images. In this way, philosophy is indispensable to the Christian life, not because it can reveal something about God, but because it can help one be self-critical in their adoption of Christian belief. Thus, interpretation of Christ's life is imaginative and poetic, while interpretation of Scripture is theological and literary.

40. Farrer, Glass of Vision, 108–9.

41. Farrer, *Glass of Vision*, 21.

42. Farrer, *Glass of Vision*, 22.

10

An Assessment of Farrer's Perspective

BENEFITS OF FARRER'S POSITION

Comprehensive Nature of Revelatory Theory

IN SOME WAYS, FARRER'S success is based on his audacity. He is not afraid of reading widely and drawing on diverse sources, even though such disparate perspectives are bound to lead to tension and require qualification. Furthermore, he has no problem seeking a type of comprehensiveness in his theories that invites criticism in a large number of different theological and philosophical areas. His motivation for seeking all-inclusive perspectives likely relates to the role he sees for metaphysics in understanding reality, as well as his desire for a rational theology. In some ways, it appears that his fear that some unforeseen issue might bring inconsistency to his position, leads him to attempt to fit as many areas of philosophy, theology, the sciences, and the humanities as possible into his theories. Such boldness, for many, would be overly dangerous, since they would not have the capacity to deal with such different topics and ways of thinking. Yet, Farrer was largely up to the task. This is not to say that he was completely successful, as there are difficulties in his view of speech and revelation. However, he was very consistent and very tempered in this thinking.

One area where Farrer's comprehensiveness bears fruit, is in his development of a theory of revelation. Whereas Wolterstorff sets revelation aside and Jüngel speaks most pointedly to personal revelation in Christ, Farrer attempts to take the diversity of events that could be described as revelatory and integrate them into a cohesive picture of God's self-disclosure. In *Glass of Vision* alone, he addresses revelation in Christ, Scripture, and particular events described in Scripture. Moreover, Farrer actually deals with general revelation, a concept that is approached with much skepticism after the inception of dialectical theology. Whether he successfully addresses the issue does not detract from the fact that whereas general revelation has a long theological history and possible exegetical backing (see Ps 19:1–6; Rom 1:18–23; 2:12–16; Acts 14:15–17; 17:22–28), it is not given sufficient treatment in contemporary theories. Yet, when dealing with such a broad swath of revelation, Farrer does not make the mistake of allowing the revelatory act in Christ to be treated as just one event amongst equally important instances of revelation. He attempts to show the reason for Christ's revelation being seen as primary, as well as how it relates to other revelatory acts.[1] In this way, he lays a broad foundation from which to investigate the relationship between human speech and divine speech and revelation.

View of Scripture

There is constant danger for a rational theologian in allowing for the emphasis on reason at the expense of the recognition of how God uses Scripture. Farrer, never falls prey to this ensnarement, even when demonstrating a rationalism that was largely unprecedented within theological circles in a post-Kierkegaardian era. Though he did not believe that Scripture was ultimate revelation, he did believe that it was the way in which revelation could occur, as Christ's life and its interpretation were allowed to interact.[2] With this emphasis, he could see a way in which Scripture could be authoritative, even though he had a proclivity for a high church ecclesiology. This leads to another facet of Farrer, one which some see as a positive and others as a negative. His view of Scripture naturally leads him to insulate it from outside criticism. Thus, he is not unlike Jüngel and Wolterstorff in having a limited role for any historical critical perspectives within his viewpoint, though admittedly with a very different rationalization. David Brown is worried about this particular facet of the Anglican's theology, claiming, "The problem rather is Farrer's attempt to make the Scriptures entirely self-contained."[3] However, he was rightly worried that some of the critical

1. Farrer, *Glass of Vision*, 39.

2. For more on how Scripture fit into his theory of revelation, see Dalferth, "Stuff," 150.

3. Brown, "Role of Images," 91. Something similar is echoed in Barbour, *Myths, Models, and Paradigms*, 18. For an analysis of Barbour's argument, see Platten, "Diaphanous Thought," 45.

methodologies may restrain too much what the writers of Scripture could be conceived of doing. In this way, he defended the centrality of the Bible to the ecclesiological outworking of the Christian faith. This also allowed him to see the significance of the historicity of events within Scripture without reducing faith to a historical question. Consequently, Evangelicalism finds parity with Farrer's view in its limitation on historical criticism while placing Scripture in a significant place in terms of divine revelation.

Another positive feature of Farrer's understanding of Scripture, is that he addresses inspiration, an idea with a significant history in theology and central to an Evangelical perspective. With Barth's arguments that Scripture is the fallible testimony to God's revelation in Christ, inspiration became a largely forgotten idea. Jüngel continues this de-emphasis, with Wolterstorff agreeing, though more because he believes his theory could make sense of God appropriating human speech without the need for God directly influencing individual writers. Two questions, though, remain unanswered if one were to reject any sort of idea of God inspiring Scripture. First, what should one do about purported exegetical evidence for inspiration? Second, without inspiration how does one conceive of God's involvement with the text? Farrer's viewpoint, though admittedly idiosyncratic, at least begins to broach the issues of how to approach traditional views of inspiration in light of their testimonial nature. Moreover, where Jüngel focuses on God's work in the readers of the texts, since the text itself is simply testimony, and Wolterstorff focuses on God's work in the appropriation of the text as the bearer of divine discourse, Farrer attempts to retain a strong sense of divine activity in both. His view of inspiration means that there is a trinitarian activity in the production of the text, while his view of the receptivity in faith also requires such trinitarian activity. Only by the Father imparting "divine life" to the believer in their faith in Christ, can they be placed in the right spiritual condition to be receptive to the text in a manner in which they would recognize its revelatory nature.

Farrer's concern with preaching, praxis, and personal piety, gave rise to an approach to Scripture that constantly sought to develop theological theories of speech and revelation in constant dialogue with exegetical concerns. When developing a theory of divine and human speech, he is reluctant to move towards what he believes to be the overly doctrinal concerns of scholasticism or the overly existential perspective characteristic of theological liberalism.[4] By referencing activities and human reactions,[5] Farrer refrains from the linguistic atomism so often derided by Wittgenstein. Thus, he is able to develop a hermeneutic that, all at once, pays attention to the author, to the text, and to the theological usage of that text.

A Rational Theology without Rationalism

A constant criticism of Barthian views of divine speech and revelation is that it can easily degrade into fideism. This, coupled with a skepticism concerning philosophy, leads Neo-Orthodoxy down a path, so some have said, towards a religious irrationalism. Farrer was unwilling to tread this path and, therefore, sought how to relate faith to reason in a way that emphasized the supremacy of the former without discarding the latter. Thus, Christianity is founded upon faith, but this faith finds confirmation in its ability to provide the foundation for interpreting the events of this world. In this way, Farrer's perspective finds marked similarity with the Reformed epistemology that Wolterstorff finds dear. Particularly in Plantinga's version, the view argues for the rationality of the Christian faith without any evidence, in terms of inferential arguments based on prior beliefs. Moreover, it would hold that evidence could be produced which would show the internal rationality of the Christian faith, without being convincing to an individual who has not previously committed themselves to Christianity.[6] Evangelicalism's similar concerns with Plantinga, consequently, will find voice in Farrer's work, specifically the belief that philosophical concerns of reason can advance without dismantling the prior event of human receptivity to the gospel message. Moreover, Farrer's view has the benefit of recognizing the distinctive nature of God as an object of investigation. God is not one to be known through scientific of philosophical investigation, but can only be known by direct personal relationship. Yet, this relationship has implications beyond one's Christian faith. Farrer, therefore, recognized that to be able to really answer questions concerning God's existence, attributes, and activities, may require a stance from within the bounds of religion before it can begin to move theologically and philosophically towards ideas outside of the faith. In

4. Farrer writes, "The Mediaeval Scholastic mind, it would seem, was (in theory, at any rate) on the hunt for theological propositions, out of which a correct system of doctrine could be deduced by logical method. If we set about the quest in that way, we close our ears to the voice of Scripture" (Farrer, Glass of Vision, 44).

5. Farrer asserts, "It is not I to whom God is revealed, it is the people of God in all their persons, times and places, and if I will not look with them I need not hope to see" (Farrer, "Revelation," 91).

6. See Plantinga, Warranted Christian Belief; "Reason and Belief in God," 16–93.

short, Farrer emphasized existential dimensions of individual faith, without neglecting the universal implications of belief in the God of Scripture.

Farrer's rational theology, also gives him a well-rounded view of metaphysics. Though claiming similar arguments against Aristotelian substance metaphysics as other theistic personalists, he does so without abandoning substance altogether. Farrer is unwilling to see metaphysics as a driving force for theological inquiry, but does not dispense with the recognition that it can be a useful instrument from a hermeneutical perspective. Thus, his self-critical attitude towards the use of metaphysics gives him a correctly limited perspective on its use and thus his reframing of it is allowed constant refining by theological beliefs. Thus, his metaphysical personalism is allowed to be servant to his picture of God as a trinitarian community in love. This gives Farrer philosophical tools to use in a theological context, without those philosophical tools overriding theological concerns.

A CRITIQUE OF FARRER'S POSITION

The Nature of Revelation

Whereas it is a benefit to Farrer's position that he gives a more comprehensive view of revelation than most, this does not prevent his perspective from being problematic in various ways. The greatest difficulty is that his defining of revelation in terms of events and interpretations does not recognize the existential nature of revelatory activity. The idea of intransitive revelation, as termed in Wolterstorff and seen as ideologically present in Farrer, is a highly peculiar way to refer to the act. This is not to say that such a way of conceiving of revelation has no place, since it typically focuses on what events must occur in order for revelation to happen. Yet, these events must refer to an observer for revelatory activity to reach its core meaning. Consequently, Farrer's understanding of revelation as the events of Christ's life along with their interpretation may be somewhat misleading. This has a few fundamental outcomes. First, it becomes difficult to relate how revelation occurred to the apostles to how revelation occurs to believers since, for Farrer, the revelatory act is apparently constituted in the "interplay between a particular event and a particular interpretation,"[7] with this primarily referring to the life of Christ and the apostolic understanding of it. Furthermore, this revelation occurs through images given to the apostles by God. Yet, for the revelatory act to occur with subsequent believers, it must occur when the apostolic imagination combined and modified those images to explicate

7. Dalferth, "Stuff," 152.

the Christ's activity. Hence, for the apostles there is a given-ness to how revelation can be expressed, based on God's direct activity, while for all other believers there is strong variance in how revelation can be expressed (at least theoretically) based on the apostolic refashioning of the images. In essence, revelation can occur for the apostles based on the inspiration that allows for the use of images. How, then, does revelatory activity work for the contemporary believer? Common in Calvinistic inspired Reformed traditions, including Evangelicalism, is to argue for illumination that is related to, though distinct, from that act of inspiration. Farrer, though, does not take this route. Instead, he appears to argue that believers after the apostolic era are bound to a natural understanding of the images, based on his paralleling the idea of a linguistic image to rational theology's emphasis on analogy.[8] Thus, revelation for the apostles appears to be the supernatural and imaginative institution of images, while revelation for others is in the receptivity to the apostolic interpretation. If this is the case, though, then it appears that the use of revelatory activity to place emphasis on God's role in an individual's knowing him would be reduced. Farrer is likely right that the divine activity in the apostles and that in other believers must be distinguished, but the transmission of revelation through images may not be the most natural place to find this distinction.

Second, the reduction of the existential nature of revelation means that the personal dimension of revelation will also be reduced. Farrer appears to recognize the impossibility of reducing the personal nature of God to an Aristotelian substance, as well as the difficulty of relating to God through a system of theological propositions. Yet, revelation appears to be depersonalized, de facto, by the manner in which interpretation enters his concept of the revelatory act. Whereas the Barthian tradition focuses on the self-interpreting Word that is able to be transmitted by testimony, such that Word is inherently personal as God's self-understanding in Jesus, Farrer's placement of the interpretation upon the apostles begins to make the linguistic reconstruction of the Word the place of revelation. If that is so, it is inherently depersonalizing in reducing the Word to thoughts about the Word. For Farrer, then, revelation becomes, in spite of his desire against it, focused upon knowledge about an individual and not about knowing that individual. This is not to say that such knowledge is not necessary, but revelation would appear to require more for personal knowledge to be achieved. Thus, though Farrer believes God must be known by being in relationship with him, he, at times, appears to reduce one's relationship to God to knowing things about him. The full existential nature of revelation, being something that includes

8. Farrer, Glass of Vision, 62.

beliefs, feelings, desires, etc., may be over-simplified. Fundamentally, this is a problem that Evangelicalism also must address.

Revelation and Interpretation

If revelation comes through images, then the issue of interpretation is naturally raised. It is in this area where Farrer is, perhaps, at his most innovative. It is also at this point where he is prone to criticism. There has never been a shortage of questions concerning the legitimacy of the manner in which he uses his understanding of revelation in biblical exegesis. In his two most extended exegetical works, *The Rebirth of Images*[9] and *A Study in Mark*[10], he displays a methodology of imaginative reconstruction of the author's use of images, which seems to be impractical. Since revelation occurs where the images allow for interpretation to come together with event, the understanding of the revelatory act requires an understanding of how these images disclose something about God. However, in order to do so, Farrer requires an ability to see connections and modifications that do not appear feasible to the lay person. Where Wolterstorff's perspective on hermeneutics, even if wrong, is at least possible for the average individual, Farrer's view requires a type of intelligence and imagination that few outside of himself possess. One can only look at his understanding of why Mark has such an abrupt ending[11] to see the innovative, and perhaps unrealistic, nature of his interpretational style.[12]

Another difficulty arises that relates to Farrer's use of images and how it relates to interpretation. In order for these images to be able to do the revelatory work that he seeks for them to do, he needs to be able to show which images are central and which are ancillary. Moreover, he needs to provide a way to interpret those images, so that he can begin to seek their conceptual relationships and how they relate to the apostolic usage. The first of these issues Farrer attempts to alleviate through the aforementioned use of the hierarchy of being in relation to images. Yet, in doing so, the only criterion that he can use is a metaphysical one that requires something similar to a Thomist view of being that may not be consistent with his personalistic

9. Farrer, *Rebirth of Images*.

10. Farrer, *Study in Mark*.

11. Farrer, *Glass of Vision*, 136–49.

12. In essence, Farrer sees a parallel between the last events of Christ and his disciples before the crucifixion and the events of Christ's body with the disciples after his death. In this parallel, which is perhaps not as easy to see as he seems to suggest, he holds that Mark is creating a poetic expectation of a non-resolute ending. See Farrer, *Glass of Vision*, 140–45.

recasting. This criterion, furthermore, may allow philosophy to dictate the parameters for interpretation in a way that will not allow for a truly theological hermeneutic. The second of these difficulties is never fully addressed by Farrer. Interpretation seeks how the apostolic imagination used images to communicate God's revelation, but the interpretive methodology is lacking. While Farrer's understanding of how images relate is "poetic" and imaginative, the way each image is to be understood is often based on orthodox interpretations, which rely on authorial intention. In this way, one could argue that he is reinstituting a multiple level style of interpretation, similar to the Alexandrian style of Augustine, whereby a literal hermeneutic is foundational for a poetic and theological type of interpretation. If one does not agree with a literal hermeneutic or a multi-level interpretive methodology, then Farrer's overall perspective will be unconvincing. However, if one is attempting to reconcile a traditional view of the significance of the apostles' interpretation to revelation with a view of inspiration that does justice to human freedom and creativity, Farrer may provide an attractive foundation for a theory even if one does not agree with all of his details. Evangelicalism, with its high emphasis on authorial intention and a literary methodology, will, then, find strong affinity towards the Anglican's perspective.

Metaphysics and Revelation

One last area of criticism is worthy to note, especially as it lays the foundation for later comparison between Farrer, Jüngel, and Wolterstorff. The Anglican, in his voluntarist reframing of metaphysics to be useful in the interpretation of Scripture, seeks a metaphysical perspective that may not be able to what he desires for it to do. Farrer, though agreeing largely with scholastic perspectives early in his career, came to become skeptical of substance views.[13] This may lead to a difficulty since the sense of stability that is offered by an Aristotelian metaphysics may be significant to interpretation. If one is attempting to interpret, that which is interpreted must not change so much that the interpretation quickly becomes obsolete. By recasting substance in personal terms, the foundation for said stability is undercut. No longer could an immutable substance prevent the type of changes that would make interpretive activity impossible. Instead, one is trusting that a person who makes choices has a fixed enough nature that interpreting his words and activities will apply beyond the instant that the interpretation is made. Yet, in a strictly personal metaphysic, it is impossible to say whether there is any grounding for this trust. Consequently, the loss of an

13. Farrer, *Finite and Infinite*, 76–78.

Aristotelian substance metaphysic may make better sense of God being person, but it may reduce the hermeneutical use of metaphysics in attempting to delve into the constancy of God as required by the scriptural depiction of God's faithfulness. Evangelicalism, though it must be granted it would be novel, could bear a dialectical metaphysic that could attempt to bring together both a substance perspective, as while as a personalist one, such that the nature of God would possess the stability necessary for belief in faithfulness and the voluntarism necessary for belief in grace.

SUMMARY OF ASSESSMENT

Farrer is nothing, if not provocative. His boldness leads to a pursuit of a comprehensive theory of revelation that takes into account many of the phenomena that are commonly seen as revelatory. He rightly places Christ at the center of his theory, while not neglecting Scripture. Though he does not take the pains to develop an understanding of divine and human speech to the degree he does with revelation, he still attempts to reckon with the multifarious nature of speaking and how it relates to God's self-disclosure. In doing so, he resists some of the excesses of scholasticism, such as a focus on propositional content and an Aristotelian metaphysics, without rejecting the hermeneutical enterprise of metaphysical thinking. In this way, he begins to move towards a pluriform metaphysic that can be used as an aid to theological thinking concerning revelation. Furthermore, his understanding of revelation possesses a high view of Scripture and its authority, without equating it with the revelatory act. In doing so, he is able to bring his Reformed tendencies together with his Catholic foundations, in a way that finds parallel in the Evangelical's continuance of orthodox formulations of Christology and theology proper with the *sola scriptura* perspective of its inherited Calvinism.

Though Farrer's view was ambitious in his attempt to bring together various strains of theology, he was also moderate in seeking mediation without simply rejecting the entirety of any given viewpoint. Yet, it is this combination of theories that makes certain facets of his perspective untenable. His theory of revelation is somewhat complicated and suffers from its inability to speak to the transitive nature of revelation. It is the lack of existential understanding that makes the revelatory act, in Farrer's view, somewhat depersonalized. Revelation is not a person in the Word, as in the Neo-Orthodox perspective, but it is the life of that person and its interpretation in conjunction. In doing so, it is possible that he reintroduces a focus on knowledge about persons without fully relating it to the knowledge of persons. Thus, though he attempts to take into account personal revelation, he does not appear to develop it enough to show why the revelatory act results in knowing God. In spite of this, Farrer's view still has elements that are ripe for use in the construction of theory of speech and revelation.

DIALOGUE AND FOUNDATIONS
FOR CONSTRUCTION

11

Scholars in Dialogue

COMPARISON OF VIEWS OF REVELATION

ANY SORT OF ECUMENICAL theological activity is fraught with difficulties and opportunities. A dialogue that crosses theological divisions requires a sensitivity to the goals and concerns of the interlocutors combined with a critical attitude that will not simply take for granted the truth or veracity of any given perspective. Moreover, it requires an entrance into methodological and theoretical concerns that will prevent any construction from being an ad hoc system whose additive nature prevents consistency and practicality. Yet, in spite of the challenges, such an undertaking holds the promise of advance beyond past endeavors since the failure to think topics anew is often related to the inability to move beyond the typical understanding of one's own tradition. Discussion with voices that contrast one's preferred perspective forces a self-critical stance to one's own beliefs, while opening the possibility of appropriating the theological thinking of others. The ensuing conversation will begin to compare and contrast the views of Wolterstorff, Jüngel, and Farrer, attempting to distill their concerns into those areas that a holistic view of revelation, from an Evangelical perspective, would need to address in order to provide a compelling systematic understanding. This will then be utilized in providing the beginnings of a constructive attempt to bring together perspectives into a consistent view of speech and revelation that can account for the various theological, philosophical, and existential concerns that have historically been broached.

Significance of Trinity to Revelation

Though revelation has a similar conceptual treatment in Wolterstorff, Jüngel, and Farrer, it does not take much effort to recognize their relevant differences. They all agree that revelation and hiddenness are necessary correlates and that the term "revelation" is used to cover a set of diverse phenomena. Yet, their techniques of investigating said phenomena relate to the chosen set that they will conceive as normative for the understanding of the others. All three would agree that Christ can be revelatory, with Farrer and Wolterstorff agreeing that miracles and Scripture could also be. Jüngel is difficult to discern on the issue of the latter two categories, since his singular focus on self-revelation makes him reluctant to attach the moniker of "revelation" beyond the trinitarian activity at the cross. Yet, he does not seem necessarily opposed to the belief that God could reveal something in other ways, as long as the central activity is seen in Christ and that all other aspects of revelation relate strictly to understanding something about God and not to knowing God himself.

Though agreeing with Farrer and Jüngel on the occurrence of revelation, Wolterstorff conceives of it playing a lesser (and perhaps ancillary) role in his theorizing. Believing that past exploration had sacrificed God's speech on the altar of revelation, he attempts to treat divine discourse *sui generis*. In doing so, he does not see a necessary connection between the two. This has obvious differences from Jüngel and Farrer. Jüngel, coincidentally, believes that divine speech should take a central position in one's understanding of God. Yet, he conceives of this speech differently than Wolterstorff, focusing more on personal revelation in Christ than on the text of Scripture. Moreover, Jüngel sees speech as indispensable to the investigation of revelation, since he believes that the Word of God is the locus of the revelatory activity which constitutes the divine being. To attempt to speak of divine discourse without revelation, for him, would be like dealing with speech without recognizing that there was a speaker. Farrer is also distinctive from Wolterstorff on the significance of divine revelation to understanding God's speech, in spite of his Reformed tendency in emphasizing the role of the scriptural texts in a human coming into and continuing relationship with God like his American counterpart. For Farrer, the biblical texts may be God's speech, but even if so, it only is able to be this based on the revelatory activity of God. Thus, revelation is the foundation upon which divine and human speech can be built.

The Paradigmatic Revelatory Events

The difference between Wolterstorff, Jüngel, and Farrer concerning revelation can be understood as the diverging emphasis they place on the
categories of phenomena they see as the paradigmatic cases of divine
revelation. Whereas Jüngel focuses clearly on Christ, it could be argued
that Wolterstorff emphasizes Scripture and Farrer focuses on miraculous
activity. It is true that Wolterstorff attempts to separate divine speech and
revelation, but this can only occur since the revelatory activity is primarily
understood in terms of biblical texts. His analytic of revelation concerns
primarily information concerning a person, which then becomes the basis
for his understanding of how revelation could relate to Scripture.[1] Yet, since
he believes it to be a distinct occurrence from divine discourse, he considers
revelation to be an issue that does not require treatment if one is examining
the text. Thus, Wolterstorff's focus on the text as revelation gives his view
its distinctiveness.

Farrer, on the other hand, accentuates miracles when he examines
revelation. It should be noted that he does claim the centrality of Christ
in his understanding of revelation[2], but it can only occur when combined
with the miraculous activity in the apostolic witness that allows for its interpretation. For Farrer, as mentioned previously, revelation encompasses
the whole process of Christ's life and its subsequent understanding as dis-
seminated in the scriptural witness. Both he and Jüngel, contra Wolterstorff,
emphasize the significance of trinitarian distinctions in the revelatory activity. However, where Jüngel focuses on the Father revealing Himself in his
self-interpretation in the Son, Farrer holds that the Father sends the Son
to reveal Him by providing the foundational life and death that offer the
content for the interpretation found in the New Testament writings. For this
reason, Jüngel has a somewhat lesser role for the text than Farrer since any
way in which Christ is presented can become the Word. Christ is not just
another prophet, since his life and speech provide the material and linguistic foundation for subsequent revelatory activity. Thus, the broadening of
the scope of revelation to be more than the Word, as in Jüngel, means that
Farrer has to include a strong view of inspiration[3] and that the miraculous
or "supernatural"[4] activity that is at the foundation of inspiration must converge with meaning. He claims,

1. Wolterstorff, *Divine Discourse*, 19–31.
2. Farrer, *Glass of Vision*, 39.
3. Farrer, "Revelation," 104. See also Farrer, *Glass of Vision*, 36.
4. Farrer, *Glass of Vision*, 30.

Any [supernatural] knowledge would be so, which transposed us, as it were, to the divine centre of activity: which gave us to know, not the bare idea of such a centre, but anything about the way in which the life there lived is exercised and enjoyed at its own divine level: anything which reveals to us the activity of God in God.[5]

Thus, for Farrer, it was in the miracle that the revelation of God's activity in himself can occur whereby the faculties of human understanding are elevated beyond their natural employment. He, therefore, has an emphasis on Christ in revelation, but not as a person to be known so much as a life to be understood.

The consequence of the different loci of revelation is that all three scholars conceive of the Trinity's relationship to divine revelation differently. For Jüngel, as in Farrer, there is no concept of revelation without trinitarian understanding, since his hermeneutical assumption of a Barthian view of Christ prevents any schism. This is not completely novel, nor completely traditional, since Protestantism has historically viewed revelation in trinitarian context, but without emphasizing the constituting nature of revelatory activity. For, Jüngel, revelation is central to who God is as the Father, Son, and the Holy Spirit, not just as a way of knowing God or how he acts. By seeing Christ as the primary revelatory act, there is no way of developing a concept of revelation, nor of divine speech, that is not trinitarian at its core. Thus, he asserts:

> Jede Rede von Gott, die das Dasein Gottes isoliert von seinem trinitarischen Selbstverhältnis, seinem Wesen und seinen Eigen- schaften (Wesenszügen) zur Sprache zu bringen versucht, verfehlt das Sein Gottes und abstrahiert in illegitimer Weise von der Sprache des Glaubens.[6]

Farrer's focus on Christ means that he sees a stronger relationship between the Trinity and revelation, but not nearly to the degree that Jüngel does. There are structural similarities between their views in that both see event and interpretation as significant to revelatory activity, with Farrer emphasizing Christ and his life's interpretation by his own words and that of the apostles, while Jüngel focusing on the self-interpreting nature of the Word in Christ. Yet, the attenuation of the relationship between Trinity and revelation in Farrer, in contrast to Jüngel, is based on two significant factors. First, his unwillingness to break from orthodoxy means that he does want

---

5. Farrer, *Glass of Vision*, 30.
6. Jüngel, "Thesen zum Verhältnis," 254.

to see revelation as constituting divine being, since it would likely imply a mutability that he is unwilling to concede. Second, by focusing on the miraculous activity of revelation as the supernatural interpretation, through images, of Christ's life, then revelation becomes more of an issue of knowing something about Christ than knowing God in Christ. Thus, even if revelation can lead to an understanding of the Trinity, revelatory activity is not developed as a trinitarian activity. Wolterstorff, by focusing on revelation in speech, does not require any sort of trinitarian understanding when he develops a theory. For him revelation is centralized on knowledge and, thus, personal revelation receives a secondary treatment. This is not to say that the personhood of the members of the Godhead do not matter at all to his understanding, but he assumes God's personhood in revelation and advances the matter no further. Thus, God being person is required for the revelation with which he was concerned, but God being three persons is not necessary. It is in this way that Westphal can claim that Wolterstorff's project was to attack the ontotheological "depersonalizing"[7] of the scriptural text, without the personhood of the members of the Trinity taking a central role in his theory.

Also significant to the manner in which Wolterstorff, Jüngel, and Farrer differ in their treatment of revelation is the manner in which they approach the issue of self-revelation. For Jüngel, Christ as the revelation of God is significant for the fact that the central type of revelation is God's revelation of himself. Thus, even where Farrer emphasizes and Wolterstorff admits of personal revelation, their lack of focus on God's manifestation of self will give them a greater emphasis on the conveyance of knowledge in revelatory activity. In many ways, Farrer is the mediating point between Wolterstorff and Jüngel, since he retains trinitarian distinctions as does the latter, but with a greater emphasis placed on Scripture in line with the former. He holds that God does reveal Himself in Christ, but only when the events of his life are brought into interplay with the interpretation of this life. Thus, unlike Jüngel, the Father does not reveal Himself in the Son apart from the understanding of His significance being provided in the image-oriented activity of the apostolic imagination. However, Jüngel's understanding of Christ as the one who reveals God, and his belief that God himself is seen in the event of the life, death and resurrection of said Christ, means that knowledge is insufficient to encompass revelation. Jüngel's understanding of self-revelation appears to have affinities to Kierkegaard's analysis of the self, in that the very idea is relational. Thus, God's self-revelation is a type of relationship to himself that is constitutive of divine being. Yet, in construing

7. Westphal, "Review Essay," 526–27.

it so, Jüngel holds that the divine being and the revelatory function are inseparable such that for revelation to occur, God's presence must also be recognized. Hence, Christ is the very presence of God and thus can reveal God by being the self-attesting Word, but can only be understood as divine presence in his entirety, such that knowledge is not enough to exhaust revelation. Consequently, Farrer and Wolterstorff will differ with Jüngel on the importance of divine presence.

Though Jüngel does not explicitly develop a theology of presence, it is assumed and can be seen in his sacramental view of language and manner in which God is present in the word event. Farrer appears to have a foundation for an understanding of divine presence in his emphasis on God's work and ability to reveal himself in any historical event. Yet, though some connection is drawn between revelation and divine activity, he does not move onto arguing for God's actual presence in his revelation. Thus, Farrer sees the interplay between event and interpretation as revelation, but such an interplay cannot be confused with divine presence. Wolterstorff, without a trinitarian foundation for revelatory activity, is not concerned with God being present, so much as it assumes that God is present and therefore can speak. Thus, the differing approach of Wolterstorff, Jüngel, and Farrer towards divine presence further separates the manner in which they relate Trinity to revelation.

COMPARISON OF VIEWS OF SPEECH

Divine Speech

Wolterstorff, Jüngel, and Farrer's divergence concerning the nature of divine speech is strongly related to their understanding of revelation, while their differences in the area of human speech is more tangential. Wolterstorff does not explicitly disagree with Jüngel and Farrer due to the hypothetical nature of his enterprise in developing an understanding of God's discourse. In fact, his explicit criticism of the overly reductive nature of Barth's perspective,[8] displays an implicit belief that divine speech is multifarious and thus explanations may require a circumscription of a particular aspect of divine speech in order to begin. As he attempts to understand whether God could use human words to produce his own speech, he relies on a speech act model that lends itself to appropriation. In doing so, he never actually defines what divine speech is, so much as arguing that God could speak in a manner similar to humans in the generation of illocutionary acts.

8. Wolterstorff, *Divine Discourse*, 58–75.

Significant to this model is that Wolterstorff broaches the possibility of a "double agency discourse."[9] Yet, unlike Farrer, this double agency very simply separates, in the discourse act, the activity of God and that of humans. Where Farrer wants to see a more intimate relationship between the activity of God and that of the writers of Scripture, especially in his development of an idea of inspiration, he is reluctant to delve into the afore mentioned "causal joint"[10] between human and divine actions. Wolterstorff, however, has no such qualms, placing the work of the writers of Scripture squarely in the locutionary area, with God appropriating it to produce an illocutionary act. Though recognizing that a theology of inspiration may be important to fully develop his theory, he brackets off its discussion since he believes appropriation is sufficient to deal with the biblical text. Of importance to Wolterstorff's work are the analogies between human discourse relationships and that between God and the authors of Scripture. Were they not to hold, then his analytic of human speech would not be able to make the considerable move towards representing divine discourse.

Farrer's view of divine speech is similar to Wolterstorff in that it is centered on the instrumentality of speech to do what God desires. For Wolterstorff, this is a matter of the way that God uses human speech acts, while for Farrer there is a less defined manner in which divine discourse works. He does, contra his Calvinist interlocutor, hold to some degree to a communicative theory of speech,[11] whereby God is attempting to convey truth concerning himself in the act. There is a note of irony that Farrer's career-spanning accentuation of the activity of God carries over less into his theory than that of Wolterstorff. The reason that he is not tempted to move in the direction of speech act theory appears to be his emphasis on revelation, whereby the instrumentality of divine speech gains communicative significance in its relaying of the authoritative understanding of Christ's life, death, and resurrection necessary for revelatory activity to occur in the interaction of event and interpretation. Thus, where Wolterstorff treats divine speech independently of revelation, Farrer draws the relationship between the two such that revelatory activity occurs through divine speech.

Jüngel's view distinguishes himself from his dialogue partners both by a more extreme stressing of the relationship of revelation and speech

9. Wolterstorff, *Divine Discourse*, 38.

10. Farrer, *Faith and Speculation*, 65, 172, 174–75.

11. The reason for the tentative nature of this argument is related to the manner in which Farrer changes his characterization of speech depending on the context. He tends to hold a communicative understanding when speaking of texts, but when he deals with thinking, he characterizes also as discourse, where communication is either absent or present in a much more idiomatic sense. See Farrer, *Saving Belief*, 63.

than that of Farrer and by the employment of the speech event category of his hermeneutical predecessors to see a more constructive nature to divine speech. Jüngel strongly disagrees with Wolterstorff on the separability of speech and revelation, since he views the divine Word as the primary activity of speech, to which revelation refers. For Jüngel, divine speech and revelation are essentially the same act, viewed from two different standpoints of analysis. Divine speech focuses on the manner in which Christ is God's self-interpretation, while revelation emphasizes the trinitarian act whereby the Word in relation to the Father, by the Spirit, constitutes divine ontology. Thus, the revelatory act is the act where God is the God who reveals himself in the cross of Christ, while divine speech is the divine self-identification with the event of the cross. In this way, divine speech is constitutive of the nature of God, in a manner that starkly contrasts Wolterstorff and Farrer's views. Moreover, this view of the nature of the Word as the primary speech event whereby God is who he is, means that speech has a sacramental nature which will carry down into Jüngel's analysis of human speech. This also means that, similar to Barth, he is not keen on drawing distinctions between the form and content of revelation.[12] In order for Jesus Christ to be the self-interpreting Word, the content of revelatory activity is inseparable from its form. Thus, the cross of Christ becomes not only the event of God's revelation, but also becomes the interpretive framework by which God's activity is to be understood.

Human Speech

The variance in the manner in which Wolterstorff, Jüngel, and Farrer address human speech relates not only to their view of revelation and divine speech, but also their methodology of analysis. Wolterstorff's assumption of a philosophical stance, employing an analytic that begins with normal language usage, leads to his development of a theory of discourse wherein the divine is parasitic off of the human. Thus, for God to speak, at least in the case of the Bible, is for God to perform human speech acts. In this area, Wolterstorff is an intriguing mixture of humility and boldness. In spite of the limited nature of his endeavor, he attempts to not only explain the functional nature of speech, but also begins to provide an ontology of speech, which is somewhat of a rarity in the analytic tradition.[13] Wolterstorff's

---

12. Jüngel, *God's Being*, 27–28.

13. One may speculate as to its cause, though Wittgenstein's complicating of the nature of speech and its relationship to thought and life may be part of the reason that analytic philosophers have become unnerved.

normative theory of speech attempts to explain what speech is through the manner in which it is used to effect changes in relationships, a concept he explains in terms of rights and obligations. Thus, when God uses human's speech, he is taking up a relationship with those to whom he speaks in a public sphere. This view will overlap with the relational concerns of Farrer and Jüngel in speech, but is developed differently in that it is essentially independent of theological concerns.

Farrer is sympathetic to some of Wolterstorff's methodology, especially in his willingness to investigate typical occurrences of speech in the everyday life of the individuals as a gateway to understanding human discourse. However, he is more willing to heed theological concerns in his development of a systematic understanding. Consequently, even when he eventually departs from a Thomist view of analogy, he still attempts to use the idea of inspired images to preserve the type of metaphorical speech that he believes necessary to do justice to the Christian concern of retaining a distinction between the human and the divine.[14] Farrer maintains a communicative element in speech, but draws a much stronger connection between speech and thought. His developmental view of humanity and language gives rise to a view where speech was compelled by external social circumstances, which preceded the development of thought.[15] Thus, he agrees with Jüngel that thinking is after talking, whereas Wolterstorff does not draw that connection to the forefront of his writing. In fact, Farrer begins to understand thinking as a type of inner discourse. In doing so, he has certain similarities to his Lutheran counterpart in developing his perspective under the principle that God speaks prior to human speaking. By seeing thinking and speech as having such an intimate relationship, Farrer develops a view of discourse that he believes can make sense of the manner in which thought occurs in diverse ways. Thus, he attempts to deny the supremacy of propositional content, without attacking the significance of assertorial language. Moreover, like Jüngel, the significance of metaphor in speaking about God, especially as it relates to the recognition of possibilities, is emphasized. However, in contrast, Farrer never appears to move towards the continental views of language as exemplified in Jüngel's appropriation of Heidegger.

Jüngel's employment of the speech event compels him to seek a type of holism in his view of human speech that has both benefits and difficulties. His perspective prevents the loss of the speaker, in contrast to views that abstract the act of speech from the one producing it. Moreover, Jüngel

14. Farrer, *Finite and Infinite*, 7.

15. On this view, though never explicitly mentioned, he is presumably speaking of discursive thought.

wants to retain a teleological and not functional view of speech. Since he believes divine speech is primary, he is disinclined to analyze speaking as a way of performing activities, since it would be somewhat difficult to apply that concept in relationship to God. For Jüngel, speech cannot just be a contingent way that God acts, but must be more essential to his being. Thus, whereas divine speech is constitutive of the divine ontology in the primary speech event, human speech, in the secondary speech event, must similarly perform a function whereby one's being is enacted through discourse. Thus, human speech is a way for one to specify their relationship to the world and thus conceive of reality. Intriguingly, though Jüngel parts ways with Wolterstorff concerning speech act theory,[16] they converge on the importance of the declarative aspects of speech. Wolterstorff, in centralizing speech on declaration, comes close to certain continental understandings of language in that speaking will always affect reality. Thus, though he never subscribes to a constructivist approach to linguistic activity, he does want to see reality as an issue closely tied to such activity.[17] In summary, Jüngel's view that God is the primary speaker, similar to Barth, means that human speech reflects the manner in which divine speech is related to divine being, but differentiated in that humans can never, as created, completely determine their own being.

Inspiration and the Scriptural Text

Wolterstorff, Jüngel, and Farrer, though different in many respects, are unified in their concern for systematic consistency in their thinking. That is not to say that they feel compelled to adhere to every aspect of a particular system even if they come to conclusions that contradict it. Wolterstorff's broad form of Calvinism, Jüngel's willingness to depart from orthodoxy, and Farrer's drift away from Thomism is enough to demonstrate a willingness to break from the normal constraints that systems may pose. Yet, even with such willingness, they will tolerate tension but not contradiction. One area that is notably unusual, in light of this tendency, is their view of Scripture. It is in discussion of texts that these scholars are most willing to depart from

16. It must be admitted that Jüngel makes allusions to and possesses a limited appropriation of speech act theory. However, he never fully ascribes to its tenets or its implications. See Jüngel, *God as the Mystery*, 10–12.

17. As was mentioned earlier, Wolterstorff is not inclined to constructivist views of language since he poses a strong correlation between reality and realism. Yet, he believes that, as part of reality, humans can affect reality. Thus, his philosophy of language as related to ontology could be seen as an attenuation of continental perspectives that humans actually construct reality linguistically.

philosophical and theological concerns, such that their conclusions are, in many ways, predetermined by external scholarship. The most prevalent example of this is that in spite of their large differences concerning the nature and purpose of the Bible, they all attempt to reconcile their perspectives with historical criticism. Even though the work of historical critics plays little role in their interpretation of texts and they trend towards traditional explanations, they all attempt to show why historical criticism is significant, differing on its role based on their view of the relationship between revelation and Scripture. Wolterstorff's canonical perspective focuses on the received form of the text and thus any questions as to what lays behind the text, whether in oral tradition or previous textual traditions, are largely ignored. Farrer, in relating historical activity to significance, does believe that the events contained in Scripture can be examined in terms of their actuality, but not in terms of their meaning or importance. The latter is the purview of theology and thus historical criticism cannot overturn doctrines of Scripture, even when, from his view, it purifies the understanding of the events of the text which are given theological interpretation. Jüngel has certain similarities with Farrer in that God's self-interpretation in Jesus Christ is not open to scrutiny, since it does not have a purely historical meaning. He, thus, followed Barth in preserving some role for historical-critical studies, but limited their application to the testimonial record of the writers of Scripture and not the Word that was contained therein.

Wolterstorff, Farrer, and Jüngel could be categorized in terms of the degree to which they deviate from traditional views of Scripture. Farrer is perhaps the most traditional with an overall theory that includes a reason for preferring New Testament texts without preferring only the gospels, a theology of inspiration, and a hermeneutical methodology that plays close attention to the literary features of the text. In terms of preferring particular texts or types of texts, he is willing to explicitly give ascendancy to portions of Scripture, namely, texts that refer to the life and death of Jesus Christ. This preference, unlike many traditional hermeneutical methods, is not based on the literary characteristics found in groups of biblical texts. Instead, the preference is content oriented. Since Farrer understands revelation as including both events and their interpretation in relationship[18] and his belief that Christ is primary revelation,[19] Scripture that deals with the events of his life, death, and resurrection are given primacy. This is also the reason that he is not unwilling to call Scripture revelatory, similar to traditional conceptions. Since events require interpretation, and the Bible can provide this, then it

18. Farrer, *Glass of Vision*, 38.
19. Farrer, *Glass of Vision*, 38.

can be called, in some sense, revelation. He also comes closer to traditional views than Wolterstorff and Jüngel in that he believes in the indispensability of inspiration when understanding Scripture and its relationship to divine speech and revelation. Like both of his dialogue partners, Farrer recognizes that one's understanding of the relationship of God's speech/revelation to the text will influence one's hermeneutical methodology. Yet, where both Wolterstorff and Jüngel believe that the relationship of the divine to the text can be explained without inspiration, Farrer believes that it is a central distinctive of the Christian Scriptures. Granted that his perspective on what it means for the authors of Scripture to be "inspired" is very different from previous positions, but his view on its necessity is not. Furthermore, his view of inspiration, in terms of the prophetic and apostolic development of divinely sanctioned images means that his view will pay strong attention to the literary features of the text. Though not agreeing with the tradition, both Jewish and Christian, concerning the approach of the literary analysis, he does argue that the revelatory activity that can occur in the interpretive activity of the apostles is not independent of the features of the text.

Wolterstorff is the next closest to a traditional view of the Bible in that he assumes that Scripture is "one book,"[20] attempts to retain a significant role for the author in understanding interpretive activity, and takes a canonical perspective that privileges the New Testament without explicitly privileging any particular, group, or genre of texts.[21] However, he takes certain positions that distinguish him from views that were historically prevalent. His surmising that Scripture should be understood as God's illocutionary actions being performed through human locutionary and/or illocutionary acts is obviously non-traditional, simply because it is contemporary. However, his lack of a developed theology of inspiration is somewhat peculiar. Since he sees appropriation as sufficient to describe the relationship between God and the human author of a scriptural text and since this appropriation is understood in terms of analogy with situations containing only human agents, inspiration plays very little role in his theorizing. He claims:

> Of course it would be bizarre to think of God as just finding these books lying about and deciding to appropriate them; the appropriation model calls for supplementation with some doctrine of inspiration. But what's worth noting is that, on this way

20. Wolterstorff, *Divine Discourse*, 53.

21. It is possible, however, to argue that functionally, Wolterstorff privileges certain genres of Biblical literature. Since he focuses on propositional content and the self-interpretive nature of words, one might be tempted to claim that he gives precedence to prose. Yet, whether this is true or not does not detract from his refraining from explicitly preferring a genre in a way that distinguishes his view from Farrer and Jüngel.

> of thinking of the matter, a doctrine of inspiration really is a supplement. However these books came about, the crucial fact is that God appropriates that discourse in such a way that those speakings now mediate God's speaking.[22]

Wolterstorff believes that the content of Scripture is incidental, though not necessarily arbitrary. Hence, inspiration may help to explain the peculiarity of God using the particular texts of the Bible, but is not necessary to explain that God uses the text or how he appropriates them. Also, since Wolterstorff believes that one can address the idea of God speaking in Scripture without also broaching the issue of revelation, he contends that Scripture can be revelatory of items of knowledge about God, but this is secondary to what God is doing through the text.

The view that God uses Scripture to perform illocutionary acts means that his view of biblical interpretation will mirror traditional perspectives without coinciding with them. He agrees that there will be dual foci in interpretation, similar to the speed at which historical exegetical works have moved between claims that "the author said" and claims that "God said." Yet, he deemphasizes authorial intention and attempts to blunt criticisms concerning the author's psyche by arguing that authorial discourse interpretation is dealing with words used in the public sphere. Thus, the type of historical-literary exegesis at the foundation of both Alexandrian and Antiochian schools of interpretation is not fully retained.

Jüngel is the least similar to historical styles in his employment of an essentially Barthian view of Scripture, with some modification to bear the weight of his speech event analysis of Christ's activity in revelation. He understands the Bible to be the authoritative testimony concerning the work and person of Jesus Christ, who is the revelation of God. In emphasizing its testimonial nature, he is willing to part ways with tradition by not understanding the inspiration of the authors of Scripture to be a substantial factor in one's view of the text or the hermeneutical methodology implied thereafter. One area where he substantially diverges from Barth, which is also a way in which he is differentiated from Farrer and Wolterstorff, is in his preference for the gospels in exegesis. His dialectical predecessor had a greater propensity to show the continuity between the Old and New Testaments, which finds echoes in Wolterstorff's "one book" understanding. Farrer, similarly, wants a larger canonical birth even when preferring the New Testament. Jüngel, on the other hand, continues the trend he instituted in his doctoral research of highlighting the sayings of Jesus, especially in the parabolic accounts. The self-interpretive nature of the Word of God

22. Wolterstorff, *Divine Discourse*, 187.

means that Jesus has the first say concerning his relationship to God and his kingdom. Thus, Jesus Christ, as the primary Word event, becomes the hermeneutical locus for adjudicating the importance of different texts in being the bearer of the secondary word event and, thus, his self-attestation in the gospels gains a central place in theological exegesis. Yet, in spite of his differences with Barth, Jüngel's belief that the revelation of God in Christ requires historical representation for subsequent Christians, means that he will agree with his predecessor that Scripture has an important, though secondary, role in revelation.

The God who Speaks

Similar to the manner in which Wolterstorff, Jüngel, and Farrer could be distinguished in their views of revelation by investigating their paradigmatic cases of revelatory activity, so, it could be argued, that some of their relevant differences can be made manifest by looking at the manner in which they highlight particular characterizations of the divine speaker over others. Wolterstorff, in his fundamental agreement with what he terms the "classical Western conception"[23] of God, trends toward portraying God as "Lord" in speech. When God speaks through Scripture, it is a matter of him acting through the text to perform the acts he desires. Thus, his choice of appropriation, the fact that the success conditions for speaking are solely under his control, and his ability to unilaterally impose normative stances through Scripture, points to the centrality of lordship to Wolterstorff's position. This is given further credence by his mentioning and general defense of a divine command metaethical theory.[24] This has specific consequences for Wolterstorff's theory, in that there is less of an emphasis on the soteriological aspects of the Scripture than in either the work of Farrer or Jüngel, with the former seeing it as necessary and the latter seeing it as both necessary and central. To some degree, with the trinitarian nature of revelation being held in abeyance in Wolterstorff's theory, as well as his setting aside of personal revelation from his address, it essentially means that the Father's traditionally conceived role as superintendent of the world and its history will be brought to the forefront. Thus, speech becomes a method for the extension of God's rule over the world.

Farrer, in contradistinction from Wolterstorff, has a much stronger soteriological strain in his later work. In his earlier scholarship, God's role as agent and actor were much more prevalent. His attempts to provide a

23. Wolterstorff, *Divine Discourse*, 15.
24. Wolterstorff, *Divine Discourse*, 97–113.

substance metaphysic based on divine activity draw attention to the centrality of God's work and will. In the evolution of his perspective, he grew to reject certain of the more Thomist features of his earlier work, but divine choice never receded from view. Consequently, Farrer conceived of God as "savior" in his speaking. In the role of savior, Farrer is both able to bring together the gracious activity of God's free choice to save with his communicative theory of speech whereby God interprets his own salvific activity through the words of Christ and the apostles. Central to his view, which is what will distinguish him from Jüngel and bring him closer to previous orthodoxy, is that God being savior assumes a rudimentary *ordo salutis* that attempts to protect divine independence. Divine speech follows divine ontology, such that God assumes the role of saving speaker based on his prior trinitarian being. He, therefore, conceives of God as savior who speaks to save.

Jüngel is similar to Farrer in holding a strong place both for trinitarian distinctions and the saving work of God in his analysis of speech. He also stresses God as savior when he speaks, but in a manner in stark contrast to Farrer. Jüngel believes that God can only be characterized as speaker in his actual speaking. God is not savior first and then speaker subsequently, but God is savior in and through his speech. Only in the speech event of God identifying with the Christ on the cross can he be understood as a savior. Thus, even though Farrer focuses on divine free choice, he does not want to see God as being able to make choices that affect divine being. Jüngel has no such qualms and thus there is only conceptual difference between saying that "God is savior" and "God is speaker," with both ideas being inseparable. For Jüngel, God is savior because that is how he has spoken. Thus, he parts ways with Farrer concerning the possibility of divine self-definition and, consequently, differs with his Anglican interlocutors' position even when both emphasize God's saving work.

In spite of the differences concerning inspiration, texts of concern, etc., Wolterstorff, Farrer, and Jüngel have certain areas of broad agreement. All are going to distance themselves from Catholic perspectives in claiming the centrality of the authority of Scripture to their perspective. Wolterstorff's Calvinism and Jüngel's Lutheranism appear to influence them towards a *sola scriptura* position, whereas Farrer, notwithstanding his brand of high church Anglicanism, appears to side, to some degree, with the practical piety of his Baptist roots. Thus, all would claim that exegesis is a centrally Christian practice and, consequently, should be related to one's overall theological perspective. Furthermore, they would all agree on the interpretive nature of being approached by God and though they understand such interpretation differently, all would see Scripture as significant to said activity.

Metaphysics and Speech

The differences between Wolterstorff, Jüngel, and Farrer on Trinity and revelation also has the implications concerning their relationship to metaphysics. Wolterstorff's lack of emphasis on personal revelation, with its related
development of a view of divine discourse outside of trinitarian concerns,
allows him to assume a metaphysical view of divinity that both Farrer and
Jüngel come to criticize. This perspective is a gift from his Calvinist background and its willingness to appropriate certain philosophical categories
from scholasticism. Thus, he conceives of God in terms of his characteristics, which he terms the "classical Western concept of God."[25] In this way,
God is viewed in terms of a divine nature, and his revelation in terms of
knowledge of that nature and its attributes. Jüngel, believing in the centrality of personal revelation in conceiving of revelatory phenomena, strongly
opposes those past metaphysical perspectives that cannot bear the idea of
personhood that he comes to espouse. Squarely in his view is the type of Aristotelian substance perspective that Farrer also resists. For Jüngel, substance
possesses a type of constancy that does not makes sense of God's decision
concerning himself in identifying with the man Jesus Christ. Thus, even if
substance metaphysics could make sense of God choosing, which scholastic
theologians would not deny as a divine possibility, he does not believe it
could make sense of God's self-determination in free choice. Consequently,
he agrees with Barth in questioning philosophical perspectives that does
not allow for divine grace to be understood in terms of a non-necessitated
decision to be Savior. Whereas Wolterstorff is willing to see God as a divine
nature bearing characteristics, Jüngel sees him as a trinitarian community
that is constituted in a decision to fulfill a soteriological role, with this role
bringing accompanying characteristics. Thus, Wolterstorff finds constancy
in the divine nature, with Jüngel seeking constancy in the divine choice.
Farrer, in many ways, splits the difference between his dialogue partners,
since he is both unwilling to reject metaphysics in the examination of the
being of God, but is also not content with Aristotelian views that does not
allow a sufficient role for Christ's personhood in understanding divinity.
Thus, he attempts to revise metaphysics to align it with an understanding of
trinitarian personhood, while allowing his theological concerns to branch
out into a philosophy of being that orients his examination of the world and
natural knowledge.

Though Jüngel has a tendency to reject metaphysics and Farrer seeks
to refine it, neither of them are willing to completely forego metaphysical

25. Wolterstorff, *Divine Discourse*, 15.

thinking, nor are they willing to give up completely on substance thought. This has two different outcomes for them. For Jüngel, metaphysics as a tool for understanding different subjects is a possibility, as long as it does not infringe upon theological thinking. He appears to imply its use, especially in the sciences.[26] Yet, such metaphysical thinking is more in line with attempts to "master" a subject and, in a similar vein with Kierkegaard, Jüngel does not believe that God can be domesticated as such.[27] Whereas Jüngel seems to believe metaphysics has some applicability, but not in the sphere of theology, Farrer appears to be more open to a multiform metaphysic. Similar to Jüngel in seeing it as primarily a tool, he believes that it will take a structure according to the object of its interpretation. He, therefore, argues that "a single over-all conceptual analysis will be about as useful for the interpretation of the Apostle's writings as a bulldozer for the cultivation of a miniature landscape-garden."[28] Farrer, then, will attempt to refine the metaphysic that speaks concerning God, while allowing Aristotelian substance talk to stand in impersonal areas.

26. Jüngel, God as the Mystery, 177.

27. It might be argued that there is a parallel here to a Heideggerian view of science and technology and their relationship to speech. In the same way that metaphysical speech may imply mastery over its subject, so could technology imply mastery over nature as individuals cause resources be placed in a state of "standing-reserve." See Heidegger, Question Concerning Science.

28. Farrer, Glass of Vision, 45.

12

Principles of Construction

With a comparison of Wolterstorff's, Jüngel's, and Farrer's views in place, some analysis of how their perspectives can be fruitful for a systematic construction from an Evangelical position can begin. This will include both a criticism of their views and a retrieval of those aspects of their scholarship that can serve to clarify the relationship between divine speech and revelation and human discourse. Specifically, there will be an emphasis on those aspects of their views that could serve to buttress the traditional Evangelical support for a verbal plenary inspiration of Scripture. Following this, a brief proposal will be made as to a possible understanding of divine ontology that may be useful in the attempt to draw together a revelatory theology with a philosophy of language.

DIVINE REVELATION

Though Wolterstorff, Jüngel, and Farrer possess commonality on the idea inherent in the term "revelation," there is less agreement as to the conceptual role it plays in their thinking. Farrer and Jüngel appear to be in accord on the idea that divine revelation is integral to accentuating God's activity in humans coming to know him. The former's suspicion (developed later in his career) towards the possibilities of natural theology, which coincides with a similar skepticism in the latter, appears to be related to the mode of receptivity necessary for the conveyance of divine intention. Whereas natural theology, though speaking as to the stamp of God on creation, points to a seeking inherent within humans such that they can gain certain understanding of the divine by their unaided faculties, revelation implies a mode of passivity such that the credit for the activity is given to the divine. Farrer and Jüngel conclude that there is a need for such a receptivity for many of the same reasons. They both rightly see such to be implied by the role of faith in the Christian life, as well as the New Testament emphasis on grace. For Jüngel, who retains the Lutheran belief in the centrality of understanding humans as *simul justus et peccator*,[1] justification and grace are of great significance both to his theological anthropology and to his Christology. For this reason, being defined by grace and impaired by sin requires divine initiation if any reconciliation between divinity and humanity is to occur. Thus, both Farrer and Jüngel make the fateful, and likely correct, decision to give revelation a central position in their understanding of the Christian's relationship to God.

Wolterstorff, in contradistinction to Farrer and Jüngel, believes that revelation is separable from the question of God speaking and from one's view of the scriptural text. The difficulties with this have already been mentioned, but a note of defense for the philosopher is in order. Wolterstorff's appropriation model, though perhaps idiomatic and not uncontroversial, can perform a similar conceptual function to revelation (in a more limited sense) in the work of his dialogue partners. He argues that though there may be authorized and deputized representatives for God, he, potentially, could use the writing of someone who has no relationship to him at all. If that is the case, then the human author loses significance compared to the divine work of appropriation. Moreover, since one's purpose, on Wolterstorff's model, is to understand what God says in a text, there is a recovery of a mode of receptivity. It will be admitted that certain aspects of this may be difficult from the Christian perspective, since a discussion of inspiration and faith are lacking. Yet, one might be able to argue that he is attempting to philosophically construe language such that God can speak through it in a way that safeguards similar values as are found in revelatory perspectives. Moreover, in his theorizing, he never disregards the possibility of multiple forms of speech or the significance of revelation to the Christian view. Thus, though he may be incorrect that revelation is separable from the question of divine speech, he holds similar values to Farrer and Jüngel and the hypothetical nature of his product means that his perspective, by his own admission, is limited. Thus, his viewpoint may be significant to an overall construction seeking the relationship between human and divine speech since he gives the most in depth treatment of the philosophical concerns of normal language usage. Moreover, the provisional nature of his work

1. Jüngel, "On the Doctrine of Justifiction," 45.

naturally solicits interaction with a theological perspective that can begin to fill in the gaps necessary to make his perspective specifically and uniquely Christian.

Wolterstorff's view that revelation is separable from an understanding of Scripture and divine speech is reflective of a significant difference between his work and that of Farrer and Jüngel. All three recognize that a diverse set of phenomena is understood in the Christian faith as being revelatory. Yet, they all choose a different particular type of revelation to be central to their theoretical development. Wolterstorff gives his most extensive emphasis to revelation of an "item of knowledge"[2] concerning an agent. In setting aside revelation in Christ, revelatory activity revolves around propositional content and can be conveyed through assertorial speech acts. Since Wolterstorff removes assertion from its traditional place of prominence in scriptural exegesis, a theology of revelation, likewise, becomes less pronounced. Whereas the personal nature of revelation is central to Farrer and Jüngel, Wolterstorff is concerned with personhood merely tangentially since only persons, in his view, speak. Thus, he never really examines what it means for a person to be revealed. Farrer, on the other hand, places personal revelation at the center of his theory with his concentration on Christ. In doing so, he assumes that revelation of knowledge can occur, since it is necessary for the authoritative interpretation of Christ to be conveyed. Consequently, he is similar to Wolterstorff in singling out the literary nature of revelation in Scripture. Jüngel, though not neglecting the possibility of revelation of knowledge and personal revelation, focuses on God's self-revelation in Christ. Since the Christian life is a committed life, whereby its inception is an encounter with God in the Word event, a third person understanding of God's revelatory act is insufficient. One must not just know that God is person, but must know the person who is God.

A constructive attempt to address divine speech and revelation must, then, determine which revelatory event is primary and how it relates to any other revelatory phenomena. Such a decision is difficult since it will often be dependent on one's position on a myriad of theological areas. Though Wolterstorff, Farrer, and Jüngel are not in perfect agreement theologically (as no three scholars could be), they are in accord in terms of their belief in the centrality of Christ to faith, as well as the soteriological significance of the event of Christ's crucifixion and resurrection. These values, in conjunction with a recognition of some of the existential elements of Christianity as well as the exegetical concerns revolving around Jesus self-understanding, would point to Jüngel's emphasis being central. The exclusivity of Christ's

2. Wolterstorff, *Divine Discourse*, 23.

claims, though often directed towards the question of universalism, appears to be, foremost, a matter of the centrality of Christ towards any relationship with God. Thus, soteriological debates aside, claims such as, "I am the way, and the truth, and the life. No one comes to the Father except through me. If you know me, you will know my Father also. From now on you do know him and have seen him" (John 14:6–7) begins to draw a connection between an exegetical sense of "knowing" and the centrality of Christ to the revelatory act. Moreover, it is the significance of self-revelation that makes the Trinity integral to the development of an understanding of the divine revelatory act.

Thus, Barth's trinitarian structure is fundamentally correct, though perhaps incomplete. Whereas he was willing to apply the moniker "word of God" beyond Christ, he was not willing to do so to the term "revelation." However, self-revelation could not occur without personal revelation and personal revelation could not occur without the revelation of some knowledge. God, in Christ, reveals himself as one who comes into relationship with humanity. That relationship, as Farrer argues, is given definition by his activities and decisions for his people. Consequently, personhood is not understood primarily as a characteristic that is possessed, but a manner of relationality. Without some understanding of this, though not necessarily thematically, a Christian could not really approach God as the one who has acted in her behalf in the event of the crucifixion. Yet, personal revelation requires the conveying of some knowledge, since one could not have understanding of one as person or be able to identify said person, without some sort of understanding of them. Thus, God's self-revelation comes in Christ, who is personal revelation that requires interpretation, but that interpretation can only come through the transmission of knowledge. Thus, there is a fundamental inseparability between Wolterstorff's, Farrer's, and Jüngel's view of revelation, with Wolterstorff's coming first if one were to take the *ordo cognoscendi* and Jüngel's being primary in terms of *ordo essendi*. An understanding of revelation must, then, center itself on God's self-revelation, while not reducing all revelation to self-revelation.

Moreover, this perspective, is consistent with Jüngel's view that, though God does not need humans, He chooses not to be God without humans. Though God is capable of self-revelation without the need of humans to be involved with the revelatory activity, He chooses not to reveal Himself, at least in the present economy, without the involvement of human activity in terms of the production of Scripture. Ironically, the Evangelical position that God can speak through Scripture, even as it is the production of human agency, may assume of ontological openness to humanity that is vital to Jüngel's claims concerning the "humanity of God." Thus, perhaps an incarnational foundation for bibliology is in order, to which Barth hints, whereby the willingness of God to assume the role of Savior for his self-revelation is mirrored by his willingness to assume flesh for his personal revelation and willingness to be inscripturated in human words for the revelation of knowledge about Himself.

Similarly, Farrer's perspective of a revelatory holism without the reduction of the foundational significance of Christ's life, death, and self-explication, would admit of the possibility that Scripture could be a manner in which God reveals and speaks, without dismissing central Christological insights. In this way, the Evangelical belief that God can reveal through Scripture cannot be dismissed out of hand, though admittedly it must be refined beyond many of its previous self-understandings. When revelation is reduced to being that which is found in Scripture, there is an overreaction that is mirrored by Jüngel's simplifying revelation to being Christ. Yet, the frequent failure to recognize the centrality of Christ to the revelation of God must be remedied by a reexamination of the relationship of God's speaking in Christ and God's speaking through the prophets and apostles.

A final issue of note relates to the conception of the Christian life and how it relates to revelation. All of the scholars in discussion, though admittedly drawing from different influences, would agree that Christianity is something to be lived. The question, then, naturally arises as to how one is to live the Christian life. This becomes significant in that it forces one to recognize that the question of God's revelation is not just related to the soteriological implications of the Christ's coming, but on the implications of confession of the resurrected Christ on the sanctification of the believer.[3] Wolterstorff, Jüngel, and Farrer would all appear to agree on the normative nature of Scripture to the church and the individual believer, but the mode of its normativity is not an area of accord. It appears that Jüngel sees this normative nature as a function of the usage within the church, whereas Wolterstorff would believe that usage is a function of normativity. Farrer tends towards Wolterstorff's side, since the normativity appears to be a product of the revelatory nature of Scripture in their bearing not only accounts of Christ's life, but also the authorized interpretation of said life by apostolic representatives. Jüngel's perspective, as compelling as it is in its

---

3. It is recognized that there are instances in Scripture where sanctification is given a positional treatment similar to the Protestant view of justification. However, this does not detract from those instances where sanctification is recognized as having progressive aspects that will only reach culmination in eschatological consummation. The scope of this work will prevent the addressing of the question of the nature of sanctification, and will assume for the remainder that sanctification is both progressive and unfinished previous to the *eschaton*.

ability to support a view that has fruitful interaction with modern critical scholarship, will appear to have certain difficulties on the practical level. For Farrer and Wolterstorff, the authority of Scripture is not independent of the qualities of Scripture, and therefore its usage is not enough to define its delegated right to direct the Christian life. Jüngel may have some recourse in arguing that the life of the Christian is meant to reflect the life of Christ. Yet, this runs afoul of both an exegetical and a theological difficulty. Exegetically, it appears that there are some things that Christ is able to do that Christians are not. Theologically, some disjunction between the life of Christ and the life of the believer may be necessary in order to guard the uniqueness of the former. This criticism will also be applicable to Jüngel's rejection of a two natures Christology. Moreover, even as Christ's life is supposed to be a model, to some degree, for the Christian, it can only be so when it is interpreted to display those aspects central for emulation. Even if Jüngel's view of revelation can make sense of an individual coming to faith in Christ without the need for Scripture being revelatory, he would still need to make sense of how the believer can continue the Christian life without some sort of direct instruction with divine authority. Consequently, an Evangelical perspective would be warranted in agreeing with Wolterstorff and Farrer, contra Jüngel, that Scripture itself could be revelatory in some significant sense.

DIVINE SPEECH AND DIVINE ONTOLOGY

It would not be difficult to argue that, in terms of divine speech, Jüngel's perspective is the least similar to the other positions. His theologically informed understanding of the Word of God, in conjunction with his hermeneutical understanding of speech events, provides an indivisible connection between divine ontology and divine speech. God is who he is in identification with Jesus Christ on the cross. Thus, the divine self-interpretation of the Father in the Son is none other than what makes the Father who he is. Since this self-interpretation is not, as Barth thought, located in the choice of self-election in eternity's past, but in the historical event of the life of Christ, especially in terms of the crucifixion and resurrection, God must be understood as going through change. He is historical being in his identification with Jesus and thus is defined by the eschatological nature of Christ's activity. While Wolterstorff and Farrer reside closer to orthodoxy in their assigning greater primacy on being over becoming, Jüngel is the exact opposite. Jüngel's view is further unique, in comparison to Wolterstorff, because speech cannot be examined apart from the revelatory act. Since, as was demonstrated, the Word is a moment in the entirety of the event of revelation, they cannot be separated. The Word, as God's self-identification shows that God is the God who reveals himself in love. Farrer, similarly, sees revelation and divine speech as inseparable, since it requires both event and interpretation.

Jüngel's view is both helpful and problematic. It is helpful in drawing into question the issue of God's being, which is a concern he shares with his Anglican counterpart. Farrer's shift from his earlier substance metaphysic, related to the greater role that choice and activity played in his thought. Even in his earlier works, he attempted to redefine the attributes of God in terms of the qualities exhibited in divine activity. Thus, the character of God becomes more of the character of his choices and chosen set of actions. Jüngel, similarly, redefines the role of the divine attributes. In both cases, their perspectives help to make sense of exegetical information that points to the ability of God to choose who he is for his people. Moreover, an analytic of grace appears to require contingency, such that seeing graciousness as a necessary aspect of the divine essence appears to be an awkward way of describing God's ontology. Thus, grace should be understood in terms of his choice to be savior and thus involved with who he is. Jüngel and Farrer's work help to bring out the role of divine voluntarism in divine being. Moreover, they help to show the significance of the Christian emphasis on divine speech, since it is more than just the contingent conveyance of knowledge of God, but is central to God in that he, as Barth would argue, is the Lord over his own being.

Jüngel's view, however, has three difficulties that would need to be surmounted if a larger appropriation of his event-oriented view of divine speech were to be sought. First, there are certain exegetical difficulties, since some scriptural texts, from a traditional perspective, appear to point to the immutability of God, were immutability be properly qualified.[4] Even if one were to deny it, there are still questions whether his speech event interpretation will bear the Biblical evidence. For Jüngel, this may not be a particularly damaging criticism, since he believes that the Word of God is the criterion of significance for the Scriptures. Yet, where too many texts diverge from his depiction of the event of the crucifixion and resurrection, it could produce an insuperable tension within his argumentation that the understanding of the Word could be had in the word of God in the Bible. Moreover, Jüngel's

---

4. The nature of this qualification is up for debate. Many historical perspectives have largely associated immutability and impassibility. However, the Reformation gave rise to questions as to the latter, with the Swiss and German sides of early Protestantism differing on the status of God's ability to suffer. Immutability, however, if qualified to questions of nature and plan, appear separable. If it is given a broader definition, then impassibility will also require treatment before decisions are made on immutability and those proof texts traditionally used to support it.

view may be too reactionary to the Catholic view of substance metaphysics, since he simply argues that the perspective is philosophically motivated and does not give proper treatment as to whether there are exegetical reasons to hold that God can speak about himself in terms of immutable attributes. The repeated claims in Scripture of God possessing a characteristic that has no possibility of changing would appear to militate against the reduction of all divine ontology into the speech event.

Second, even if one sets aside immutability, there appears a lack of stability in Jüngel's perspective that seems applicable to any perspective, including Farrer's, where divine choice is given primacy. Traditionally, *essentia* and *natura* talk had various motivations, philosophical and theological. At least one significant theological reason that such a manner of speaking would be justified, is to provide a stable basis for relational language of trust. For example, the *Luther Bibel* and the *Vulgate* differ on the manner in which they translate the Hebrew:

אהיה אשר אהיה[5]

Luther emphasized the nature of God's becoming with his rendering, "*Ich werde sein, der ich sein werde*"[6] while Jerome pointed to the constancy of God's being by translating, "*ego sum qui sum*."[7] Contextually, however, the significance of God's faithfulness to his promise is in view. Thus, whatever one's interpretation of God's declaration to Moses through the burning bush is, it requires that God's being possesses the stability necessary to guarantee faithfulness. Aristotle's substance metaphysics, though perhaps unable to give proper voice to God's ability to choose concerning his own being, does at least provide the grammar for divine constancy. Jüngel's view also requires stability in God, since eschatological hope plays a structural role in his thinking. However, his retraction from traditional views on immutability broaches the possibility that the divine ontology would change such that there is no guarantee of the promises of God. Jüngel's answer would likely be in the finality and paradigmatic nature of the divine speech event, whereby God displays his resolve to be for humanity in his orientation towards Jesus Christ at the cross. Yet, that would just push back the question as to whence that resolve came from. Traditional views would retreat to immutability, which, though perhaps not optimum in every way, at least could prevent divine faithfulness from being a desire but not a scriptural hope. Jüngel has no such retreat. Thus, a constructive attempt to use his work would have to

---

5. Elliger and Rudolph, *Biblia Hebraica* (Exod 3:14b).

6. Luther, *Die Bibel* (Exod 3:14b).

7. Weber and Gryson, *Vulgata* (Exod 3:14b).

investigate the exegetical and theological implications of placing the locus of divine stability on God's will.

The Evangelical perspective, in light of this difficulty, has both benefits and area for improvement. By often defending divine immutability[8] it will at least have the stability necessary to argue for hope, the faithfulness of God, the significance of the covenant, etc. Yet, this benefit has often come at the cost of downplaying God's ability to choose concerning Himself. Thus, were Evangelicalism to adopt a more dialectical perspective, that would allow for a tension between object/characteristic-oriented speech that provides stability and the subject/act-oriented speech that provides relationality, it may have a perspective that can address the concerns of Wolterstorff, Farrer, and Jüngel concerning divine ontology. Such a view may not, from the perspective of some, be philosophically satisfying in that it will not necessarily seek resolution between those two types of speech. Yet, such discontentment could perhaps be somewhat mitigated were it to be recognized that a lack of resolution does not mean the view is wrong, nor does it mean that the view would be ineffective in allowing for a believer to think and speak concerning God. Furthermore, it appears at times that the nature-oriented language of substance metaphysics and the act-oriented language of a relational metaphysic can be translated into one another. Yet, this translation would probably require a theological substructure and not a philosophical one. For example, one might be able to argue that different ways of speaking about God are related to the tension found in the Trinity between the unity and diversity of God. If one were to begin to clarify the manner in which the unity and diversity relate in the Trinity, one may be on the road to clarifying how substance and personalist metaphysics are related as hermeneutical aids by which Christians interpret and speak about God. In any case, an Evangelical position, properly guarded against oversimplification of speech and improper reification of the being of God, can make sense of the type of stability necessary for other theologically necessary concepts.

Finally, an appropriation of parts of Jüngel's perspective would appear to involve one scrutinizing whether his idea of "identification"[9] could perform all of the functions which he desires. If self-revelation requires personal revelation, then identification would need to pay attention to the personal nature of Jesus Christ and his relationship with the Father. Identification, in underscoring the sacramental nature of the speech event, appears

---

8. It must be admitted that not all who would claim the moniker of "Evangelical" would agree with immutability, as a recent survey of literature in open theism would show some diversity among Evangelicals. Yet, historically, this is both a relatively recent and relatively rare position.

9. Jüngel, *God as the Mystery*, x.

to depersonalize the relationship between the Son and the Father. It is not at all clear if God's decision to be Jesus Christ at the cross would require either to personally relate to the other. Jüngel has a simple recourse to his questioning of the "personhood" language, since he appears to follow Barth in criticizing how the early church used the concepts contained therein. Yet, even if one were to allow him this concern, it would still make the gospel accounts of God's interactions with Jesus Christ superfluous. Thus, even if identification could draw some relationship between the Father and the Son, it is not obvious that it could do justice to the personal nature of said relationship. Consequently, identification would require greater support if it were to be used as a way of constructing a view of divine ontology as it relates to the historical event of Jesus Christ's crucifixion.

Jüngel's view, though complex and not impervious to criticism, does provide a compelling relationship between divine discourse and revelation in a thoroughly trinitarian context. Though Wolterstorff and Farrer's views do not have this advantage, they still provide reasonable arguments as to how God's speech could be construed in alternative manners. Even if the primary speech of God is in the Word, that does not necessarily require rejection of the appropriation model of speaking, as long as the latter is not considered the only mode of divine discourse. Moreover, Farrer's communicative view, which may or may not cohere well with Wolterstorff's theory, provides a method of bringing a traditional view of Scripture in conversation with a perspective on divine discourse that places a premium on God's revelatory activity. Moreover, both Wolterstorff and Farrer's views provide a simple way of relating divine and human speech. Jüngel's view, as theologically ambitious as it is, is only inconsistently related to the manner in which humans speak. This causes him to assume a Barthian testimonial view of Scripture without much argument. A constructive theory of divine speech and revelation would appear to require not only a manner in which they relate, but also how this relates to human speech. Moreover, a strong connection between divine speech and divine ontology does not require understanding the prior in a singular fashion even if one does so with the latter. In other words, a stable and single divine ontology does not necessitate one opposing a polysemic view of divine speech. Furthermore, a comprehensive theory may require a paradigmatic sense of divine discourse to provide unity for the various ways to construe speech. Through this, a closer and more consistent relationship between divine and human speech may be possible than the Word of God-word of God view of Barth.

The Evangelical view, which rightly recognizes that God could speak through Scripture and indeed reveal (at least items of knowledge) in it, could benefit from interaction with Jüngel's perspective for a few reasons. First, there is often an inability to speak about divine ontology with Evangelicalism beyond the listing of characteristics, since there is some ambiguity as to the relationship between nature and choice within the movement. The Word event understanding of Christ helps to make sense of the self-interpretive nature of Christ that has a long history within the Christian faith. Second, a strong benefit to Jüngel's perspective is that it provides a natural movement towards answering questions concerning the nature of history, since God's historicity is found in his identification with the event of Christ's crucifixion. Whereas Evangelicalism has an often, ambivalent relationship to the purpose and essence of history, Jüngel has an inroad to answering the questions posed by God's decision to act in history. With these benefits in mind, Evangelicalism could seek refinement without complete reconstruction, since it has strong exegetical and theological reasons for holding to a more diverse perspective on revelatory activity, as well as, for retaining a belief that Scripture can speak for God in a substantial sense.

HUMAN SPEECH

The nature of human speech is an unusual field of inquiry for Wolterstorff, Jüngel, and Farrer, in that their approaches have a note of similarity. Fundamentally, each of the scholars finds recourse to a philosophical examination of human discourse. This is particularly unusual for Jüngel, in that he is driven towards a theological anthropology and understanding of divine speech, but resorts to a largely Heideggerian account of speaking. Wolterstorff and Farrer's views are similarly philosophical, with both drawing much on the resources of early analytic philosophy. They differ in that the former has an obvious penchant for speech act theory, while the latter is more influenced by those views that draw a strong relationship between speaking and thinking. In any case, their view of discourse is not developed theologically. This is not, per se, to the detriment of their theories, but perhaps a common recognition that the Christian tradition has not a provided a theological view of human speaking, but instead assumes such speech in its endeavors. To understand, therefore, what it is to speak may require a philosophical analysis into the manner in which humans normally perform it. Thus, all three scholars trend towards normal language usage in their theoretical development.[10]

---

10. This can be seen in Wolterstorff and Farrer by their common practice of approaching human speech by examining various examples that they perceive to be ordinary. Jüngel, though perhaps less consistent in its employment, also displays normal language analysis, especially in his attraction to philological concerns in language.

Wolterstorff's view is unique in its attempt to give an ontology of human speech. Farrer's employment of a communicative view of speech and its relationship to thinking provides a way of understanding the latter, but not an explanation of what the former is. Thus, though he understands discursive thinking as an inner discourse,[11] he is much sparser as to the nature of speaking. Jüngel's theologically developed view of speech events would see divine speech as the way in which God is in his self-determination. However, such a perspective can only be partially applicable, since no human who, whether consciously or unconsciously, lives *coram Deo* can claim similar self-determination. Thus, he tends to widen his scope towards Heidegger's account, with speaking being the manner in which one relates herself to the world. Wolterstorff's normative view, though perhaps not perfectly sufficient, does draw interesting points of contact with Jüngel. If Ward's interpretation of Wolterstorff is correct,[12] and it appears to be, then centrality of declaration to his version of speech act theory means that all speech is reality altering. In this, it does not appear to be overly distant from a continentally influenced view of language as the manner in which reality is constructed, though it must be noted that Wolterstorff would not like to describe this activity in terms of reality. Furthermore, the terms that Jüngel uses in describing the primary speech event appear to be very similar to those used by Wolterstorff to explain declaratives. For example, Jüngel's writes, "Or is it not at least partially possible that the thing, about which words are spoken, is not what it is without the word? Is there some existing thing which exists only or chiefly in the word event?"[13] Similarly, Wolterstorff agrees with Searle as to the unusual nature of declarations in that the actuality of the propositional content only comes to be in the act of speech. Thus, there appears to be a parallel idea in Jüngel's word event and the declarative nature of speech in Wolterstorff.

Whether a theory could combine their views in a manner that retains their particularity will likely be related to how one is convinced on the normative nature of speech. As was mentioned previously, this is not altogether unproblematic. Two further difficulties deserve mention, especially as they relate to the work of Farrer and Jüngel. First, Wolterstorff's view will have to answer the question of how this normativity works, since the deontological nature will appear to require a theory as to the nature of obligation in discourse. Why, for instance, should one treat another's assertion as what they actually believe? From whence comes this *shouldness*? Second, Farrer seems

---

11. Farrer, *Saving Belief*, 63–4.

12. See Ward, *Word and Supplement*, 98–100.

13. Jüngel, *God as the Mystery*, 10.

justified in drawing the strong connection between speech and thinking. If thinking is a sort of inner discourse, then Wolterstorff's view becomes highly difficult, since normativity appears highly foreign to this situation. It is true that the Calvinist philosopher could argue that the ways that words are used in thinking are different than how they are used in speaking, but that would at least require an argument and an alternative proposal. Otherwise, it is likely that his view is a successful examination of one way in which speech is used, but is not as successful in its attempt to give an overarching theory as to what speech is. It is perhaps this metalinguistic theory that Jüngel's theological concerns could address. Consequently, Wolterstorff's view of speech must be reckoned with in that it is likely right concerning some of the ways in which human discourse is used, but would require strong interaction with other views to provide a more comprehensive theory. Jüngel's linguistically constructive view of reality and Farrer's understanding of how speaking is primary over thinking may be part of the solution.

For an Evangelical perspective to be viable, it does not need to produce a comprehensive theory, since the fact that none of the three scholars in discussion have been able to do so, shows its difficulty. Yet, the strength of such a perspective could be seen if it were able to accommodate the insights from Wolterstorff, Jüngel, and Farrer without significant revision. Wolterstorff's commonality in theological background with Evangelicalism makes their reconciliation the most straightforward. The normativity necessary in the former's view of speech finds affinity with common ethical perspectives within the latter, especially the use of divine command theory. Yet, his speech act understanding of speech will be insufficient as shown in Farrer's attempting to draw a more considerable relationship between speaking and thinking. Speech act theory is significant in describing how language is used in inter-subjective activity, but has greater difficulty to describe the manner in which speech occurs in thought. Jüngel's understanding of language, since it necessarily understands the speaker and listener being brought into a single event, allows for a type of teleology that draws an intimate connection between both activities. Thus, were an Evangelical perspective to be able to bear a Heideggerian view of language, or at least one where the purpose of language in its revelatory function is retained, then it will allow Wolterstorff's speech act theory to be brought into contact with an expanded treatment of language that accounts for thought. Evangelicalism will typically be reluctant to agree with Heidegger's perspective, though perhaps a greater examination of that possibility should be undertaken.

That language has a strong revelatory function is fundamental to the viewpoint that Scripture is understood as always, in both direct and indirect manners, revealing something about God. Thus, an Evangelical perspective could take insights from speech act theory, while still claiming that language has a primary function of revealing something about the speaker. In order to account for thinking, however, it would either have to modify its perspective on speech towards a Heideggerian view, or at least recognize the semiotic nature of speech. The latter would require very little movement, as the sign nature of language that allows it to represent knowledge concerning God could be understood as foundational for the conceptual use of thinking. In other words, the semiotic nature of language would be tied to the semiotic nature of thinking, both being necessary for the revelation of God to humanity.

Another area where Wolterstorff, Jüngel, and Farrer disagree, but may be useful in constructive dialogue, is concerning the status of metaphor, poetic language, and propositional content. All three appear to have a peculiar reluctance to letting theoretical concerns dominate their theorizing. Thus, all recede from approaches to discourse that make speech merely a way to make assertions and convey information concerning entities. None would subscribe to a purely referential view of language, though none of them would appear to deny that language can refer. Farrer's emphasis on the poetic and Jüngel's focus on metaphors make them both hesitant to separate the form and content of sentences as is often the case in analytic philosophy. Though not explicit, Jüngel appears to connect human speech to the metaphorical nature of the primary speech event. If this is the case, then metaphors, though not the only type of speech, are primary in terms of their significance to address the subject of divinity. Since the revelatory event in Jesus Christ does not permit the content to be understood apart from form,[14] then parabolic literature takes a central position in his view as irreducible metaphorical presentations of the kingdom of God wherein the secondary speech event can occur.

The significance of poetry to Farrer means that he looks on propositionalizing speech with suspicion. Just as a Psalm could not be reduced to a list of truths concerning humanity's relationship with the divine, without substantial loss, so one should also question the validity of such a division between form and content. Wolterstorff, on the other hand, sees the possibility of finding propositional content within a sentence to be central to his mode of analysis. As was mentioned earlier, his view can only be seen as deficient if it could be shown to be reductive of speech in a way that is problematic to the issue being discussed. Even if propositions are reductive, they may still be warranted depending on the particularity of the situation.

14. Such a perspective also relates to Jüngel's view on the inseparability of the economic and imminent Trinity, as well as his usage of a Heideggerian/hermeneutical view, which resists such a dichotomy.

Moreover, since Wolterstorff removes the assertive speech act from its philosophical primacy in terms of human discourse, he is apparently not attempting to follow the trend of Enlightenment thinking concerning the supremacy of objective reasoning. For this reason, Farrer and Jüngel's concern with linguistic reduction should be heeded, while not denying the possibility that some simplification, as a reflection of the necessary simplificaiton of all thinking, should be retained.

An Evangelical perspective on speech has, at times, been enamored with assertorial speech in Scripture, giving primacy to prose when the development of doctrine and practice is in view. Yet, this is not necessarily so, as is evidenced by the many attempts within the movement to push to a greater heeding of genre differences in literary analysis. Evangelicalism would agree with Wolterstorff that the propositionalizing of a text may be necessary for the type of simplification that is foundational for certain significant Christian endeavors, especially in the *kerygmatic*, catechetical, and dogmatic functions of Scripture. Yet, such a use of propositional content would require two qualifications, one of which Wolterstorff himself addresses. First, as the philosopher notices, one must recognize that the relation of the speaker to the content must retain a type of diversity that can account for the many ways in which speech is presented in Scripture. Thus, even if one can take a particular sentence and separate it into a proposition and an illocutionary action, the types of illocutionary acts that can be performed are numerous. Second, it should also be understood that in an attempt to propositionalize a text, which will include some loss, what type of loss is allowable will depend on the situation. Thus, in performing a theological function, a text will require a greater emphasis on propositions such that the conceptual content necessary for comparison, construction, defense, argumentation, etc. is brought to the forefront. Yet, certain religious functions, which are meant to treat the whole of the Christian person, including desires, emotions, and volition, may cause the text to resist simplification, since, for example, the emotional impact of a text would be reduced or destroyed by an attempt to reduce a poetic statement to a propositional one.

Significantly, there is no central facet about Evangelicalism that would prevent it from taking note of these qualifications. The movement would believe that there are times that propositions may be helpful, but not that it is necessary in every case, nor that there could not be significant loss in the simplification of the text. Evangelicalism also does not require that form and content be separable, but that the combination of form and content be interpretable. Thus, Farrer and Jüngel, though resisting propositionalizing, tend towards the practice in their explanation of the text. It could, then, be argued that the content of Scripture could not be understood apart from its form,[15] without arguing that the combination of form and content could be explained "in other words." The Evangelical's emphasis, then, on the literary features of the text, while retaining a strong distinction between the text and its subsequent interpretation, can argue for a strong connection between form and content without rejecting all prospects of propositionalization.

The reconciliation of human speech to divine speech and revelation may be aided if two questions are answered. First, what is the proper understanding of reality as it relates to discourse? Second, what methodology has the best chance at bringing together the differing, but related phenomena of human and divine discourse? The prior should be answered along the Heideggerian lines, but without the excesses that postmodernism has exercised. Jüngel rightly notices that Christianity requires some sort of realism, since God would not be able to hold his rightful place if he did not possess some sort of independence from humanity and the world. Yet, the idea of reality may not be exactly the same concept. If reality has to do with one's relationship to the world, the semiotic nature of human life would mean that reality is mediated through language. Thus, language must be given a larger function than reference, since reality is dependent on it to be real.[16] It will be admitted that this would be an unusual concession for Evangelicalism. However, the movement is concerned with reality because of its belief in the necessity of historical realism, as well as a cognitivist view of truth. Yet, neither of these facets of the perspective are in essential contradiction to Jüngel's view, were one to separate the question of reality from realism as he does. Thus, one could argue for the historical actuality of the bodily resurrection, as well as the objectivity of truth, while still retaining the view that one's relationship to history and truth will be constructed through language.[17] Thus, the resurrection would be an actual event, but only being part of one's reality by confession of the resurrected Christ. In this way, Evangelicalism can retain the type of historicity and realism that has been traditionally held within Christendom until the attacks of the Enlightenment on the former

15. It is noted that there are Christological implications to this perspective, since Jüngel is driven by his understanding of Christ in the question of form and content. For the sake of brevity, this will be left unaddressed except to say that Evangelicalism still could agree with Jüngel's view of the significance of the incarnation, as long as they reject his retreat from orthodox Christology in terms of the hypostatic union.

16. There appears to be some relationship to this and Heidegger's idea of the spiritual. For Heidegger, animals possess no *Welt* or *Umwelt*, because they are not spiritual. Similarly, from a neo-Heideggerian perspective on language, animals would not recognize reality since they are not speakers. See Heidegger, *Introduction to Metaphysics*, 49–50.

17. This has obvious parallels with the discussion of contextualization within contemporary theology.

and Postmodernism on the latter, while recognizing insights into the nature of speech and reality as found in more recent philosophies.

It should be noted that if Wolterstorff's view is to be brought into contact with his dialogue partners, it will require some modification to allow for the sign function of words to be integral to one's interaction with the world. Furthermore, if reality is significant to the manner in which language is construed, then metaphysical questions may be relevant. Yet, with the constructive nature of reality, metaphysics will not be able to possess the monolithic character it has possessed since Aristotle. Instead, it may require, as can be seen in Farrer's work, that metaphysics possess a more provisional and hermeneutical function than previously recognized. Though some Evangelicals would be hesitant towards this movement, there is nothing that would prevent it. Since the perspective already has some suspicion of metaphysics, it may be more willing to question it. Yet, it must be recognized that Evangelicals continue some of the metaphysical terminology of Catholicism, especially as it relates to the early ecumenical councils. Hence, a view that can employ metaphysics, without submitting to its supremacy in theological matters, would be preferable. In this way Evangelicalism appears to be amicable to Farrer's insights without the excesses of Jüngel in the rejection of metaphysics and thus many orthodox doctrines. Farrer's view appears to be opposed to the traditional attractiveness of metaphysics as a principle of unity and may compel a seeking of unity elsewhere. Yet, said unity does not necessarily have to be philosophical, especially, as was argued previously concerning the Trinity, if a dialectical methodology which resolves a thesis and antithesis in favor of the prior is held. This leads to the second question of methodology.

Jüngel's revised dialectic treats as significant the manner in which the nature of the speaker is intrinsically related to the act of speaking. Thus, it appears prudent to investigate the dialectical relationship between God and humans with the result that humanity is taken up into divinity in a way that does not remove the uniqueness of either party. Since that relationship is defined by Christ at the cross, a crucicentric understanding of how God and humans come together is integral to connecting divine and human discourse. Moreover, each side of the dialectic must be investigated on their own terms. Thus, before humans are given a theological interpretation in terms of their humanity, a phenomenological description of human life appears warranted. This is why Jüngel can make the claims:

(a) Man and his world are interesting for their own sake.

(b) Even more so, God is interesting for his own sake.

(c) God makes man, who is interesting for his own sake, interesting in a new way.[18]

Since humans are given speech and thinking for their relationship to God, but this speech and thinking may also address that which is not God (i.e., the world), then the free subjectivity of humanity allows human discourse to be a topic for discussion apart from God. Yet, as Jüngel claims, it is given new import when redefined in terms of God. Jüngel's perspective, then, can serve to be the overarching method that brings together Wolterstorff and Farrer's normal language usage and theological views about the being of God. Hence, even if one disagrees with Jüngel concerning God's being, his methodology still retains significance as a way of seeking unity between human and divine discourse.

Evangelicalism would obviously have difficulty agreeing with Jüngel's use of identification in construction of the doctrine of the Trinity, but his dialectic is fundamentally in agreement with the movement's hermeneutical methodology. Verbal plenary inspiration is, centrally, an attempt to show how God and humanity can come together for the production of the scriptural texts, such that there can be a definite relationship between phrases such as "Paul wrote" and "God speaks." With this foundation, the literary methodology of Evangelical exegesis corresponds to the manner in which humanity, in freedom, can speak of its own within its writing. Yet, a theologically construed understanding of divine speech allows for the Bible to be approached in a "new way,"[19] such that it is recognized as Scripture. Furthermore, if Scripture is to be understood as, in some sense, the word of God, then it must be approached in a fashion parallel to one's approach to the Word of God. Dalferth recognizes that Jüngel has an essentially tripartite hermeneutic when it comes to Scripture.[20] However, whether he intended it or not, the movements necessary for the revelatory act are mirrored in his hermeneutical methodology. When approaching the text, a literary methodology leads to an understanding of authorial intention, which then lends itself to application in terms of existential impact. Thus, a tripartite hermeneutic similar to what Jüngel, de facto, uses, may actually be a viable way of mirroring the fact that the word of God comes to humans in a manner similar to the way the Word of God comes to humans. Where Barth believed that the inspiration of Scripture could functionally parallel the hypostatic union, it could be argued that similarly the interpretation of the Bible should mirror the interpretation of Christ as the Word of God.

18. Jüngel, *God as the Mystery*, 34.
19. Jüngel, *God as the Mystery*, 34.
20. Dalferth, "God and the Mystery," 96.

Thus, traditional methods, including that of Evangelicalism, dealing with the literary features of the text and focusing on the significance of the author, should not be treated with as much skepticism as has been common in liberal and post-liberal theology.[21]

SCRIPTURE, INSPIRATION, AND HERMENEUTICS

Wolterstorff, Jüngel, and Farrer have certain broad areas of agreement concerning Scripture. All believe that the Bible can be used by God, that it has a special place of authority in the Christian life, and that it gives rise to significant hermeneutical questions. Yet, the commonality gives way to differences related to the systematic distinctions in their understanding of divine and human speech, as well as revelation. Wolterstorff and Jüngel are in agreement against Farrer, that inspiration is not necessary to account for the human authorship of Scripture. Wolterstorff's appropriation model does not require that the authors of the text be inspired, but he admits that it would be unusual for God to simply use any text. Moreover, it is debatable whether one could hold to Scripture being "one book"[22] without some sort of theory of inspiration. Though, perhaps, not a viable theory in and of itself, Wolterstorff's view does appear to at least show that there is a way in which Scripture can be substantively said to speak for God, even if it is not inspired. Thus, verbal plenary inspiration leading to the view that the text of the Bible can be understood as the word of God, is not unheard of. In other words, Wolterstorff making a powerful argument that there is a way in which God can speak through a text only serves to aid Evangelicalism in its argument that Scripture is to be understood as divine discourse.

Jüngel, in contradistinction, holds to the testimonial nature of the text since he focuses on the speech event in Jesus Christ. Since the Word of God is self-interpreting in his view, it requires no further interpretive action. Thus, the apostles are simply recording their experience of the Word event, with the possibility that God uses this to become the word of God for the reader. Farrer, on the other hand, holds to a strong, though non-traditional, view of inspiration. He, like many philosophers and theologians in the history of Christendom, holds that the uniqueness of Scripture is tied to its inspired nature. Thus, he agrees with Wolterstorff that it would be questionable whether God would use a text as Scripture in which he had no

21. Intriguingly, the summary of Evangelical hermeneutics as an issue of observation, interpretation, and application is nearly identical to Jüngel's three-part hermeneutic.

22. Wolterstorff, *Divine Discourse*, 53.

involvement in regard to its production. However, unlike the Calvinist philosopher, he is unwilling to bracket the discussion of inspiration. One aspect
of Farrer's theory that is surprising is that he possesses a concept of double
agency with an unspecifiable causal joint between agents, but he does not
appear to genuinely consider any of the post-Reformation compatibilist
views of inspiration. Instead, he takes a view of inspiration that focuses on
creative imagination based on authorized images.

In spite of the weight of the argument of Jüngel, Farrer has a stronger
position for the significance of inspiration and one that backs the Evangelical perspective. That he has Wolterstorff generally on his side is no small
support. If one were to go with a purely testimonial approach to Scripture,
it would require a constellation of other beliefs that may not be convincing.
Included among these would be that the text has nothing that recommends
it as unique over and against any other testimony to Christ, except for the
fateful choice of the church to use it normatively. Yet, such a perspective
would, perhaps, cause ecclesial concerns to weigh too heavily on the text
that is supposed to be the authority in matters of the body of Christ. Moreover, Scripture claims itself to be "inspired" (2 Tim 3:16), which would
require some explanation if one were to move to a strictly testimonial or
appropriation model. Of importance is that the term θεόπνευστος is not
applied to the authors of the Bible, but to the text itself. This is not to say that
Jüngel's view has no benefits, as the self-interpretive nature of Christ being
the Word can help make sense of the divine ontology and also the manner
in which the preaching of the gospel can lead to salvation without direct
reference to the Scriptures. However, it is probably not sufficient to explain
the entirety of the text.

Farrer's view of double agency appears to have exegetical and theological warrant and his humility in refraining from attempting to delve too
deeply into the details of how such agency works is probably wise. Moreover, it dovetails well with the compatibilist views of the production of
scriptural texts by the activity of both God and humans that is often held
by Evangelicals. His imaginative view of inspiration also appears to have
merit, though it is probably not sufficient to account for the whole of the
text. Farrer himself holds that God must provide those images, which are
interpreted, combined, and refined, but is not clear how such images are
provided. Thus, poetic imagination may be significant for some of what is
going on, but other modes of production of the scriptural text may be necessary. Evangelicalism can fill this gap in that God may provide the images in
some direct way (e.g., visions, direct speech, prophetic consciousness, etc.),
which can then serve as the foundation for the poetic movements of the
authors of Scripture. Such a view would allow one to glean insights from

Farrer's use of poetry and categorize them under a larger umbrella of inspiration that both accounts for divine and human activity in the inception of the text. Furthermore, Wolterstorff's perspective concerning the manner in which God speaks through a text may be similarly helpful. For example, if God were to want to issue a command, the philosopher's view of speech act theory may be close to what is occurring. Jüngel may protest, since this does not appear to be close enough to the soteriological significance of the Word of God. Yet, in defense of Wolterstorff, the dialectic theologians often, in their well-intentioned attempt to concentrate the Christian faith on the cross of Christ, reduce the Christian life to the question of salvation. Even if the primary speech event is central to the life of faith, the believer's life cannot be reduced to an event. Thus, even if the dialectical theologians were justified in moving away from salvation history to an understanding of the salvation event, this does not, in turn, validate the reduction of the Christian life. Thus, if salvation and sanctification are strongly tied, as both Catholics and many Reformed theologians would agree, and if Scripture has strong ecclesiological implications, then at least some of its normativity for the individual and corporate existence appears to be from God's direct speech through the text. Therefore, even if Wolterstorff's view is not comprehensive, it may be a viable way of viewing the fact that God still uses Scripture to direct Christians and churches, a concern he shares with Evangelicalism.

SUMMARY OF THE PRINCIPLES OF CONSTRUCTION

A constructive attempt by Evangelicalism to bring Wolterstorff, Jüngel, and Farrer into conversation is not simple, but is potentially fruitful. A theory of divine and human speech appears to require an accompanying view of revelation. Furthermore, revelation must be understood in its diversity, whereby self-revelation may be given primacy, but will include ideas of personal revelation and the revelation of knowledge. In giving self-revelation a central place, a revelatory theory should be developed in a trinitarian context and a speech event understanding provides a natural bridge to divine speech. Furthermore, the relationship between divine and human speech will likely take on more than one form, with a theory of inspiration necessary to protect Scripture's self-claimed uniqueness. In bringing together divine and human speech, a dialectical methodology is preferable that allows for the human and the divine to retain their distinctiveness even when they are drawn together in discourse and reconciled theologically in terms of the divine. Such a dialectical methodology would require both a theologically derived view of divine discourse and a philosophically informed view of human discourse. In doing so, the humanity of speech, in its free subjectivity, is given its due credence without attacking the Lordship of God in using speech and revelation. These concerns appear to be either addressed in Evangelicalism or, at the very least, not incompatible with the Evangelical perspective on divine discourse.

13

Conclusion

THE SCHOLARS' CONTRIBUTIONS

IT COULD BE ARGUED that the twentieth century was a time of great flourishing and great turmoil in philosophy and theology. A combination of worldwide human events, the existentialism of the previous century, and a continued engagement with the natural sciences led to a diversity of academic movements, some lasting only decades. Thus, though the modernist paradigm in philosophy had finished drawing to a close after centuries of dominance, no subsequent school of thought has achieved such lasting appeal. Theology, similarly, underwent upheaval as the ravages of the World Wars and the accompanying existential angst had to be reconciled with a Christian tradition that itself had to deal with the internal struggles accompanying theological liberalism and the rise of historical critical methodologies. Yet, upheaval is not always bad. Just as no crop can be planted without breaking up the soil from which it can grow, often constructive thought is most greatly encouraged from the chaos of disrupted traditions. And yet, just as no crop can grow by completely discarding the soil, so theological thinking would be prudent to not simply cast aside traditional understanding. Perhaps, then, Gadamer was right in arguing that there are right prejudices to be had and that one's thinking could not even start down the path towards greater understanding without being founded on the testimony and scholarship of times past. Wolterstorff, Jüngel, and Farrer stand out for their thoughtful combination of gentle iconoclasm and intentional retrieval of Christian tradition. None of them are willing to simply explicate and combine traditional theories and ideas. Yet, they are also unwilling to see themselves as islands in a vast theological ocean. Instead, they exemplify some of the best qualities in scholarship in bringing together forward-looking innovation and contemplation of the past. Wolterstorff, Jüngel, and Farrer know they stand on tradition and thus do so with a consciously self-critical attitude. It is this quality, when added to their acute theological and philosophical acumen, that allows them to be fruitful dialogue partners for the Evangelical scholar.

Wolterstorff's Calvinistic influenced brand of analytic philosophy provides intriguing ways to handle the traditional claim that God speaks through Scripture. His theory is incomplete, by his own decision, and thus appears to be a helpful or, perhaps even, integral part of an overarching theory of divine and human speech. In his work, Evangelicalism has a powerful argument for the possibility that God could speak, in some ways, directly through a text. Moreover, his hermeneutical methodology has certain affinities with the movement. His ontology of speech, though perhaps inadequate to account for the theological depictions of divine speech, does provide a foundation for reconciling normal language usage with a theology of the Word. It is this facet that helps to draw connections between an Evangelical's theological understanding of the being of God and the literary understanding of the meaning of Scripture.

Jüngel's methodological considerations and examination of speech events clarify questions concerning divine ontology and how it relates to revelatory concerns. He and Farrer rightly defend the centrality of revelation to an understanding of God's manifestation to humans, a concern that Evangelicalism shares, without disregarding the significance of speech, both human and divine. Jüngel, furthermore, provides a view of divine discourse that takes seriously that God is the primary speaker. The Reformed strains in Evangelical theology, especially in its Edwards-mediated Calvinistic skepticism towards humanity's natural capacities, finds a compelling voice in a neo-Barthian emphasis on revelation. Moreover, Jüngel's dialectical methodology, which seeks correlation in favor of God's activity, appears supportive of Evangelicalism's similar *modus operandi* in terms of Scripture. Though he claims a theologically defined hermeneutical approach, his actual practice is very similar to the Evangelical's move from literary to theological exegesis. Of significance, is that this approach mirrors Jüngel's usage of Barth's revelatory trinitarian understanding. In this way, Evangelicalism provides a method of interpretation that can use Christ as a paradigmatic understanding of how God comes to man (i.e., *Immanuel*), with the attendant implications on inspiration. Finally, Jüngel's emphasis on God's self-interpretation, with its basis on God's lordship over his own character, finds parallels within Evangelical theology, even when they do not find perfect correspondence.

Farrer's examination of inspiration provides an intriguing account of how to reconcile human imagination in poetic consciousness with divine agency in such a way that a traditional view of dual authorship can be retained. Even if one does not agree with his work, he does demonstrate the possibility of God being active in the production of Scripture without removing human free subjectivity. Thus, his perspective buttresses the Evangelical argument of a compatibilist view of divine and human activity in inspiration. Moreover, Farrer's act-oriented view of divine ontology coheres well with Jüngel's understanding of the Word of God. In this way, the acts of God and the character of God are drawn together in the revelatory act. If this is so, then any revelatory activity can lead to conclusions concerning God, even if it is indirectly through propositional revelation. Thus, Evangelicalism can assume a traditional understanding of how God can speak through Scripture, without having to deny the supremacy of Christ in self-revelation.

In summary, Wolterstorff, Jüngel, and Farrer provide the foundation for a comprehensive view of divine speech and revelation, as well as how they relate to human speech and the scriptural text. Their various emphases alternately support the Evangelical perspective and refine it. However, it could be argued that the substance of their positions, when purified to their most basic concerns, cannot successfully oppose the core of the view. Even if some modification is necessary, there is no good reason, as has often been the case in theology at large, to dismiss Evangelicalism as not being a viable systematic position.

AN OUTLINE OF CONSTRUCTION

It is nearly a truism that in philosophy and theology, destruction is not nearly as demanding as construction. To criticize, complicate, and problematize is the first and simpler work. To retrieve, appropriate, and integrate is the second and more dangerous task. Wolterstorff, Jüngel, and Farrer are courageous in their undertaking to do the more difficult work and it would border on being unfair to criticize their labor without at least giving a hint at how their perspectives would actually come together in construction. Consequently, a short outline of one possibility of how their viewpoints can be brought together will be given, with the understanding that it will be simply a sketch without much defense.

If one were to agree with Jüngel that God is who he is in the Word event, then a Barthian view of the trinitarian revelatory structure fits well with Christ as the Word of God. This should be done without the use of identification idea found in Jüngel. Even though he is probably correct as to the sacramental nature of Christ, he too easily comes to reject the two natures Christology of orthodox confessionalism. Granted, both he and Farrer's criticisms would require an explication and elucidation of the term "nature," but this appears to be a worthwhile endeavor especially if one were to agree with Jüngel and his forbearer Luther in arguing for a strong sense of realism in the Christian faith. That Christ has two natures is easier, in a certain sense, from a substance view, but does not as easily deal with the voluntarism that Farrer rightly holds dear. Substances can make choices, but are not defined as such, and thus it is more fitting for the objectifying talk of scientific investigation. Yet, as Jüngel notices, God objectifies himself in Jesus Christ. Thus, it may be the case that the Father opens himself up to the grammar inherent in substance metaphysics by choosing for historical being in the Son. Yet, a personal and/or relational metaphysics is required to supplement such substance speech. Thus, metaphysics should be understood in the hermeneutical and provisional fashion that Farrer depicts, with the admission that there will neither be a singular nor simple grammar of speech about God. An inherent difficulty with an argument for a pluriform metaphysic is that the unity that metaphysics has historically afforded would be lost. Thus, substance and personhood should be understood as regional metaphysics that requires further unity. The most natural, though not perhaps the most philosophically satisfying answer, would be in the doctrine of the Trinity itself. Thus, the creedal formulations of the scriptural material concerning the Trinity would be understood as an early attempt at providing a metaphysic for dealing with the difficult and controversial topic of the ontological status of the Father, Son, and Holy Spirit, as well as an attempt to provide a grammar for speaking about them.

Assuming the speech event structure of the hermeneutical theologians as a way of construing divine speech, one would have to reconcile it with human speech. Moreover, one would have to reintroduce the stability that appears in the textual depictions of God's faithfulness, but could be removed by giving primacy to becoming over being. Thus, Jüngel moves from the Barthian focus on the incarnation as seen in the claim that "God's being is in becoming" and moves towards an eschatologically defined idea of being seen in the claim that "God's being is in coming." This movement is an improvement, but still suffers from a specific difficulty. One of the weaknesses of Barth's view, at least in its theoretical formulation,[1] is that it

1. It should be noted that at times Barth borders on a biblical theological perspective in showing how the person of Jesus Christ connects to the Old Testament promises of God.

attempts to reduce Christ to one event. Jüngel performs a similar reduction, though he is closer with his crucicentric focus. Yet, a view that gives the cross centrality to understanding Jesus Christ without reducing the latter to the former would be preferable. Furthermore, a crucicentrism that would not entail an entirely mutable God would mitigate the aforementioned problems concerning trust in divine faithfulness. One possibility would be that God's being is in his promise. In the idea of promise one has the constancy of being necessary for the absolute claim of God's faithfulness, but the contingency necessary to argue that God determines himself in the primary speech event. Promise also helps to bring together the covenantal talk of biblical theology with the forward looking ideas in an eschatologically oriented view of divine futurity.

With the promissory nature of God in place, the reconciliation of human discourse to divine speech has a foundation. The Word of God in Jesus Christ is not only the event of God's self-determination, but it is, as was argued, the transcendental foundation for human speech about God. Thus, human speech would find its ontology in relation to the paradigmatic speech of the Word. Though Wolterstorff's declarative-central version of speech act theory appears to fit together well with Jüngel's understanding of the speech event, a revision of the speech event in terms of God's promissory nature would mean that speech act would require similar revision. Thus, speech would not be understood as a way for acquiring normative stances, but speech is a way to enact being in promise. This would be able to better stand against criticisms concerning destructive speech and speech without listeners.

If human speech mirrors divine speech, the next move is to understand how the primary Word event relates to the secondary word event. The self-interpreting Word in Christ, though sufficient in itself, does require two movements for it to be revelatory for the individual. There is first an understanding of Christ, which is then interpreted in terms of the intention of the Father. This intention then has existential impact as the Spirit allows the believer to recognize her life *coram Deo*. Scripture's role in this could be for the presentation of the information concerning the interpretation of the Christ necessary for the first movement. This, by the work of God can be a revelation of God's self as a Christian recognizes in faith that she knows God in Christ. The secondary speech event, then can occur only based on the primary speech event which is given interpretation and received by the Spirit. This has hermeneutical implications, including the aforementioned tripartite interpretational style that is held by both Jüngel and Evangelicals.

The preceding sketch has some weaknesses that could be remedied by elaboration. However, it would be arrogant to believe it to be unassailable. Yet, at the very least, it shows that a constructive approach that is built off a dialogue between Wolterstorff, Jüngel, and Farrer could both seek innovation, while honoring the scholarship and beliefs of the past. At a time that there is an almost pathological obsession with novelty, a contemplative look at tradition appears to be a necessary antidote. Yet, interaction with tradition cannot give way to slavery and, thus, a self-critical usage of the past in meeting the situation of the present appears to be the best course of action. Wolterstorff, Jüngel, and Farrer appear to be adept at just that. Consequently, though diverse in background, methodology, and overall perspectives, they possess unity in their boldness in holding their beliefs up to criticism and attempting to refine them without rejecting their Christian convictions. In this, they possess qualities that every theologian, Evangelical and otherwise, should aspire to possess.

Bibliography

Adams, Robert. "Divine Command Metaethics Modified Again." In *The Virtue of Faith and Other Essays in Philosophical Theology*, by Robert Adams, 128–43. New York: Oxford University Press, 1987.

———. "A Modified Divine Command Theory of Ethical Wrongness." In *The Virtue of Faith and Other Essays in Philosophical Theology*, by Robert Adams, 97–122. New York: Oxford University Press, 1987.

Allen, Paul. *Theological Method.* New York: Continuum, 2012.

Alston, William P. *Perceiving God: The Epistemology of Religious Experience.* Ithaca, NY: Cornell University Press, 1991.

American Bible Society. *The Holy Bible, Containing the Old and New Testaments.* Revised Standard Version. New York: American Bible Society, 1962.

Aquinas, Thomas. *Faith, Reason and Theology.* Translated by Armand Maurer. Toronto: Pontifical Institute of Mediaeval Studies, 1987.

———. "Quaestiones Disputatae de Veritate." Corpus Thomisticum. http://www.corpusthomisticum.org/qdv02.html#52389.

———. *The Summa Theologica.* Translated by Fathers of the English Dominican Province. Reprint. 5 Vols. Allen, TX: Thomas More, 1981.

Aristotle. *The Complete Works of Aristotle: The Revised Oxford Translation.* Edited by John Barnes. Princeton, NJ: Princeton University Press, 1984.

Asiedu, F. B. A. "Illocutionary Acts and the Uncanny: On Nicholas Wolterstorff's Idea of Divine Discourse." *Heythrop Journal* 42.3 (2001) 283–310.

Audi, Robert, and Nicholas Wolterstorff. *Religion in the Public Square: The Role of Religious Convictions in Political Debate.* Lanham, MD: Rowman & Littlefield, 1997.

Augustine. *The Enchiridion on Faith, Hope, and Love.* Chicago: Regnery Gateway, 1961.

———. "Letters." In *A Select Library of the Nicene and Post-Nicene Fathers of the Christian Church,* edited by Philip Schaff, 251–53. Translated by J. G. Cunningham. Vol. 1. Buffalo, NY: Christian Literature Company, 1886.

———. *On Christian Teaching.* Oxford: Oxford University Press, 1999.

———. *The Trinity.* Edited by Edmund Hill. Translated by John E. Rotelle. New York: New City, 1991.

Austin, John L. *How to Do Things with Words.* Cambridge, MA: Harvard University Press, 1962.

Barbour, Ian G. *Myths, Models, and Paradigms.* New York: Harper & Row, 1974.

Barth, Karl. *Church Dogmatics*. Edited by Geoffrey William Bromily and Thomas F. Torrance. Translated by Geoffrey William Bromily, et al. Edinburgh: T. & T. Clark, 1936–58.

———. *Der Römerbrief.* Zurich: Theologischer Verlag Zürich, 2011.

———. *Die Menschlichkeit Gottes: Vortrag*. Zurich: Evangelischer Verlag, 1956.

———. *The Humanity of God*. Richmond, VA: John Knox, 1960.

———. *Protestant Theology in the Nineteenth Century; Its Background & History*. Valley Forge, PA: Judson, 1973.

Bebbington, David. *Evangelicalism in Modern Britain*. Grand Rapids, MI: Baker, 1992.

Berry, Everett. "Speech-Act Theory as a Corollary for Describing the Communicative Dynamics of Biblical Revelation: Some Recommendations and Reservations." *Criswell Theological Review* 7.1 (2009) 81–100.

Black, Max. *Models and Metaphors*. Ithaca, NY: Cornell University Press, 1962.

Braaten, Carl, and Robert Jenson. "Trinitarian Theology." In *A Map of Twentieth Century Theology*, edited by Carl Braaten and Jenson Robert, 179–82. Minneapolis, MN: Fortress, 1995.

Brecht, Martin. *Martin Luther: Sein Weg zur Reformation*. Stuttgart: Calwer Verlag, 1983.

Brown, David. "God and Symbolic Action." In *Divine Action: Studies Inspired by the Philosophical Theology of Austin Farrer*, edited by Brian Hebblethwaite and Edward Henderson, 103–23. Edinburgh: T. & T. Clark, 1990.

———. "The Role of Images in Theological Reflection." In *The Human Person in God's World: Studies to Commemorate the Austin Farrer Centenary*, edited by Brian Hebblethwaite and Douglas Hedley, 85–105. London: SCM, 2006.

Brümmer, Vincent. "Farrer, Wiles and the Causal Joint." *Modern Theology* 8.1 (1992) 1–14.

Brunner, Emil. *Revelation and Reason*. Philadephia, PA: Westminster, 1946.

Calvin, Jean. *Institutes of the Christian Religion*. Edited by John T. MacNeill. Translated by Ford Lewis Battles. Vol. 1. Louisville, KY: Knoxville, 2006.

Dalferth, Ingolf. *Becoming Present*. Dudley, MA: Peeters, 2006.

———. *Die Wirklichkeit des Möglichen: Hermeneutische Religionsphilosophie*. Tubingen: Mohr/Siebeck, 2003.

———. "Esse Est Operari: The antischolastic theologies of Farrer and Luther ." *Modern Theology* 1.3 (1985) 183–210.

———. "God and the Mystery of Words." *Journal of the American Academy of Religion* 60.1 (1992) 79–104.

———. "The Stuff of Revelation." In *Scripture, Metaphysics, and Poetry*, edited by Robert MacSwain, 149–66. Farnham: Ashgate, 2013.

———. *Theology and Philosophy*. New York: Blackwell, 1988.

DeHart, Paul. "Eberhard Jüngel on the Structure of Theology." *Theological Studies* 57 (1996) 46–64.

Eaton, Jeffrey C. *The Logic of Theism: An Analysis of the thought of Austin Farrer*. Lanham, MD: University Press of America, 1980.

Ebeling, Gerhard. *God and Word*. Translated by James W. Leitch. Philadelphia, PA: Fortress, 1967.

———. "Wort Gottes und Hermeneutik." In *Wort und Glaube*, by Gerhard Ebeling, 319–48. Tübingen: Mohr/Siebeck, 1962.

Edwards, Jonathan. *The Religious Affections*. Reprint. Edinburgh: Banner of Truth Trust, 1956.

Elliger, Karl, and Wilhelm Rudolph, eds. *Biblia Hebraica Stuttgartensia*. 5th ed. Stuttgart: Deutsche Bibelgesellschaft, 1977.

Farrer, Austin. *A Celebration of Faith*. London: Hodder & Stoughton, 1970.

———. *Faith and Speculation*. London: Adam & Charles Black, 1967.

———. *Finite and Infinite*. 2nd ed. London: Dacre, 1959.

———. *The Freedom of the Will*. 2nd ed. London: Adam & Charles Black, 1966.

———. *The Glass of Vision*. London: Dacre, 1948.

———. *Interpretation and Belief*. Edited by Charles C. Conti. London: SPCK, 1976.

———. *Lord I Believe: Suggestions For Turning the Creed into Prayer*. 2nd ed. London: SPCK, 1958.

———. "On Being an Anglican." In *The End of Man*, edited by Charles C. Conti, 48–52. London: SPCK, 1973.

———. *The Rebirth of Images: The Making of St. John's Apocalypse*. Albany, NY: State University of New York Press, 1949.

———. "Revelation." In *Faith and Logic*, edited by Basil Mitchell, 84–107. London: George Allen & Unwin Ltd, 1957.

———. *Saving Belief*. London: Hodder and Stoughton, 1964.

———. *A Study in Mark*. Westminster: Dacre, 1951.

Flew, Anthony. *Hume's Philosophy of Belief*. New York: Humanities, 1961.

Frege, Gottlob. "Über Sinn und Bedeutung." *Zeitschrift für Philosophie und philosophische Kritik* 100.1 (1892) 25–50.

Fuchs, Ernst. *Marburger Hermeneutik*. Tübingen: Mohr/Siebeck, 1968.

———. *Studies in the Historical Jesus*. Translated by Andrew Scobie. London: SCM, 1964.

———. *Was Ist Theologie?* Tübingen: Mohr/Siebeck, 1953.

Gill, Jerry H. "Divine Action as Mediated." *Harvard Theological Review* 80.3 (1987) 369–78.

Glasse, John. "Doing Theology Metaphysically: Austin Farrer." *Harvard Theological Review* 59.4 (1966) 319–50.

Gunton, Colin. "The Being and Attributes of God." In *The Possibilities of Theology*, edited by John Webster, 7–22. Edinburgh: T. & T. Clark, 1994.

Haddock, Guillermo E. Rosado. "On Frege's Two Notions of Sense." *History and Philosophy of Logic* 7 (1986) 31–41.

Hamm, Berndt. *Frömmigkeitstheologie am Anfang des 16. Jahrhunderts*. Tübingen: Mohr/Siebeck, 1982.

Hebblethwaite, Brian. "The Experiential Verification of Religious Belief in the Theology of Austin Farrer." In *For God and Clarity: New Essays in Honor of Austin Farrer*, edited by John C. Eaton and Ann Loades, 163–76. Allison Park, PA: Pickwick, 1983.

———. *The Philosophical Theology of Austin Farrer*. Dudley, MA: Peeters, 2007.

Hebblethwaite, Brian, and Edward Henderson. "Introduction." In *Divine Action: Studies Inspired by the Philosophical Theology of Austin Farrer*, edited by Brian Hebblethwaite and Edward Henderson, 1–20. Edinburgh: T. & T. Clark, 1990.

Hedley, Douglas. "Austin Farrer's Shaping Spirit of Imagination." In *The Human Person in God's World: Studies to Commemorate the Austin Farrer Centenary*, edited by Brian Hebblethwaite and Douglas Hedley, 106–34. London: SCM, 2006.

Hefling, Charles C., Jr. *Jacob's Ladder*. Cambridge, MA: Cowley, 1979.

Hegel, Georg Wilhelm Friedric. *Elements of the Philosophy of Right*. Edited by Allen W. Wood. Translated by H. B. Nisbet. Cambridge: Cambridge University Press, 1991.

———. *Lecture on the History of Philosophy*. Translated by E. S. Haldene and F. S. Simson. Vol. 1. New York: Humanities, 1968.

Heidegger, Martin. *Being and Time*. Translated by Joan Stambaugh. Albany, NY: State University of New York Press, 1996.

———. "Phenomenology and Theology." In *Pathmarks*, edited by William McNeill, 39–54. Cambridge: Cambridge University Press, 1998.

———. *The Question Concerning Science and Other Essays*. New York: Harper & Row, 1977.

———. *Sein und Zeit*. Tübingen: Max Niemeyer Verlag, 1956.

———. *Unterwegs zur Sprache*. Pfullingen: Neske, 1959.

Helm, Paul. "What is Divine Eternity?" In *Eternal God*, by Paul Helm, 23–40. Oxford: Oxford University Press, 2010.

Henderson, Edward Hugh. "Austin Farrer and D.Z. Phillips on Lived Life, Prayer, and Divine Reality." *Modern Theology* 1.3 (1985) 223–43.

———. "Valuing in Knowing God: An Interpretation of Austin Farrer's Religious Epistemology." *Modern Theology* 1.3 (1985) 165–82.

Hick, John. "Theology and Verification." In *The Philosophy of Religion*, edited by Basil Mitchell, 53–71. Oxford: Oxford University Press, 1971.

Hodge, Archibald Alexander. *The Confession of Faith*. Reprint. Edinburgh: Banner of Truth Trust, 1978.

Holmes, Christopher R. J. "Eberhard Jüngel's Soteriologically Minded Doctrine of the Trinity: Some Commendations and Reservations." In *Indicative of Grace—Imperative of Freedom*, edited by R. David Nelson, 101–14. New York: Bloomsbury, 2014.

Jüngel, Eberhard. "Die Freiheit der Theologie." In *Entsprechungen: Gott-Warheit-Mensch*, by Eberhard Jüngel, 11–36. Munchen: Chr. Kaiser Verlag, 1986.

———. "Die Welt als Möglichkeit und Wirklichkeit." *Evangelische Theologie* 29.8 (1969) 417–42.

———. *God as the Mystery of the World*. Eugene, OR: Wipf & Stock, 1983.

———. *Gott als Geheimnis der Welt*. Tübingen: Mohr/Siebeck, 1977.

———. "Humanity in Correspondence to God." In *Theological Essays*, by Eberhard Jüngel, 124–53. Translated by John Webster. New York: Bloomsbury, 1989.

———. *Justification*. Translated by Jeffrey F. Cayzer. New York: T&T Clark, 2001.

———. "Metaphorical Truth." In *Theological Essays*, translated by John Webster, 16–71. New York: T. & T. Clark, 2014.

———. *Paulus und Jesus. Eine Untersuchung zur Präzisierung der Frage nach dem Ursprung der Christologie*. Tubingen: Mohr/Siebeck, 1967.

———. "The World as Possibility and Actuality. The Ontology of the Doctrine of Justification." In *Theological Essays*, by Eberhard Jüngel, 95–123. New York: T. & T. Clark, 1989.

Jüngel, Eberhard, and John Webster. *God's Being is in Becoming: The Trinitarian Being of God in the Theology of Karl Barth*. New York: T. & T. Clark, 2004.

Kripke, Saul. *Naming and Necessity*. Cambridge, MA: Harvard University Press, 1980.

Ledwig, Marion. *Common Sense: Its History, Method, and Applicability*. New York: Peter Lang, 2007.

Locke, John. *An Essay Concerning Human Understanding.* Indianapolis, IN: Hackett, 1996.

Luther, Martin, trans. *Die Bibel.* Stuttgart: Deutsche Bibelgesellschaft, 1996.

Luy, David J. *Dominus Mortis.* Minneapolis, MN: Fortress, 2014.

Macquarrie, John. *The Scope of Demythologization.* London: SCM, 1960.

MacSwain, Robert. "Above, Beside, Within: The Anglican Theology of Austin Farrer." *Journal of Anglican Studies* 4.1 (2006) 33–57.

———. "The Stuff of Revelation: Austin Farrer's Doctrine of Inspired Images." In *Scripture, Metaphysics, and Poetry,* edited by Robert MacSwain, 149–66. Farnham: Ashgate, 2013.

Malysz, Piotr J. *Trinity, Freedom, and Love.* New York: T. & T. Clark, 2012.

Martinich, Aloysius. "A Theory of Metaphor." In *The Philosophy of Language,* by Aloysius Martinich, 485–96. Oxford: Oxford University Press, 1985.

McClain, F. Michael. "Narrative Interpretation and the Problem of Double Agency." In *Divine Action: Studies Inspired by the Philosophical Theology of Austin Farrer,* edited by Brian Hebblethwaite and Edward Henderson, 143–72. Edinburgh: T. & T. Clark, 1990.

McGrade, A. S. "Reason." In *The Study of Anglicanism,* 115–30. London: SPCK, 1988.

Mezei, Balázs. *Radical Revelation.* New York: Bloomsbury, 2017.

Milbank, John. "The Second Difference: For A Trinitarianism Without Reserve." *Modern Theology* 2.3 (1986) 213–34.

Mitchell, Basil. "Introduction." In *The Human Person in God's World: Studies to Commemorate the Austin Farrer Centenary,* edited by Brian Hebblethwaite and Douglas Hedley, 1–13. London: SCM, 2006.

Moltmann, Jürgen. *The Coming of God.* Translated by Margaret Kohl. Minneapolis, MN: Fortress, 1996.

———. *The Crucified God.* Translated by R. A. Wilson and John Bowden. New York: Harper & Row, 1974.

———. *The Trinity and the Kingdom.* Translated by Margaret Kohl. San Francisco, CA: Harper & Row, 1981.

Muis, J. "Die Rede von Gott und das Reden Gottes. Eine Würdigung der Lehre der dreifachen Gestalt des Wortes Gottes." *Zeitschrift für Dialektische Theologie* 16.1 (2000) 59–70.

Muller, Robert A. *Post-Reformation Reformed Dogmatics.* Vol. 1. Grand Rapids, MI: Baker Academic, 2003.

Ngien, Dennis. *The Suffering of God According to Martin Luther's 'Theologia Crucis.'* Vancouver: Regent College, 2005.

Oberman, Heiko A. "Luther and the Via Moderna: The Philosophical Backdrop of the Reformation Breakthrough." *The Journal of Ecclesiastical History* 4 (2003) 641–70.

———. *The Harvest of Medieval Theology.* Grand Rapids, MI: Baker Academic, 1983.

Padiyath, Thomas. *The Metaphysics of Becoming.* Berlin: de Gruyter, 2014.

Plantinga, Alvin. "Reason and Belief in God." In *Faith and Rationality: Reason and Belief in God,* edited by Alvin Plantinga and Nicholas Wolterstorff, 16–93. Notre Dame, IN: University of Notre Dame Press, 1983.

———. *Warranted Christian Belief.* Oxford: Oxford University Press, 2000.

Platten, Stephen. "Diaphanous Thought: Spirituality and Theology in the Work of Austin Farrer." *Anglican Theological Review* 69.1 (1987) 30–50.

Putnam, Hillary. "A Problem About Reference." In *Reason, Truth, and History*, 22–48. Cambridge: Cambridge University Press, 1981.

Quinn, Philip. "Can God Speak? Does God Speak?" *Religious Studies* 37.3 (2001) 259–69.

Rahner, Karl. *Hearers of the Word*. Translated by Michael Richards. New York: Herder and Herder, 1969.

———. *The Trinity*. Translated by Joseph Donceel. New York: Herder and Herder, 1970.

Reichard, Joshua D. "Beyond Causation: A Contemporary Theology of Concursus." *American Journal of Philosophy & Theology* 34.2 (2013) 117–34.

Riceour, Paul. *Hermeneutics and the Human Sciences*. Translated by John B. Thompson. New York: Cambridge University Press, 1981.

———. "Metaphor and Reference." In *The Rule of Metaphor*, by Paul Ricoeur, 215–56. Translated by Robert Czerny. Toronto: Toronto University Press, 1977.

———. *Time and Narrative*. Translated by Kathleen Blamey and David Pellauer. Vol. 1. Chicago: University of Chicago Press, 1985.

Sailhamer, John. *The Meaning of the Pentateuch*. Downers Grove, IL: InterVarsity, 2009.

Schrenk, Gottlob. θέλω, θέλημα, θέλησις. In *Theological Dictionary of the New Testament*, edited by Geoffrey W. Bromiley, 44–62. Translated by Geoffrey W. Bromiley. Vol. 3. Grand Rapids, MI: Eerdmans, 1965.

Schwöbel, Christoph. "Theology." In *The Cambridge Companion to Karl Barth*, edited by John Webster, 17–36. Cambridge: Cambridge University Press, 2000.

Scotus, John Duns, and Allan B. Wolter. *Duns Scotus on the Will and Morality*. Translated by Allan B. Wolter. Washington, DC: Catholic University of America Press, 1997.

Searle, John. *Expression and Meaning*. Cambridge: Cambridge University Press, 1979.

Slocum, Robert Boak. *Light in a Burning-Glass: A Systematic Presentation of Austin Farrer's Theology*. Columbia, SC: University of South Carolina Press, 2007.

Smend, Rudolf. "Nachkritische Schriftauslegung." In *Parrhesia: Karl Barth zum achzigsten Geburtstag*, 215–37. Zurich: EVZ Verlag, 1966.

Spjuth, Roland. "Mystery or Sacrament? An Assessment of Eberhard Jüngel's Cruciform Ontology." In *Indicative of Grace—Imperative of Freedom*, 219–30. New York: Bloomsbury, 2014.

Steinmetz, David. *Calvin in Context*. Oxford: Oxford University Press, 1995.

Stump, Eleonore. "Eternity, Simplicity, and Presence." In *God, Eternity, and Time*, edited by Christian Tapp and Edmund Runggaldier, 29–46. Burlington, VT: Ashgate, 2011.

Sudduth, Michael. *The Reformed Objection to Natural Theology*. New York: Routledge, 2009.

Swinburne, Richard. *Revelation: From Metaphor to Analogy*. Oxford: Clarendon, 1992.

Vanhoozer, Kevin J. *The Drama of Doctrine: A Canonical Linguistic Approach to Christian Doctrine*. Louisville, KY: John Knox, 2005.

———. *Remythologizing Theology*. Cambridge: Cambridge University Press, 2010.

———. "The Voice and the Actor." In *Evangelical Futures: A Conversation on Theological Method*, edited by John J. Stackhouse Jr., 61–106. Grand Rapids, MI: Baker, 2000.

Volf, Miroslav. *After Our Likeness: The Church as the Image of the Trinity*. Grand Rapids, MI: Eerdmans, 1998.

Wainwright, Geoffrey. "Church and Sacrament(s)." In *The Possibilities of Theology*, edited by John Webster, 90–105. Edinburgh: T. & T. Clark, 1994.

Ward, Timothy. *Word and Supplement*. New York: Oxford University Press, 2002.

Weber, Robert, and Roger Gryson, eds. *Biblia Sacra Vulgata*. 5th ed. Stuttgart: Deutsche Bibelgesellschaft, 1983.

Webster, John. *Eberhard Jüngel: An Introduction to His Theology*. Cambridge: Cambridge University Press, 1986.

———. "Eberhard Jüngel on the Language of Faith." *Modern Theology* 1.4 (1985) 253–76.

Westphal, Merold. "Must Phenomenology and Theology make Two? A Response to Trakakis and Simmons." *The Heythrop Journal* 55.4 (2014) 711–17.

———. "On Reading God the Author." *Religious Studies* 37 (2001) 271–91.

———. "Review Essay: Theology as Talking about a God who Talks." *Modern Theology* 13.4 (1997) 525–36.

Whitehead, Alfred North. *Process and Reality*. Edited by David Ray Griffin and David W. Sherburne. New York: Free Press, 1978.

Wittgenstein, Ludwig. *Tractatus Logico-Philosophicus*. London: Routledge and Kegan Paul, 1975.

Wolterstorff, Nicholas. *Art in Action*. Grand Rapids, MI: Eerdmans, 1980.

———. "Can Belief in God Be Rational if it has No Foundations?" In *Faith and Rationality*, edited by Alvin Plantinga and Nicholas Wolterstorff, 135–86. Notre Dame, IN: University of Notre Dame Press, 1983.

———. *Divine Discourse: Philosophical Reflections on the Claim that God Speaks*. Cambridge: Cambridge University Press, 1995.

———. "An Engagement with Rorty." *Journal of Religious Ethics* 31.1 (2003) 129–139.

———. "Escaping the Cage of Secular Discourse." *Christian Scholar's Review* 40.1 (2010) 93–99.

———. "Herman Bavinck-Proto Reformed Epistemologist." *Calvin Theological Journal* 45.1 (2010) 133–46.

———. "Is It Possible and Desirable for Theologians to Recover from Kant?" *Modern Theology* 14.1 (1998) 1–18.

———. "Is Reason Enough?" *Reformed Journal* 31.4 (1981) 20–24.

———. *John Locke and the Ethics of Belief*. Cambridge: Cambridge University Press, 1996.

———. *Justice in Love*. Grand Rapids, MI: Eerdmans, 2011.

———. *Justice: Rights and Wrongs*. Princeton, NJ: Princeton University, 2008.

———. *Lament for a Son*. Grand Rapids, MI: Eerdmans, 1987.

———. "Liberating Scholarship." *Reformed Journal* 31.2 (1981) 4–5.

———. *Reason within the Bounds of Religion*. 2nd Edition. Grand Rapids, MI: Eerdmans, 1984.

———. "Religion in Public Life: Must Faith be Privatized." *Faith and Philosophy* 27.2 (2010) 223–5.

———. "Response to Helm, Quinn, and Westphal." *Religious Studies* 37.3 (2001) 293–306.

———. "Response to Levine." *Religious Studies* 34.1 (1998) 17–23.

———. "Resurrecting the Author." *Midwest Studies in Philosophy* 27 (2003) 4–24.

———. *Thomas Reid and the Story of Epistemology*. Cambridge: Cambridge University Press, 2001.

———. "To Theologians: From One Who Cares about Theology but is Not One of You." *Theological Education* 40.2 (2005) 79–92.

―――. *Unqualified Divine Temporality.* Edited by Gregory E. Ganssle. Downers Grove, IL: InterVarsity, 2001.

―――. *Works and Worlds of Art.* New York: Clarendon, 1980.

Yandell, Keith E. "Review of Divine Discourse." *The Journal of Religion* 78.1 (1998) 146–47.

Zwingli, Ulrich. "An Exposition of Faith." In *Zwingli and Bullinger*, by Huldrych Zwingli, 245–82. London: SCM, 1953.

Index